D1084738

International Political Economy Series

General Editor: **Timothy M. Shaw**, Professor of Commonwealth Governance and Development, and Director of the Institute of Commonwealth Studies, School of Advanced Study, University of London

Titles include:

Eul-Soo Pang
THE INTERNATIONAL POLITICAL ECONOMY OF TRANSFORMATION IN
ARGENTINA, BRAZIL, AND CHILE SINCE 1960

Henry Veltmeyer, James Petras and Steve Vieux
NEOLIBERALISM AND CLASS CONFLICT IN LATIN AMERICA
A Comparative Perspective on the Political Economy Of Structural Adjustment

Henry Veltmeyer, James Petras
THE DYNAMICS OF SOCIAL CHANGE IN LATIN AMERICA

International Political Economy Series
Series Standing Order ISBN 0–333–71708–2
(*outside North America only*)

You can receive future titles in this series as they are published by placing a standing order.
Please contact your bookseller or, in case of difficulty, write to us at the address below with
your name and address, the title of the series and the ISBN quoted above.

Customer Services Department, Macmillan Distribution Ltd, Houndmills, Basingstoke,
Hampshire RG21 6XS, England

The Caribbean Banana Trade

From Colonialism to Globalization

Peter Clegg
University of the West of England
Bristol

First published 2002 by
PALGRAVE MACMILLAN
Houndmills, Basingstoke, Hampshire RG21 6XS and
175 Fifth Avenue, New York, N.Y. 10010
Companies and representatives throughout the world.

PALGRAVE MACMILLAN is the global academic imprint of the Palgrave
Macmillan division of St Martin's Press, LLC and of Palgrave Macmillan Ltd.
Macmillan® is a registered trademark in the United States, United Kingdom
and other countries. Palgrave is a registered trademark in the European
Union and other countries.

ISBN 0–333–99849–9

This book is printed on paper suitable for recycling and
made from fully managed and sustained forest sources.

A catalogue record for this book is available
from the British Library.

Library of Congress Cataloging-in-Publication Data

Clegg, Peter, 1972–
    The Caribbean banana trade : from colonialism to globalization / Peter Clegg.
        p. cm. – (International political economy series)
    Includes bibliographical references(p.) and index.
    ISBN 0-333-99849-9 (cloth)
    1. Banana trade–Caribbean Area–History. I. Title. II. International political
economy series (Palgrave (Firm))

HD9259.B3 C273 2002
382′.414772′09729–dc21
                                                            2002020060

10 9 8 7 6 5 4 3 2 1
11 10 09 08 07 06 05 04 03 02

Printed and bound in Great Britain by
Antony Rowe Ltd, Chippenham and Eastbourne

For Veronika

Contents

Acknowledgements

First of all I must thank the friends and colleagues at the University of the West of England and the University of Southampton who have encouraged and commented on my work over a number of years. Particular gratitude must go to Professor Caroline Thomas for her guidance and support, together with Dr Paul Sutton and Professor Lawrence Grossman. I would also like to thank all those who were kind enough to give up time in their busy schedules to be interviewed, all of whom showed great courtesy and patience. More generally, I would like to express my gratitude to the many people that helped me during my travels across Europe and the Caribbean.

Special thanks must go to Professor Peter Davies of the University of Liverpool, Dr Lennox Honychurch, Dr Wayne Sandiford, Francis Leonce, and Patrick Foley for kindly allowing me to access their personal archives. I would also like to thank Alistair Smith of Banana Link, Peter Bursey of the Foreign and Commonwealth Office Library, Martina Edwin of WIBDECO, Junior Lodge of JAMCO, and David Jessop of the Caribbean Council for Europe for allowing me to access their organizations' archives.

In addition, my thanks go to Gerry Aird, Horton Dolphin, David Reid, Marshall Hall, John Ellis, Bernhard Stellmacher, Gregory Shillingford, Bill Gates, Sam Denley, Edwin Carrington, Tony Gonzales, Ann Lewis, the Atkinson family, and Steve and Judy Harle who were particularly generous with their time and assistance.

List of Tables

Conversion Table

12 fingers = 1 hand

9 hands = 1 stem

1 stem = 1 bunch

74.6 stems/bunches = 1 long ton

1 long ton = 1.0160 tonne

1 tonne = 0.9842 long ton

List of Abbreviations

ACP	African, Caribbean and Pacific Countries
APEB	Association of European Banana Producers
CBEA	Commonwealth/Caribbean Banana Exporters Association
COREPER	Committee of Permanent Representatives
DEFRA	Department for Environment, Food and Rural Affairs
DG	Directorate General
DSB	Dispute Settlement Body (of the World Trade Organization)
DTI	Department for Trade and Industry
EC	European Community
ECOSOC	Economic and Social Committee
EEC	European Economic Community
EU	European Union
FAO	Food and Agriculture Organization
FII	Fruit Importers of Ireland
GATS	General Agreement on Trade in Services
GATT	General Agreement on Tariffs and Trade
JAMCO	Jamaica Marketing Company
MAFF	Ministry of Agriculture, Fisheries and Food
SEA	Single European Act
TRQ	tariff rate quota
UFC	United Fruit Company
UK	United Kingdom
UKREP	United Kingdom Permanent Representation to the European Communities
US	United States (of America)
USTR	United States Trade Representative
WIBDECO	Windward Islands Banana Development and Exporting Company
WINBAN	Windward Islands Banana Growers' Association
WTO	World Trade Organization

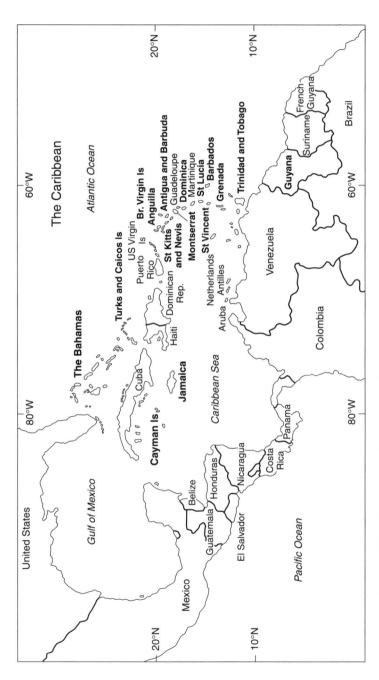

Commonwealth Caribbean banana–producing countries
Source: Payne and Sutton (2001) *Charting Caribbean Development*, Macmillan Education Ltd

1
Introduction

The present study was undertaken to investigate and analyse the detailed political interactions of the Caribbean banana trade, as an important contemporary issue within the context of the international trading system. The emphasis on the role of interest groups within the study helps us to further our understanding of the nature of the political process. At the centre of the study of this important and controversial aspect of international affairs, is an evaluation of the relationship between the traditional actors in the trade, namely governments (and government departments), private corporate interests, and producers. Within this context, an assessment is made of why the nature of Caribbean banana imports into the United Kingdom developed in the way it has, and why in the past 30 years the traditional actors within the trade have seen their influence and importance decline.

The main themes of the study are not mutually exclusive, but the development of particular themes come to the fore in each chapter. The theme of corporate ownership and monopoly control was chosen as it formed the origin of the developing interest group dynamic within the Caribbean banana trade. The role of American corporate interest, particularly in the form of the United Fruit Company, dominated the Caribbean banana trade from its inception, and the challenges to it defined the subsequent nature of the trade and the associated interest group dynamic. The theme of colonial responsibility was chosen as the nature of the relationship between the UK and its traditional banana suppliers was one based on colonial ties, a concept which underpinned global political and economic relations for much of the twentieth century. The UK governed the Windward Islands and Jamaica, and the nature of the interest group relationship within the banana trade was underpinned by that particular dynamic. Further, even when Jamaica and the Windward Islands had gained their independence, the legacy of colonial rule continued to be an important factor in defining the nature of the relationship between the actors involved in the UK banana trade.

A further theme is the gradual diminution of national control of the UK's trading policy, and the beginning of a transfer of political and economic commitments from the colonies and former colonies, to Europe. The theme was chosen because the change in the UK's political and economic priorities from its former colonial power status to the European Economic Community (EEC) was vitally important in slowly broadening the range of actors with an interest in the UK banana trade, some of which had conflicting political and economic agendas. The traditional actors in the trade had to readjust to a new, more complex interest group dynamic, which in time was to precipitate the establishment of a single European market in bananas, which superseded national controls. The fourth major theme is the influence of an empowered world-trading organization on those groups with an interest in the UK banana trade and the marginalization of those interests that have defended the merits of preferential access for certain banana producers, against those who have called for a more liberal banana trading environment in Europe. The theme was chosen as the issue of preferential access, which has underpinned banana imports into the UK, and latterly the European Union (EU), was not only one of the first issues to be dealt with at the World Trade Organization (WTO), it was the first case that was ruled to be non-compliant with the General Agreement on Trade in Services (GATS), and it was also the first case in which compliance with a WTO ruling was disputed. The development of an empowered world-trading organization thus transformed the nature of the interest-group dynamic within the banana trade, as there was now a higher level of arbitration, which superseded the influence of the traditional interest-group relationships.

The analytical framework

The study draws on interest-group literature to interpret the wealth of new empirical data. Such an approach was chosen to enable a detailed assessment to be undertaken of the actors involved in a specific area of trade. The basis of the study is to consider the motivations, actions, and relationships of the actors involved in exporting bananas from the Caribbean to the UK since the trade's inception, and to assess the resultant policy outcomes.

The interest group approach has been widely used elsewhere to assess the nature of the policy process both as it applies to the UK and the EU (including Arp, 1993; Bennington and Harvey, 1998; Bomberg, 1998; Cavanagh, 1998; Cawson, 1992; Eberlie, 1993; Kogan, 1975; Kohler-Koch, 1993; McLeay, 1998; Moon and Richardson, 1984; Richardson, Maloney and Rudig, 1992; Somsen, 1994; Visser and Ebbinghaus, 1992; Whiteley and Winyard, 1987). More particularly, interest-group analysis has also been used to assess the nature of agricultural policy making (including Averyt, 1977; Cox, Lowe, and Winter, 1986; Daugbjerg, 1998; Holbech, 1986; Self and Storing, 1962; Smith, 1991 and 1992; Wilson, 1977). Although much of the interest-group literature is American based, it tends to reflect a more open, fragmented political system than applies in the UK. As a consequence, an assessment has been made of the major theoretical approaches which have particular relevance to the nature of the policy process in the UK and the EU, which will offer a framework which will best account for the interest group behaviour within the study.

In terms of the language that is used throughout the study, the term 'interest group' is preferred, rather than 'pressure group' or any such equivalent. The term pressure group is used, particularly when attempts are made to precisely define the nature of the policy-making process between those groups that are political in nature, namely political parties and government agencies, and those groups that are not (see Alderman, 1984; Baggott, 1988; Ball and Millard, 1986; Castles, 1967; Mackenzie, 1955; Roberts, 1971). In many instances it is important to have such a definition, which provides clear parameters to assess the dynamics of a particular policy area. However, there is a risk that the term pressure group can promote a false impression of the nature of group politics. The nature of the policy process is highly complex, with compromise and negotiation at the centre of the relationship between interest groups and government. As Finer has suggested, the term pressure group can create an inaccurate impression that governments are pressurized by outside actors into following particular policies (1966, p. 3). Indeed, it can be argued that the term pressure group is disingenuous as it places too much emphasis on the government as the target of lobbying, while under representing the crucial influence governments have on groups themselves. The nature of such a complex series of relationships is illuminated by Bentley (1967), who has argued that the balance of power between groups shape public policy. Bentley also believes that government itself is a process of group interaction. Such a belief gives credence to the idea that government institutions themselves operate as interest groups, an argument supported by Latham (1953), who did not believe there was a significant distinction between the behaviour of government agencies and non-governmental groups.

The reasoning of Richardson and Jordan (1979) for a broad definition of interest groups is also of relevance to this study. They argue

> We see 'official' organisations and agencies (such as government departments) as behaving in almost exactly the same way as more conventional 'external' pressure groups. Central government departments, whilst often being the target of external pressure groups, are also playing pressure group roles themselves. By concentrating on the policy process, we begin to see just how much political activity is that of 'pressure groups' in this broad sense. [It is important to stress] the internal divisions within government itself and to highlight the degree to which 'government' is plural and not singular. Policies are the outcome of departmental conflict within government as well as the result of pressures on the government from outside. (p. 25)

Indeed, as Jordan and Richardson subsequently argued, 'the emphasis of our variant of group theory is more about pressure between bodies rather than about formal groups. Group theorists are writing about how decisions are made; group theory is about the role of groups, not merely theories about groups' (1987, pp. 15–16). The perspective of Jordan and Richardson is particularly apposite as the study is primarily concerned with the nature of the decision-making process, rather than a detailed assessment of the precise character of the actors involved in the trade. The decision to use the term interest group was therefore based on the requirements of the study to comprehensively assess the nature of the Caribbean banana trade, and the associated group interactions.

Although, a broad definition of an interest group can be seen as beneficial in helping to properly understand the complex nature of the policy process, it does have its critics, and indeed the term itself is open to challenge. A number of authors use the term interest group to describe an actor, which defends and promotes the self-interests of a section of society (see Baggott, 1995; Castles, 1967; Finer, 1966; Kimber and Richardson, 1974). In this context the term interest group is used to contrast those actors that primarily exist to protect their own interests, with those groups that promote the interests of others (cause groups). In certain circumstances the term interest group could therefore be misconstrued, as either describing a specific type of actor, or actors more generally. However, as the actors involved in the Caribbean banana trade are predominantly based on self-interest, the interest group/cause group dichotomy is of marginal significance. As a consequence, the term interest group is used as a general appellation to describe all the actors involved in the area of international trade being studied.

Another criticism is that with a broad definition of interest groups, almost any form of organization that has as its aim the influencing of public policy, and utilizes the resources at its disposal to that end could be seen as an interest group. Under such circumstances there is the risk that the term itself loses its explanatory value (see Alderman, 1984; Baggott, 1988 and 1995; Grant, 1989 and 1995; Odegard, 1958). Further, as Baggott (1995) has argued, 'the broad concept of pressure group can widen the scope of analysis to such an extent that the focus shifts too far away from the behaviour of private organisations and towards relationships between political organisations in general' (p. 11). It is true that political organizations are important elements within the study. However, there is also recognition that private organizations have a crucial role in the Caribbean banana trade, and that to disregard them would have severely undermined the study's impact. A broad concept of interest groups is therefore used in order to understand the complex nature of the Caribbean banana trade, and the important interactions that have shaped it, whether that involves governments, government departments, civil servants, parliamentarians, private companies, commodity producers, or non-governmental lobby groups. The aim of the study is to understand the nature of the policy process, and to do that the widest definition of interests is required.

Once the particular actors that are to be assessed have been identified, it is necessary to outline the theoretical concepts, which will assist in understanding the interest-group relationships and policy outcomes that are highlighted in the study. The analytical framework that has been chosen incorporates the group and network approaches, which will help interpret the particular changes that have occurred within the interest group dynamic of the Caribbean banana trade over the last century. The first part of the study utilizes the group approach in order to consider the development of the interest-group dynamic within the Caribbean banana trade, and its subsequent institutionalization. While the second half of the study uses the network approach to assess how the traditional Caribbean interest-group actors within the UK banana trade were affected by developments both at the European and international level, and what influence these had on policy outcomes.

The basis of the group approach, which emphasizes the presence of an actor in moulding the decision-making process, can be seen in Latham's *The Group Basis of Politics* (1953) and Truman's *The Governmental Process* (1962). Truman argued in his study 'the behaviours that constitute the process of government cannot be understood apart from the groups, especially the organised and potential interest groups, that are operative at any one point in time' (1962, p. 502). The early treaties on the group approach were then supplemented by the incrementalist model of policy-making, which argues that decision-making is not rational, but unplanned, disjointed and incremental (Lindblom, 1960; 1968; 1977). As John (1998) has suggested, 'Slow adjustment is the reality of much policy-making, and there is usually much interaction between the people who are involved in policy-making, both pressure groups and other policy-makers. The model helps analysts break down the conventional monolith of the state' (p. 69). Indeed, the basis of much of the early part of the study concerns the gradual formation of particular dynamics of interest, which were to have important ramifications for subsequent developments within the Caribbean banana trade.

The work of Latham, Truman and Lindblom laid the basis for what is arguably the definitive British study of the group approach, Richardson and Jordan's *Governing Under Pressure* (1979). Richardson and Jordan investigate the close relationship between interest groups and central government departments in a number of decentralized policy subsystems. The authors argue that within a so-called 'policy community' encompassing both bureaucratic and group interests, there is a natural tendency within British politics for consensus and accommodation, based on resource dependencies. The term community was chosen as Richardson (1993) subsequently noted, 'to reflect the intimate relationship between groups and departments, the development of common perceptions and the development of a common language for describing policy problems' (p. 93). Policy communities are relatively exclusive, with groups having privileged links with government, underpinned by a stable and negotiated policy environment.

In their study Richardson and Jordan conceptualize a number of ideas that are used in this study to help rationalize the nature of Caribbean banana imports into the UK. Importantly, Richardson and Jordan argue that 'the main feature of the British system is that ongoing problems and constraints force successive governments into very similar policy positions. Problems are handled similarly irrespective of what government is in power' (1979, p. 43). Further, Richardson and Jordan suggest, 'with decisions that are specific, technical, complex, managerial, then awareness of particular circumstances is all important. In such cases, the affected parties need to be contacted and their agreement sought. There is an instinctive reaction to consult' (1979, p. 43). The analysis of Richardson and Jordan helps to explain why the decision-making process with regard to the trade in bananas developed in the way it did. It should also be recognized that 'Personal networks are also regarded as important in the maintenance of group-executive relations. Shared educational backgrounds, friendships and common personal interests may all contribute to effective communication between groups and the executive' (Baggott, 1995, p. 94).

In addition, it is necessary to appreciate how interest groups attempt to maximize their influence at the structural level. Interest groups have the opportunity to influence policy at a number of stages, whether it is at the stage of formalizing the political agenda (Hogwood, 1987), or at the policy formation stage (Baggott, 1995). Interest groups can be extremely influential at the policy formation stage, with resultant changes in policy outcome (Marsh and Rhodes, 1992b). Dividing the policy process into stages not only makes it more comprehensible, but also enables us to appreciate the opportunities that are available for groups to influence policy. Moreover, this approach may help to explain the role of groups at different stages in the policy process. For example, it is often suggested that the most influential groups are those, which shape government policy at an early stage in its development.

There are also a number of places, political arenas (Jordan and Richardson, 1987) or pressure points (Baggott, 1994), within the political system where interest groups can affect the decisions that are made. In this study the main arenas include national and international decision-making institutions, as well as organizations, which mobilize and focus opinion such as the media, and other private organizations, including other interest groups. The approaches of Jordan and Richardson, and Baggott are valuable because they help us to appreciate that the policy process is a multi-layered system and that interest groups have a variety of targets that they can seek to influence.

Further, throughout the early history of the Caribbean banana trade, the nature of the interest group dynamic was shaped by two world wars, and their aftermath. In the period during and immediately after the Second World War in particular, 'outside' groups were involved in the actual administration of policies under government supervision, as opposed to undertaking its business relatively free from control. The banana companies and to a lesser extent the banana growing organizations became part of the machinery of government, directly responsible for wartime controls. As Grove (1962) has argued, in the Second World War 'trade associations were authorised, as government agents, to allocate markets, fix output and prices, and ration materials' (p. 56). Indeed, the close relationship that developed between the government and private organizations during this time is seen by some observers as paving the way for a period of increased cooperation between the actors in question (Grove, 1962, p. 61).

Within this context, the eventual development of a formalized group relationship to safeguard Caribbean banana interests in the UK trade is best interpreted in terms of Richardson and Jordan's approach. In particular, their contention that the nature of interest-group behaviour regarding a particular policy area is one

> Of a regularised, routinised relationship, which appears to be the normal response to problems that automatically reappear on the agenda ... that over time any governmental/interest group relationship on a matter of substance will evolve a special machinery ... (1979, p. 98)

Richardson and Jordan then suggest that the 'consultation phenomenon' in British government is due to a number of factors, which include

* A lack of confidence by civil servants in their own legitimacy to enforce decision.
* A realization that implementation of policies is affected by a cooperation (or lack of it) by groups.
* A recognition that in other aspects of the subject or at other times the department will depend on the interests for political support, aid in policy implementation or the provision of detailed information.
* A desire to maintain professional relations with the officers of relevant groups.

Indeed Richardson and Jordan go on to argue that

> For these and other reasons consultation takes place, and of course the development of committees is the extension of this consultative tide. By the use of committees with some continuity of existence there is administrative convenience – a process is established that obviates the need for decisions on procedure and protocol on each issue. But the formalisation of consultation has a greater impor-

tance. With a longer-term perspective, the possibility of a gradualist
solution becomes more likely. (1979, p. 98)

Despite adopting Richardson and Jordan's group approach, there are a
number of criticisms of it, which need to be addressed. John (1998)
argues that the main problem with Richardson and Jordan's approach
is that it is descriptive rather than explanatory, with little consideration of why decisions emerge when they do (p. 71). It is correct to say
that Richardson and Jordan's model does not provide sufficient explanation of why a 'regularised, routinised relationship' should develop at
a particular time. However, as the study is based on substantial empirical research, a degree of contextual support is provided which helps
sustain the adopted approach.

Once the 'regularised, routinised relationship' has been established,
John's criticisms are less pertinent as Richardson and Jordan themselves argue, 'There is evidence that it is increasingly difficult to exercise this power [to prevent decisions being made]. Much of this we
would argue, is due to the ability of new pressure groups in modern
democracies to force issues onto the agenda, whether or not governments or existing groups like it, or whether or not they are insider
groups having insider status' (1979, pp. 83–4). Further, Richardson and
Jordan consider the negotiated order approach (see Heclo and
Wildavsky, 1974 and Strauss *et al.*, 1976). Richardson and Jordan
suggest that the nature of the policy process can be appreciated 'in
terms of a complex relationship between the daily negotiative process
and a periodic appraisal process'. They argue that, 'this seems a valuable insight into appreciating how groups and departments have constant contact over policy details, but this does not prevent, in the
longer term, a change in the style of the relationship between groups
and departments to emerge' (1979, p. 102). In essence, the nature of
the policy process allows the recognized interests to conduct their business, but it does not preclude other groups and other priorities from
influencing the process, and thus altering the relative position of the
traditional interests in the established community. The criticism that
Richardson and Jordan's approach is descriptive rather than explanatory, with little consideration of why decisions emerge when they do,
is perhaps the most serious. However, a number of other issues of
concern also have to be addressed. John (1998) suggests that as
Richardson and Jordan's study was completed in 1978, a year before
the Conservative Party came into power under the leadership of
Margaret Thatcher, the study does not consider the emergence of an

ideologically based government which wanted to challenge the previously accepted consensual decision-making procedures. However, during the Thatcher era some policy areas were unaffected by the new approach and were able to continue with some degree of consensus, such as in agriculture (Marsh and Rhodes, 1992b; Baggott, 1992; and Richardson, 1993). Indeed, as will be seen the UK banana trade was one area where the established consensus remained intact.

A further criticism levelled at Richardson and Jordan is that their approach is rather broad, as Smith (1992) argues, 'a policy community seems to be nothing more than a close relationship between an interest group and officials' (p. 28). Under such circumstances, the definition loses its explanatory power. Nevertheless, even though the concept perhaps lends itself to such criticism, the study attempts to distinguish between what constitutes a policy community as opposed to a close relationship. However, John (1998) extends the criticism by suggesting 'it is hard to find any example of conflict that would undermine the idea of 'negotiated order' because everything fits into the concept except the actions of protesters' (p. 73). In defence of Richardson and Jordan, it has been argued, 'the notion of a community does not imply that there is an absence of conflict' (Grant 1995, p. 36). Indeed, as Heclo and Wildavsky point out in their seminal study of the Whitehall 'village', 'Community refers to the personal relationships between major political and administrative actors – sometimes in conflict, often in agreement, but always in touch and operating within a shared framework' (1974, p. xv). There is recognition of the potential weakness of Richardson and Jordan's approach, but within the context of the study the extent of the disagreements within the policy community are relatively unimportant.

In addition, Richardson and Jordan's approach has been criticized for under-emphasizing the role of institutions and the state in the group approach. John (1998) argues that the role of institutions of the state can have an important bearing on the interest-group dynamic within a particular area of policy, in that institutions can shape group interactions, while powerful groups can use the institutions of the state to safeguard their own priorities. In addition, Christiansen and Dowding (1994) have argued that the role of the state can depend on the policy sector under consideration, and the particular interests that are at stake. Therefore as John argues 'the group analysts' strategy of treating sections of the bureaucracy as just another group needs to be qualified by the political environment institutions inhabit' (1998, p. 77). In Richardson and Jordan's study there is recognition of the problem, and look to the 'accommodation' model of Lijphart (1968) for a solution.

Richardson and Jordan argue that Lijphart's concept of the Government's right to govern is a useful corrective to parts of their study where they argue that the government is just another group. The government is involved in the policy process, but it has a special status. As Richardson and Jordan argue, 'the government can indulge in coercion, in 'elective dictatorship', and it is often important to realise that there is this right in the background' (1979, p. 105). However, within this context they suggest it is important to remember Heclo and Wildavsky's (1974) adage that 'coercion has its uses and is not to be despised. Far better, however, to create a nexus of interests so that cooperation flows from a sense of mutual advantage' (quoted in Richardson and Jordan, 1979, p. 105). More particularly, it is important to recognize that policy communities are not always established because of the demands of 'outside' groups, as such a course of action can be precipitated by government action, if it decides on an interventionist agricultural policy (Smith, 1992).

The study attempts to meet the concerns that are raised by the perceived lack of emphasis within the group approach on the institutions of the state. Within the context of the Caribbean banana trade, it will be shown that the state always has interests to defend, and these interests have determined the nature of its involvement. On some occasions this has led the state to take a pro-active role in the banana trade, while at other times it has taken a more relaxed view. As Smith (1992) argues in his work on the agricultural policy community, a government's perception can change depending on the success or failure of a particular paradigm (p. 37). However, irrespective of the nature of the state's involvement, its place in the interest-group dynamic of the Caribbean banana trade has not been neglected. Further, Christiansen and Dowding's observations are of less significance than would be the case in other circumstances, as the study is primarily concerned with one sector of policy. Indeed, as Grant (1995) has argued 'policy communities tend to form around government departments' and that 'although pressure groups will have contacts with a range of departments, they tend to have particularly close contacts with one department' (p. 58). Such close cooperation with government then 'enables groups to express an opinion about policies at an early stage in their development. This may save much effort at a later stage when the government's policy has become more concrete' (Baggott, 1995 p. 101).

The important relationship between the state and the other actors with an interest in the Caribbean banana trade is reaffirmed by the suggestion of Rose (1976) that once a policy has been adopted, the groups who benefit, be they bureaucrats or 'outside' groups, will make every effort to retain their benefits. Rose argues that it is always more difficult to take away benefits from groups than to refuse to grant those benefits in the first place (1976, p. 262). As Bachrach and Baratz have suggested, 'individuals and groups, both liberal and conservative, who are bent upon maintaining the correct allocation of values are likely to focus on preventing demands for reallocation of values from reaching the deci-sion-making stage, rather than running the risk that hostile demands will not be voted down when they are ripe for decision' (1970, p. 57). So state officials as well as 'outside' groups play a crucial role in pre-venting the removal of issues and policies from the political agenda.

The issue of clientelism, whereby government departments identify with their 'lobby' is also considered (Christoph, 1975). As Wilson (1977) has argued, 'it is only natural that a community of shared beliefs and attitudes should develop between the officials (of the actors) in such close contact' (p. 45). Further, Crenson's (1971) sugges-tion that actors can exercise influence simply by being there, is impor-tant. Crenson argues that politicians are aware of groups and the attitudes they are likely to adopt in a given situation and will often avoid action that is likely to provoke the groups into greater activity. Crenson concludes from his study that 'Decision-making activity is channelled and restricted by the process of non-decision making [and that] the power reputations of people within a community may deter action on certain sensitive or politically unprofitable issues' (1971, p. 178). Such descriptions of the policy process prove to be apposite as the study progresses, particularly in regard to how colonial and post-colonial related interests were able to influence the UK government to sustain preferential access for Jamaican and Windward Islands bananas, despite challenges from other international trading interests.

However, despite correctly attempting to reassure critics of Richardson and Jordan's approach regarding a perceived lack of emphasis on the institutions of the state, it is important to stress that 'outside' groups retain an important role in the policy process, and par-ticularly when it comes to the process of problem identification. As Richardson and Jordan argue 'the first stage in any national policy process must be effective problem identification, and groups may well be more efficient at this than official policy-making structures such as central government departments' (1979, p. 85). Finer (1973) has also stressed the important role of 'outside' groups in forcing issues onto the political agenda. He argues that 'firms and trade unions actively seek the intervention of the political power in one shape or form. It is not so much the politicians who interferes with the market as the market – firms and unions – that interferes with the government' (1973, p. 397).

Further, it is important to recognize the development of 'umbrella or coalition groups' (Richardson and Jordan, 1979, p. 180). As Baggott (1995) argues 'pressure groups often form broad coalitions in an attempt to influence public policy'. Further, he suggests that although the coalition may be divided on certain matters, coalitions can coordinate the activities of groups in order to present a united front on general issues of policy. Baggott goes on to argue that 'Coordination is essential to avoid the duplication of lobbying efforts ... [and] by pooling resources, the coalition may be able to achieve more collectively than any group acting alone' (p. 72). The observations are particularly apposite when considering a number of seminal moments in the history of the Caribbean banana trade.

Once an assessment has been made of the developing interest-group dynamic within the Caribbean banana trade, the study considers how the traditional interest-group actors within the trade were affected by developments both at the European and international level. The UK's membership of the EEC, and the subsequent Single European Act, together with the development of a powerful international trading body in the form of the WTO, all had important ramifications for the traditional banana interests involved in the UK trade. In order properly to understand the particular interest-group dynamic at the levels of European and international policy-making, the resultant policy outcomes, and the nature of the interactions between the different layers of influence, a supplementary analytical framework to that of Richardson and Jordan is required that is less static.

The increasing importance of the policy-making process at the European level, as it applies to the banana issue is considered within the analytical framework. It can be argued that in many ways, European Community (EC) lobbying is similar to national lobbying, in that 'the most successful groups tend to be those which exhibit the usual professional characteristics – namely resources, advance intelligence, good contacts with bureaucrats and politicians, and an ability to provide policy-makers with useful information and advice' (Mazey and Richardson 1993b, p. 206). However, it is clear that the policy-making structures and processes of the Community are quite distinct. Mazey and Richardson have identified the openness of decision-making, its multinational character, and the important role of national politico-administrative elites in the process (1993b). As a consequence of these characteristics, interest groups have to cope with an unstable and complex environment, which has important ramifications for interest group strategies. As Streeck and Schmitter have argued, the European policy process is characterized by 'a profound absence of hierarchy and monopoly among a wide variety of players of different but uncertain status' (1991, p. 159).

The process of EC lobbying therefore is necessarily complex, with interest groups needing to coordinate their efforts both at the national and European levels. Mazey and Richardson (1993b) argue a sole dependency on the national level strategy is important but not sufficient to influence the policy process. Therefore, the relative significance of a national strategy and a 'Euro-strategy' in influencing European decision-making is assessed. A national strategy, where actors maintain close links with national politicians and bureaucracies, is important. As Baggott argues, 'the relationships which exist between pressure groups and national governments are stable, well-developed and reliable channels of representation ... [and that] most pressure groups carry more weight with their own government than with European institutions ...' (1995, p. 212, also Greenwood, Grote, and Ronit, 1992, pp. 22–3). Indeed, as Spence has argued, 'where a lobby can persuade government of its cause, the efficiency and the strength of the machinery of the UK European policy-making makes UK officialdom a very strong ally' (1993, p. 71). The nature of Community decision-making means that groups have to rely on national politicians and officials to defend their positions when policies are finalized. As Mazey and Richardson suggest

> Somewhat paradoxically, the growing importance of EC legislation has in many cases reinforced the dependency which exists at the national level between groups and 'their' ministries, since the latter are effectively intermediaries between groups and the EC in the final stages of Community decision-making. (1993b, p. 211)

Nevertheless, the need for a 'Euro-strategy' to allow groups to undertake representations at the European level should not be neglected. As Baggott argues, '[Groups] need to adopt a much broader strategy which enables them to influence European institutions such as the Commission and the Parliament when necessary' (1995, p. 218). The institutions of the European Commission, the European Parliament, the European Court of Justice, and the Economic and Social Committee all play a significant role in the policy process, with the

European Commission being the most important because of its central position in all stages of policy formulation through to implementation (Mazey and Richardson, 1993c and Nugent, 1994). The relevance of a 'Euro-strategy' has become more important since the Single European Act, and the expansion of qualified majority voting (Mazey and Richardson, 1993c and Kohler-Koch, 1994). Any group that depended solely on its well-established contacts with national government could regret not accessing the other avenues of influence both within the institutions of the Community, and amongst the other member states (Butt Philip, 1991; Mazey and Richardson, 1992; and Spence, 1993). The study assesses the complementary national strategy and 'Euro-strategy' of the traditional actors based in the UK banana trade, and considers why such a combination of strategies was relatively successful in safeguarding their interests.

However, it is also important to recognize how the different position of certain interests in the decision-making process at the national and European levels can affect policy outcomes. The study acknowledges the contention that the complex, fragmentary, and more open nature of the European policy process has meant 'that there is not the intimate knowledge that often exists between policy actors at the national level, and neither is there sufficient common interest between them to under-pin the development of stable agendas and processes' (Mazey and Richardson, 1993a, p. 23). There is a competitive agenda-setting process, which causes problems of uncertainty and unpredictability. Further, it is important to acknowledge the nature of agricultural policy communities, and that the dynamics of them can be altered by EC involvement. As Smith (1992) has highlighted, an agricultural policy community has an inner and outer circle of members. The actors within the inner circle 'are intimately involved in policy making on a day-to-day basis, whereas the secondary community includes groups which have access to the department only when an issue which specifically affects them is being considered' (Smith, 1992, p. 31). Within the context of the study there is an assessment of what effect membership of the EEC, and later the Single European Act, had on the relative position of the inner and outer circle of members traditionally involved in the UK banana trade. The suggestion is that a 'negotiated order' that can exist in a well-defined national policy community (Richardson and Jordan, 1979 and Strauss, 1987) is absent at the EC level.

Indeed, when considering the effect of the WTO on the traditional banana interests within the UK market, a number of the concepts used at the European level can be applied. For example, as with the EC there are a much larger number of actors who have a potential interest in the banana issue, than at the national level, which means the level of negotiated order is much less (Richardson and Jordan, 1979 and Strauss, 1987). In addition, as the WTO is an organization, which is government-based, the dependency between groups and 'their' ministries (including the European Commission) is reinforced (Mazey and Richardson, 1993b). However, in other ways the nature of the WTO supersedes the analysis at the national and European levels, particularly its rule-driven framework, the effects of which are considered in some detail.

In order to explain the changing nature of the interest-group dynamic between the traditional relationships at the national level, and the new challenges at the European and global levels, an additional set of theoretical perspectives is needed. Within this context the network approach to public policy has been chosen to supplement the group approach, which helps to interpret the first part of the study. The network approach suggests 'the different types of relationships between group representatives, bureaucrats, politicians and other participants in decision-making account for the various ways in which political systems process policy' (John, 1998, p. 78). The network approach differs from the group approach, in that the latter emphasizes the presence of an organization in shaping the policy process, while the former considers the particular relationships between decision-makers. However, both concepts look beyond the formal nature of the policy process and consider the informal and associative aspects of decision-making.

The network approach originated in the late 1960s, when the American system of consensus politics between producer groups and bureaucracies began to break down, exacerbated by the growth in 'outside' interests such as lobbyists and policy advisers. Heclo's (1978) account of the policy process argued that things were becoming more unpredictable, with the state being called upon to carry out more tasks, buffeted by an ever-increasing number of interests. Since then a number of British approaches have been developed, including Rhodes (1986, 1988 and 1997), Marsh and Rhodes (1992a and 1992b), Marsh and Smith (1996), Wilks and Wright (1987), Wright (1988) and Smith (1993). Within this context, the theoretical perspective of Marsh and Rhodes (1992a) will be used in the second part of the study. They argue in *Policy Networks in British Government* that with an emphasis on different policy networks, namely policy communities and issue networks, the nature of interest-group relationships can be determined, with consequent implications for the policy process, policy outcomes, and policy change.

Marsh and Rhodes in their study characterize a policy community as having an exclusive membership, stable relations between members, close relationships between groups and government, frequent contact, a high degree of consensus, and interdependence between groups and governments. While in an issue network, there is a large number of participants, unstable relations between members, weaker and less regular contacts between groups and governments, much conflict, and little interdependence between groups and governments (1992a, p. 251). It can be argued that Marsh and Rhodes' description of a policy community is compatible with the concept as referred to by Richardson and Jordan in their study *Governing Under Pressure* (1979). Richardson and Jordan's approach helps to explain the gradual institutionalization of Caribbean interests within the UK banana trade, while Marsh and Rhodes' model assesses the changing position of the traditional interests within the context of an extended policy-making framework, and the resultant consequences for policy outcomes.

However, as with the group approach there are certain criticisms of the network approach, some of which are more important than others (Dowding 1995; John 1998; Kassim 1994; Mills and Saward 1994). The most fundamental criticism of the network approach concerns its lack of explanatory power, which needs to be addressed. As John argues, 'the concept is hard to use as the foundation for an explanation unless the investigator incorporates other factors, such as the interests, ideas and institutions which determine how networks function' (1998, p. 85). The strongest criticism of the network approach comes from Dowding who argues that the approach fails as a model 'because the driving force of explanation, the independent variables, are not network characteristics per se but rather characteristics of components within networks. These components explain both the nature of the network and the nature of the policy process' (1995, p. 137). Dowding argues that it matters little whether networks are said to be open or closed, as their structure and operation are shaped by other changes affecting the policy sector, such as the resources and bargaining strategies of the actors. In short, Dowding argues that decision-making is determined not by networks, but by the bargaining strategies and the various interests at play.

The criticisms of the network approach by John and Dowding are important as they show that there is a tendency for networks only to explain policy in the context of other factors, and as a consequence the concept itself lacks explanatory power. In order to address this serious criticism, the approach of John (1998) will be adopted. John has argued that one way of providing a degree of explanatory power for the network approach 'is to argue that network properties have an effect independent of other factors, like group resources. As networks specify a particular structure of linkages the way in which that structure influences communication between actors can affect the way in which issues are processed' (1998, pp. 90–1). In addition, John highlights that another aspect of networks, which is important in explaining policy, is their multidimensional nature. He argues, 'Relationships on policy matters are often an amalgam of professional, propinquitous and friendship associations. Policy-makers relate to each other in different ways, and the network idea captures how different aspects of relationships reinforce each other' (1998, p. 91). Heclo and Wildavsky (1974) investigated this idea in their account of the Whitehall 'village'. They argued that relationships within an area of policy-making are more fundamental than just a direct exchange of resources; rather they result from long-standing cooperation between actors. As John argues 'the personal character of networks is important, as participants in networks invest in relationships with each other. They network to seek cooperation and information. These consciously evolved relationships impact on policy choices because decision-makers value their contacts with each other when they make decisions' (1998, p. 91).

However, there also needs to be recognition that policy network structures have a close relationship with institutions, group structure and resources, ideas, and other networks. As Daugbjerg and Marsh (1998) argue 'policy outcomes are not just a function of what occurs in the network; they are also strongly influenced by the economic, political and ideological context within which the network operates' (p. 54). Similarly John (1998) suggests that 'network structures can affect how institutions work and the way political actors make choices; but institutions in turn structure how networks function, and political choices affect the long term relationships political actors have with each other, and both paths of causation occur at the same time' (p. 89). Further, as Marsh and Smith (1996) argue that if network analysis is accepted as a meso-level concept, which examines the relationship between interest groups and governments/government departments, the role of macro- and micro-level factors must be integrated in order properly to understand the association between networks and outcomes (p. 13). While, Marsh and Smith (2000) contend that 'the context within which networks operate is composed, in part, of other networks and this aspect of the context has a clear impact on the operation of the network, upon change in the network and upon policy outcomes' (p. 8).

The acceptance of Marsh and Rhodes' model is supplemented by a recognition that analysis is required of the role of the state, of the actors, which interact within a particular network, and the influence of other networks, in order to provide the approach with some explanatory power.

As John has suggested

> Networks are research tools for identifying relationships whose structure is mainly determined elsewhere. But that does not mean that they have no effect. The research strategy must identify the structure of networks first, then ascertain the reasons why those structures function in the manner observed. Then it may be possible to deduce network effects after researchers have explored the main power relationships. (1998, pp. 90–1)

The account of networks by Marsh and Rhodes (1992a) supplemented by the work of John (1998) in particular, provides the basis for attempting to understand the changes in the nature of the interest-group relationship since the actors who were traditionally based within the context of the UK banana trade were forced to readjust to the demands of the more expansive arenas of decision-making. To supplement the work of Marsh and Rhodes, and John an additional analytical approach is needed to explain how the influence of the traditional interests has been altered by the structure of the different levels of decision-making.

In order to explain the exact dynamics of the trend between the different levels of decision-making May and Nugent's (1982) account of 'thresholder' groups, where groups oscillate over time between insider and outsider status will be used. The 'thresholder' group approach is an adaptation of Grant's (1978) 'insider/outsider' group paradigm, which distinguishes groups on the basis of their interaction within the policy process. The work that Grant, and May and Nugent undertook has been more recently extended by Jordan, Maloney and McLaughlin (1992) who have divided the categories of insider status more specifically. However, within the context of this study there is value in maintaining a broad insider/outsider distinction, which maintains the validity of the two earlier theoretical concepts. For Grant, insider groups are considered to be legitimate by government and are consulted regularly, thus being highly effective in influencing the policy process. Outsider groups either have no wish to become formally involved with officials, or are unable to gain recognition. The insider/outsider model is based on the belief that by pursuing a particular strategy, the group concerned is able to determine the type of relationship it achieves with government. Thus strategy and status are mutually self-reinforcing, whereby for example the undertaking of an insider strategy is a necessary element in gaining insider status.

However, Whiteley and Winyard (1987) suggest that Grant confuses strategy and status, in that a group might have insider status, but could pursue a broader political strategy that does not rely solely on contacts with Whitehall (see also Judge, 1990, and Baggott, 1992). Thus insider groups often undertake a combination of both insider and outsider tactics. In addition, the close relationship between strategy and status has been criticized by Jordan, Maloney and McLaughlin (1992), as assuming too much in that pursuing an insider strategy is sometimes not sufficient to achieve insider status. Jordan, Maloney and McLaughlin suggest that 'the key variable is that of resources' which can cover 'knowledge, technical advice or expertise, membership compliance or consent, credibility, information, implementation guarantees'. In their view, 'The logic of accommodation leads inevitably to certain behavioural norms. Grant's emphasis on the deliberate selection of behavioural norms then is an over-emphasis on the degree of choice' (1992, p. 25). In response Grant has argued that, 'While not denying the force of the logic of the bargaining process in a policy community, groups can make choices which can either improve an initially weak bargaining position or undermine an initially strong bargaining position' (1995, p. 16).

Within the context of the study, the approach of those that suggest that status and strategy should be separated is taken on board. It can be argued that Grant's approach can be applied in certain cases, but on occasion the particular nature of the arenas in which the banana issue is considered has fractured the link between strategy and status. Nevertheless, the value of the insider/outsider distinction is that it focuses attention on the choices that have to be made by groups and government, and on the exchange relationships that develop between them. Further, the approach can highlight the changes in status and strategy when the nature of the political environment undergoes change. In this context the 'thresholder' approach of May and Nugent, adapted from Grant's insider/outsider group paradigm, can help us to understand the changing position of vulnerable and peripheral states like Jamaica and those of the Windward Islands in the new trading environment.

The theoretical approach used to underpin the study is comprehensive in its analysis. However, two other concepts, that of 'advocacy coalitions' and 'epistemic communities', have also been applied to help explain the relationships and interactions between different actors in policy-making. These two approaches consider how professional and technical experts generate policy and how government subsequently adopts these ideas. In particular, 'advocacy coalitions' (Sabatier, 1988 and 1998; Sabatier and Jenkins-Smith, 1993, 1997 and 1999; and Cairney, 1997) and 'epistemic communities' (Haas, 1990 and 1992; Adler and Haas, 1992; and Dunlop, 2000) consider the ways in which networks, coalitions and communities promote their views during policy formulation. The 'advocacy coalitions' approach attempts to explain the influence on policy formulation of groups, which have contending beliefs, values and ideas. While the idea of 'epistemic communities' concentrates on how groups utilise their knowledge and expertise to shape policy outcomes. The additional concepts mentioned do not supersede the interest-group/policy-network approach, rather they can provide a supplementary means when attempting to understand policy development and related outcomes within the context of the Caribbean banana trade over the last century.

Structure

The main purpose of Chapter 2 is to establish how an interest-group dynamic developed within the context of a newly established trade with the UK, involving the banana interests of the colony of Jamaica, the UK government, and private corporate interests. The chapter considers the issues of monopoly power, foreign ownership, and colonial responsibility. It establishes that there were two separate policy issues addressed by the UK government that of the control of banana exports from Jamaica, and their destination.

Chapter 3 analyses how the effects of the Second World War and its aftermath fundamentally altered the position of Caribbean interests in the UK banana trade. The chapter assesses how the interest-groups reacted to the exceptional circumstances of the Second World War, and the subsequent effects on the nature of the UK banana trade. The chapter establishes that, owing to the nature of the interest-group dynamic of the banana trade at this time, a greater understanding of the respective roles of the actors involved developed which laid the foundations for a closer working relationship in the future.

Chapter 4 assesses the significant change in the interest-group dynamic of the UK banana market as a result of the establishment of a new source of colonial banana supplies in the Windward Islands, and the development of the General Agreement of Tariffs and Trade (GATT) in challenging preferential access for colonial banana supplies to the UK. The chapter examines the issues of colonial rivalry, corporate expediency, and the beginnings of a liberalizing influence in international trade. It demonstrates that despite colonial preference, competition within that context seriously compromised the stability within the UK market, which necessitated the establishment of an institutional mechanism involving all the main actors to oversee the banana trade. The chapter also establishes that despite the differences that existed between Jamaica and the Windward Islands as regards UK market share, both countries were united in resisting market liberalization.

Chapter 5 evaluates the impact on the Caribbean banana interests of the UK's membership of an organization exhibiting both intergovernmental and supranational characteristics, the EEC. The chapter considers the gradual diminution of national control of the UK's trading policy, and the beginning of a re-focusing of political and economic commitments from the colonies and former colonies, to Europe. The chapter demonstrates that despite the significant changes related to EEC membership, the UK was able to sustain its colonial and post-colonial trading relationships.

Chapter 6 focuses on the Single European Act of 1986. It assesses the impact of the Act on the Caribbean interests involved in the UK banana trade as national trading controls came to an end. The chapter assesses the complex political process by which the twelve highly distinctive banana regimes of the member states were organized as one. The chapter establishes that although the traditional interest group actors within the UK banana trade successfully defended the concept of preferential access, greater challenges lay ahead.

Chapter 7 analyses the position of the UK's traditional Caribbean banana suppliers within the EU's banana regime, with the institutionalization of a liberal trading orthodoxy in the guise of the WTO, the successor of the GATT. The chapter considers the conflict within the world-trading environment between different centres of political, economic and legal power, and the marginalization of those interests that have defended the merits of preferential access in international trade. The chapter demonstrates that the national and regional commitments to retain long-term trading patterns were superseded by the institutional nature of the existing international trading environment.

The concluding chapter highlights the results of the study. It utilizes the analytical framework together with the four themes of the study, to assess the changes that have taken place within the interest-group dynamic of the Caribbean banana trade over the last century. The chapter examines the reasons why the traditional interest-group dynamic in the Caribbean banana trade developed in the way it did, and why in recent years this dynamic has fragmented, with serious consequences for policy outcomes.

2
The Effect of Monopoly Power and the Establishment of Imperial Preference

The origins of the banana export trade in Jamaica

As regular trading links were established between the Caribbean and North America from the middle of the nineteenth century, ships from the United States would take on board small quantities of those tropical fruits, which could endure the journey. As a consequence the possibilities of the banana as an export crop was becoming increasingly appreciated. For example, in 1867, the Governor of Jamaica, Sir John Peter Grant stated in his annual report that the island might have great potential in developing a significant banana export trade (West India Committee Circular, 9 April 1912). However, the most important encouragement given to Jamaica's banana export industry came from American businessmen, such as George Busch and Lorenzo Dow Baker, who began regular banana shipments from the island in the early 1870s.

By the 1880s, there were a large number of companies involved in exporting the Gros Michel variety of banana to America, however the environment was highly competitive, and the opportunity for profitability was scarce. As a consequence a rationalization of the industry took place. Of greatest significance was the merger between the Boston Fruit Company, whose business was based primarily in Jamaica, and the interests of Minor C. Keith who was developing a fruit trade between Central America and the US. On 20 March 1899, the two companies, together with 12 smaller fruit companies, were merged into one organization and registered as the United Fruit Company (Rodriquez, 1955, p. 27). It has been argued, 'the organisation of the United Fruit Company marked the end of the era of pioneering, of risks and hardships, easy profit as well as total failures, and the beginning of a new era that converted the highly perishable tropical banana into an important item of world trade' (May and Plaza, 1958, p. 7).

The development of a large-scale UK banana trade and a challenge to American corporate power

A new market for Jamaican bananas

The first source of bananas for the UK came from the Canary Islands. Bananas of the smaller and more delicate Cavendish variety were shipped to the UK free of competition from growers further abroad, which at the time were faced with the problems of carrying bananas over long distances without refrigeration. In the mid-1880s when port facilities on the Canary Islands had been improved, a number of British shipping companies began to realize the potential for exports from the islands, including bananas. One shipping company that developed an interest in the Canary Islands was based in Liverpool and headed by Alfred Jones. The company Elder Dempster ran routes from Britain to West Africa bringing its vessels close to the islands. With the British public's increasing taste for new produce, it became apparent that there was a potentially large market for bananas. By 1886, banana exports from the Canary Islands to the UK had reached 50 000 bunches (Davies, 1990, p. 49 and West India Committee Circular, 9 April 1912). From these beginnings, the banana business grew in size and importance.

As a regular but rather limited banana trade was developing between the Canary Islands and the UK, the Jamaican banana trade to the US was developing into a substantial business. As a result attempts were made by private interests to develop a banana-shipping route to the UK, to challenge the position held by the Canary Islands banana. In early 1897, the Jamaica Fruit Importing and Trading Company was established with the support of a group of West Indian businessmen. A number of shipments were made between Jamaica and the UK, but the quality of the fruit on arrival was extremely variable. However, there was hope that the shipping difficulties could be overcome so a more regular service could be developed (West India Committee Circular, 22 February 1897). The significance of the establishment of the Jamaica Fruit Importing and Trading Company lies in the fact that it was private commercial interests that first saw the possibility of developing a trans-Atlantic banana trade, rather than the colonial authorities. Indeed, the role of private enterprise has been central in shaping the interest-group dynamic of the Caribbean and UK banana trades over the last century.

Despite, the increasing banana exports to the US and the embryonic trade to the UK, there was increasing concern on Jamaica that the dominant position of American corporate interests exporting bananas from Jamaica, in the form of the Boston Fruit Company, might not be sufficient to sustain the long-term future of the banana industry in the British colony. Indeed, during the summer of 1898, those Jamaicans with an interest in the banana industry became increasingly concerned that land the Boston Fruit Company had bought in Cuba would be used for bananas, as Cuba was nearer to the main banana markets in New York and Boston than was Jamaica. There was disquiet in Jamaica that the company might divest its interests in the island, and concentrate its operations in Cuba. The perceived ability of corporate interests to transcend the nation-state is important, reflecting the influence of private enterprise in shaping the economic development of a country. Indeed such concerns helped to define the nature of the Caribbean and UK banana trades, as throughout the twentieth century there has been a necessary accommodation between corporate power and political expediency.

In addition to the concerns regarding the Boston Fruit Company, shipments by the Jamaica Fruit Importing and Trading Company to the UK had come to an end in May 1897, and this seemed to indicate that Jamaica would continue to be dependent on capricious American interests. These circumstances led Bishop Gordon, the Roman Catholic Bishop of Jamaica, to visit the Colonial Secretary, Joseph Chamberlain, in London to ask if he could use his good offices to investigate the possibility of developing an alternative market in Britain to absorb the banana surplus the Bishop thought would quickly emerge (Stockley, 1937, pp. 25–6). The interests based in Jamaica recognized the need for government assistance to challenge the power and influence of American commercial interests, appreciating that state action was probably the best means by which corporate power could be counterbalanced.

Although Joseph Chamberlain had in the past supported the concept of free trade, he had come to accept the benefits of 'constructive imperialism', underpinned by closer economic ties between Britain and her colonies. Chamberlain believed that if this was achieved the resources at the Empire's disposal could be utilized to maximum effect, and as a consequence he was well disposed to Bishop Gordon's approach (Saul, 1957, pp. 173–5). In an attempt to stimulate an interest in a Jamaica–UK banana trade, Chamberlain approached Alfred Jones, a natural choice because of his work in the development of West Africa and his past experience in the Canary Islands banana trade. Jones agreed to investigate the situation in Jamaica, and sent a colleague,

A.H. Stockley, to the island in order to report on the situation. Stockley found that the Boston Fruit Company was the most important company on the island, but that Bishop Gordon had over-stated the risks of Cuban competition and there was little likelihood that this would have a significant effect on the Jamaican fruit trade. Stockley believed that the opportunities for Elder Dempster in Jamaica were limited, and advised Alfred Jones not to become involved in such an endeavour (Stockley, 1937, pp. 26–30). The importance of personal contacts and individual judgements are well exemplified here. It is interesting that such an important decision, that of deciding whether a banana shipment link should be established between Jamaica and the UK, was taken by such a small group of individuals. Indeed, the advice of one man was sufficient to end the immediate hopes of those in both Jamaica and the UK who saw the benefits of establishing a banana export trade between the two countries. The decision disappointed Joseph Chamberlain who continued to believe that Jamaican bananas should have an alternative to the American market. However, in December 1898 after the return of the West India Commission which had assessed the needs of the islands in the region with particular reference to the decline of the sugar industry (West India Royal Commission, 1898), the Colonial Office acted by publicly inviting tenders for a fortnightly fruit steamship service between Jamaica and Britain, which included in its remit the carrying of substantial volumes of bananas. The Royal Mail Steam Packet Company tendered a bid, costing £40 000 a year for five years. However, it was reported that 'at an interview which the Directors had with the Secretary of State for the Colonies, they were informed that £40 000 was out of the question, and that the service could be done for perhaps £10 000' (West India Committee Circular, 15 October 1901). When negotiations broke down with the Royal Mail Steam Packet Company, the government considered tenders from other companies and subsequently signed a contract with the Jamaica Fruit and Produce Association for a direct fruit and passenger service between Jamaica and the UK to commence in May 1900, with the British and Jamaican authorities providing a total subsidy of £10 000 per annum (West India Committee Circulars, 15 May 1899 and 10 July 1899). Stockley, who had been following developments, stated 'It seems incredible that such an unbusiness-like arrangement could ever have been made' (Stockley, 1937, p. 31). Stockley's comments were well founded as it was announced only a few months later that the scheme had fallen through (West India Committee Circular, 30 October 1899). Joseph Chamberlain had never been entirely comfortable with this arrangement, as he feared that the company would not be able to fulfil its obligations due to a lack of capital on its part, although the Colonial Secretary did seem to think there was sufficient subsidy for the endeavour.

Despite the failure of the first shipping service, a meeting was held in Jamaica under the auspices of Archbishop Gordon, on 17 November, where it was resolved to persuade the British government and the Colonial Office to begin negotiations with Elder, Dempster and Company to establish a direct fruit shipping service. It was reported, 'that the whole island is in favour of it' (West India Committee Circular, 27 November 1899). Under pressure from interests in Jamaica, and to repair his credibility on the issue, Joseph Chamberlain again approached Alfred Jones. However, this time the tone of the negotiations was different, with the British government willing to concede more than it had in the past. After discussions where the amount of subsidy was again a sticking point, Chamberlain was able to persuade Jones of the merits of the enterprise both on a corporate and personal level. Chamberlain was quoted as saying to Jones, 'I can promise you that should this service be started in 1901, I could then see that your patriotic action was rewarded, and I hope that will be some inducement to you' (Stockley, 1937, p. 33).

Further, Elder, Dempster and Company was a member of the West India Committee, and Alfred Jones the company's president was on the committee's executive. The committee was created in the eighteenth century as a permanent association of London merchants engaged in West Indian trade and absentee West Indian landowners who lived in London. Owing to the range and importance of its members, the committee had a degree of respect and influence within government circles. The committee was concerned with the prevailing trading conditions in the West Indies, and it seems likely that the committee would have played a role in encouraging an accommodation between the company and the government over the banana issue, particularly as the negotiations were potentially so important both for the future of the colony, and for those members of the West India Committee with an interest in Jamaica, and indeed elsewhere in the Caribbean. From this moment the West India Committee was to play an important role in acting as an intermediary between the different commercial and colonial interests that were present within the UK banana trade.

The terms of Elder Dempster for the establishment of a direct service to Britain was a subsidy of £40 000 annually for ten years. The Colonial Secretary sent word to Jamaica that the British Treasury would pay half if the colony contributed the remainder. The Governor of Jamaica was instructed to confer with the main interested parties on the island to gauge their opinion. It was reported that, 'the mercantile community whose interests lie in the US wished the terms to be rejected, but the great body of producers favoured the acceptance, saying they were willing to pay a tax on fruit to meet the subsidy' (West India Committee Circular, 2 February 1900). The contract was subsequently signed, and it was agreed that the service should begin in January 1901. It was also agreed that the company would purchase bananas at the market rates of the day, with not less than 20 000 bunches of bananas to be carried on each shipment (West India Committee Circular, 28 May 1900 and Jamaica Annual Colonial Report, 1900–1901, p. 20). It has been stated that, 'All the government officials we had to deal with were more than kind, and we had every possible assistance and information given us in connection with the arrangements for both the ships and the fruit' (Stockley, 1937, p. 44). The Imperial Direct West India Mail Service Company Limited, a sub-sidiary of Elder Dempster, began shipping bananas to the UK under the new agreement in March 1901 (West India Committee Circular, 2 April 1901).

The establishment of the Jamaica–UK banana trade link well illustrates the various and sometimes conflicting position of the different interested parties. Although the British government's role in the creation of such a link in the end proved crucial, it could be argued that the manner in which business was conducted was rather *ad hoc* with little coherence of planning. After the first failure by the Jamaica Fruit and Produce Association, the British government seemed to ignore the procedures it had followed before, particularly the tendering process, and offered terms to Elder, Dempster and Company, that they had refused to give previously. On Jamaica, meanwhile, it is important to recognize the increasing power of banana producers of all sizes over the mercantile class, the increasing importance of the banana in the Jamaican economy, and the growers' need to organize another market for their produce, other than the American one. Indeed, it can be argued that even at this early stage the dynamics of the interest-group relationship that underpinned the Caribbean and UK banana trades for the rest of the century was now in place. The importance of American commercial interests, the role of colonial interests, both in terms of the banana growers and the broader economic considerations, as well as the interests of the UK government itself, were to provide the core of the relationship within the banana trade. However, it is important to recognize that the nature of the interest group relationship at this time had not yet developed the characteristics of a policy community as stipulated by Richardson and Jordan (1979), where a 'regularised and routinised' relationship exists between the actors involved in a particular area of policy. The dynamics of the interest-group relationship within the UK banana trade were still evolving, and the precise circumstances that would eventually lead to the development of a policy community were not yet in place. However, by considering in detail the circumstances that led to the establishment of a policy community, a serious criticism of the group approach can be mitigated. Smith (1992) has argued that 'a policy community seems to be nothing more than a close relationship between an interest group and officials', and as a consequence the definition loses its explanatory power (p. 28). In highlighting the process by which a policy community is established within the context of the UK banana trade, an attempt can be made to differentiate between a close relationship and a policy community, and so address the particular criticism of the group approach.

Despite the agreement on the shipping route, there were some criticisms of the way the UK government had in essence handed the contract to Elder Dempster. The Royal Mail Steam Packet Company, in particular, were aggrieved that the Colonial Office had not approached them about putting in a further bid, but rather went straight to Elder Dempster and agreed a subsidy of £40 000 per year, an amount that was rejected by the government as excessive only a year before (West India Committee Circular, 15 October 1901). It is clear that these arrangements were not made via an open tender, but after the failure of the previous tendering process, the UK government and the Colonial Secretary were keen not to lose further political credibility on the issue, and so re-approached the company with a proven record in shipping bananas. However, even for a company with a proven record the undertaking to ship bananas from Jamaica to the UK was extremely difficult, with the result that Elder Dempster had to fundamentally rationalize the nature of its operations.

Corporate consolidation: Elders and Fyffes and the United Fruit Company

Despite the potential for a growing Jamaican banana trade with the UK, there were a number of constraints. Elder Dempster found that particularly during the summer months when banana prices in the US rose, it was very difficult to procure the necessary quantities of fruit at moderate cost, despite growers being under contract to the company. Further, it was apparent that with Elder Dempster now importing Jamaican bananas into the UK, albeit under difficult circumstances, in addition to the existing supplies from the Canary Islands, at least a further half million bunches of bananas per annum would need to be marketed. Arthur Stockley concluded that what was required was a 'large, integrated, importing, handling and distributing organization' (Davies, 1990, p. 95). The result was a merger between the fruit division of Elder Dempster, and Fyffe, Hudson and Company Limited, a fellow importer of Canary Islands bananas, and in May 1901, the firm Elders and Fyffes Limited was incorporated. The shipping division of Elder Dempster continued to operate as an independent entity, although it did provide much of the shipping capacity for Elders and Fyffes' banana business, operating alongside Elders and Fyffes' own newly developed shipping service.

However, notwithstanding the merger, the United Fruit Company (UFC) still had contracts with the vast majority of the Jamaican growers, which meant that Elders and Fyffes continued to have problems in getting regular supplies of bananas from Jamaica at prices that were acceptable to the UK market. As a consequence the company's capital base was stretched, and by February 1902 Elders and Fyffes was facing a liquidity crisis, with the future of the company under threat. In order to safeguard the company's future, Arthur Stockley attempted to organize a guaranteed supply of bananas from Jamaica. As the UFC was the major banana shipper in Jamaica, Stockley approached the American company for assistance. After discussions between the two parties it was agreed that the UFC would take a 45 per cent share in Elders and Fyffes, and in return provide full cargoes of bananas as required. The signing of the 'American Agreement' in August 1902 finalized the settlement. The opportunity for the UFC to take an interest in a possible rival in Jamaica was readily taken. In principle Elders and Fyffes remained a British entity, but in reality the UFC was involved in the decision-making process at every stage (Davies, 1990, pp. 103–4).

The relationship between the UFC and Elders and Fyffes was extended further when, in 1903, a hurricane destroyed much of Jamaica's banana production. When bananas were scarce in Jamaica, the US took most of them, and to compensate the UFC allowed Elders and Fyffes to ship fruit from its Costa Rican plantations to the UK. As a consequence, the amount of Jamaican bananas entering the UK at this time was relatively small. For example in February 1905, out of a total of 260 000 bunches imported into Britain, only 50 000 came from Jamaica (West India Committee Circular, 28 March 1905). This was a significant moment as bananas from Latin America were now supplying the UK market for the first time, and in later years the respective merits of the Latin America banana as against the Caribbean banana would come to define the nature of the banana trade both in the UK and across Europe. Further, the commercial relationship between the UFC and Elders and Fyffes was highly significant in two respects. First of all, despite the fact that an alternative market for Jamaica bananas was now in existence, the attempt by the UK government, precipitated by concern in Jamaica, to challenge American corporate power had proved unsuccessful, with the balance of power within the Jamaican banana industry fundamentally unchanged. Secondly, the influence of the UFC meant that a significant part of the UK's banana sourcing was now in the hands of 'foreign' interests. Owing to the particular commercial priorities of the UFC, bananas from Jamaica were still being sent to North America in large volumes, while the UK market was beginning to receive bananas from Latin America, a source the UK government had no control over. In essence, therefore, the UK government was beholden to foreign interests both for sustaining a banana export industry in Jamaica, and for the supplying of bananas to the UK from Latin America and the Canary Islands.

A change in political and commercial priorities

After putting so much political capital into the undertaking to establish a UK-based banana-trading link with Jamaica, Joseph Chamberlain was deeply disappointed that Elders and Fyffes was now part owned by the UFC, particularly as half of the 10-year subsidy for the Imperial Direct Line provided by the UK government was now helping to support an American-based company. However, it can be argued that despite Chamberlain's disappointment, there was little else the government could do. Although the government was prepared to provide a 'banana subsidy', it was not prepared to safeguard the independence of Elders and Fyffes by becoming more actively involved in the trade itself. Such a scenario would not only have proven highly costly in direct financial terms, but would have antagonized the UFC, thus perhaps putting at risk the company's entire involvement in Jamaica with serious ramifications for the colony's economic well-being. Nevertheless, by 1905 the idea of 'constructive imperialism' was to lose support with the defeat of the Conservative government at the hands of the Liberal

Party under Campbell-Bannerman at the general election of that year, which meant that concerns over American influence in Jamaica slipped down the political agenda. The new government was relatively relaxed about the role of the UFC in Jamaica, and the increasing volumes of Latin American bananas in the UK market. However, the Liberal government was unable to disregard the legacy of 'constructive imperialism' entirely, as it was obliged to continue payment of the 'banana subsidy' to the Imperial Direct Line until the end of the decade.

In February 1910, towards the end of the contract between the British government and the Imperial Direct West India Mail Service Company Limited, the Crown Agents for the Colonies instigated a new tendering process for the direct steamship service between Jamaica and the UK. The only tender to be received was one from the Imperial Direct Line, which offered to maintain the existing service if the £40 000 per annum subsidy was continued. However, the Colonial Secretary made it clear that the British government would not be justified in asking Parliament to sanction the £20 000 subsidy contribution. In assessing the situation the Colonial Secretary stated that

> The service was originally started as an experiment, and as you can observe, it has shown that a trade in bananas can be carried on between the colony and the UK. To that extent the experiment has been justified by success and has achieved its object. Further, I am glad to recognise that the condition of Jamaica is not now such as to call for exceptional measures. (West India Committee Circular, 30 August 1910)

The authorities in Jamaica were also reluctant to pay their share of the subsidy, and believed that under these circumstances the contract should not be renewed. The Colonial Secretary did not think any steamship company would be willing to undertake the service without such subsidy, and concluded that, 'in these circumstances it is obvious that the renewal of the contract is not practicable' (West India Committee Circular, 30 August 1910).

The exchanges between the UK and Jamaica authorities are significant in that both seem to have been more concerned with the overall economic situation in Jamaica at that time, rather than whether banana shipments from Jamaica to the UK should continue. It is also interesting to note the language used by the Colonial Secretary, suggesting that the shipping link was only an 'experiment' and an 'exceptional measure', rather than how it was originally intended as a serious and long-term attempt to reduce American corporate power on Jamaica. With the ownership of the shipping service now increasingly under American control, and the fact that a majority of bananas from Jamaica were still sent to America, while the UK was being supplied with bananas from Central and South America, there seemed to be little point in continuing the subsidy. In addition, the Liberal government may have been influenced by the opposition of some in the UK fruit trade to the 'banana subsidy' who resented the intrusion of a low-priced fruit in such large amounts (West India Committee Circular, 30 August 1910).

However, despite the ending of the banana subsidy to the Imperial Direct Line, Elders and Fyffes and the UFC not only continued their service, but also extended it, as the overall demand for bananas in the UK was growing, a demand the Canary Islands could not meet. Fruit was brought in from Costa Rica, Colombia, and Jamaica, the vast majority of bananas coming from the former two countries. In 1913, 6 713 000 bunches of bananas were imported into the UK from all sources. The number of bunches imported into the UK from Jamaica in that year, however, was only 584 000, making up 8.7 per cent of the total (West India Committee Circular, 1 July 1926). Also in 1913, the inevitable happened when Elders and Fyffes became a completely owned subsidiary of the UFC, although the UFC agreed in principle that its subsidiary would retain some degree of operational independence.

The differences in approach between the Conservative and Liberal governments regarding the concept of 'constructive imperialism' should be recognized. The Conservatives seemed to be much more proactive in terms of colonial relations, and were prepared to support attempts to undermine American corporate power on Jamaica, while the Liberals seemed less inclined to act in this way. However, it can be argued that once the UFC had taken an interest in Elders and Fyffes, the scope for government action was in reality constrained, as both the Liberal and Conservative administrations were unprepared to interfere directly with the commercial aspects of the trade. There was an acceptance within government circles of American corporate influence in determining the destination of banana exports from Jamaica, and the origin of banana imports into the UK. However, it has been argued that the ambivalence on the part of the UK authorities meant that the UFC was able 'to expand and to stretch its tentacles over [Jamaica] mainly on account of a policy of indifference on the part of past governmental administrations in the colony [by the] failure on the part of the Government to curb the monopolistic aspirations of the United Fruit Company' (Parker, 1925, p. 6).

The First World War: a time of retrenchment

During the first two years of war, the Liberal and Coalition governments, both headed by Asquith, were disinclined to impose
significant controls on foreign trade, believing that the war effort
could be run by private enterprise, thus allowing Britain's banana
trade to continue at an acceptable level, despite the fact that enemy
action was taking its toll on UK shipping. In 1915, 8 143 092
bunches of bananas were imported, of which 2 828 454 came from
the Canary Islands, 2 790 559 from Costa Rica, 2 067 392 from
Colombia, and only 455 927 bunches from the British West Indies,
thus sustaining the pattern of trade in the immediate pre-war years.
The total imports in 1914 had been 9 007 001 bunches (West India
Committee Circular, 24 August 1916). The majority of the bananas
imported during this time were under the auspices of Elders and
Fyffes who in 1914 handled more than 90 per cent of the bananas
that were imported (Davies, 1990, p. 129).

In Jamaica meanwhile, the banana trade was suffering on three
fronts, from the effect of drought, hurricanes and war. At a meeting
held between a number of growers and the Governor of Jamaica to
discuss the situation in August 1916, 'it was pointed out that the
banana industry, the staple industry of the island, was in a very grave
position'. The situation was not helped by considerable grower dissatisfaction over the shipping arrangements of Elders and Fyffes. The
Jamaica banana growers were upset that most of the company's
bananas for the UK market were coming from Costa Rica, and its ships
were bypassing Jamaica. However, because Jamaican production levels
were so low, the Governor of Jamaica stated, 'the necessity for shipping
no longer exists'. After consultation with the Board of Trade and Elders
and Fyffes, the Colonial Secretary at that time, Bonar Law, stated that
he was generally satisfied with Elders and Fyffes' shipping policy (West
India Committee Circular, 7 September 1916).

The government had little choice but to accept Elders and Fyffes'
policy, as the company had in reality little room for manoeuvre as
the government was now using the great majority of Elders and
Fyffes' shipping capacity for other purposes. Indeed, from a fleet of
22 at the beginning of the war, only one Elders and Fyffes vessel was
being used for company business at the war's conclusion (Parsons,
1988, p. 23 and Beaver, 1976. p. 58). The continuing pressure on
resources meant that by the beginning of 1917, the British government decided, albeit reluctantly, to introduce a system of import

licensing to conserve foreign exchange and shipping. As a consequence, the exportation of bananas from Costa Rica was halted, and with Canary Islands imports having been terminated in December 1916, the supply of bananas to the UK fell dramatically. For example, during 1918 only 816 938 bunches of bananas were imported into the UK (West India Committee Circular, 5 January 1922). The decision to end the importation of Costa Rican bananas was significant in that it was the first example of government action to control the importation of certain sources of bananas, while allowing other sources continued entry. Such action was to form the basis of the UK's banana import policy during the early part of the Second World War, when government controls were imposed from the outset.

After the ending of hostilities the UK government quickly abolished its wartime controls, and Elders and Fyffes began to increase its banana imports to the UK. Despite, the problems that Jamaica had experienced during the war, there was enough of a production base for shipments to the UK to be resumed on a regular basis. In 1919 Jamaica was able to contribute 37 100 tons of the 65 600 tons which were imported into the UK that year (Black, 1987, p. 107). The attempt to restore Canary Islands banana exports to their pre-war level proved to be more difficult. This added to the limited quantities of bananas available in Jamaica, meant that supplies from Central America were again necessary. However, shipments from Central America were only partially successful, owing to the lack of suitable specialized shipping. It was not until December 1920 that bananas from Costa Rica were again imported into the UK (West India Committee Circular, 6 January 1921). When Central American imports began to increase, together with a new source of cheap bananas from Brazil, the relative importance of Jamaica's banana imports in the UK declined to its pre-war levels, with a market share of around 15 to 20 per cent during the 1920s (Black, 1987, p. 107). Despite the upheaval particularly during the latter part of the First World War, the nature of the UK banana trade quickly resumed its pre-war state when hostilities ended. The dominance of American corporate interests continued, and the pattern of trade with the majority of bananas from Jamaica being sent to the US, while the UK market was supplied with bananas from Latin America was sustained. However, over the next decade the status quo was to be challenged by a number of important developments, which altered the nature of the trade, though not the interest-group dynamic underpinning it.

The push for a new approach: the Imperial Economic Committee and further challenges to American corporate power

Despite Elders and Fyffes' attempts to recover lost ground, there was residual bad feeling in Jamaica because of the company's perceived poor shipping service during the war. As a consequence, the Jamaica Imperial Association began to consider how the dependence on American companies (the UFC, as well as the smaller Atlantic Fruit Company) for the shipment of Jamaican bananas and other fruit could be challenged. The first successful attempt to provide competition by a Jamaican company came in September 1919, when the Jamaica Fruit and Shipping Company was formed, making independent shipments of bananas to the US. Although this was only made possible with the aid of the Di Giorgio Fruit Corporation, an American shipping concern. Nevertheless, the 1920s were to see an emergence of a degree of competition, which led to prices for the growers rising to a more acceptable level. It was noted that, 'with the advent of trade competition in the buying of bananas, the prices have been raised to a fairer standard and the growers consequently have been encouraged to cultivate their fruit' (West India Committee Circular, 11 November 1920). Even though the establishment of the Jamaican Fruit and Shipping Company did not affect who imported bananas into the UK, it was important as an indication of a developing challenge to American influence in the Jamaican banana business. However, the colonial authorities were still reluctant to support private attempts to reduce American corporate power, although this apathy began to change with the work of the Imperial Economic Committee.

The Imperial Economic Committee Report of 1926

The Imperial Economic Committee was established by the short-lived Labour goverment of 1924, headed by Ramsay MacDonald, which was sympathetic to Colonial demands that access to UK markets should be improved. The terms of reference for the Imperial Economic Committee were

> To consider the possibility of improving the methods of preparing for market and marketing within the UK the food products of the overseas parts of the Empire with a view to increasing the consumption of such products in the UK in preference to imports from foreign countries, and to promote the interests both of producers and consumers. (First Report General, 1925, p. 2)

The Committee considered the situation for meat and fruit and within the fruit report there was a section on the banana. The Committee assessed the banana issue in some detail, and made a number of observations that helped to set the context for the formation of a growers' co-operative in Jamaica, and for changes in the banana supply situation for the UK market. In general terms the Committee commented 'the banana trade has drifted into certain channels not wholly advantageous to the Empire. British [that is Jamaican] supplies are sent largely to foreign markets, and so far as they are consigned to the UK, are subject to foreign control' (Third Report Fruit, 1926, p. 242). While the Committee also noted that 'the UK market is almost entirely dependent upon foreign supplies, over 84 per cent at present being obtained from the Canary Islands and from Central America and Colombia' (Third Report Fruit, 1926, p. 242).

The Committee accepted 'that the Jamaican producers suffer from an undoubted disability in the fact that they are unable to ship their fruit by a "free" line to the UK for marketing through independent channels'. However, the Committee recognized that 'the development of the banana trade in Jamaica has been largely due to the efforts of the United Fruit Company ...'. The Committee also gave credit to the UFC for the benefits it had brought to Jamaica and the generally good way the company was conducting its affairs on the island (Third Report Fruit, 1926, pp. 249–50). Nevertheless, the Committee stated 'the main aim of the Jamaican producer is an alternative means of access to the UK market. But no shipping service can subsist on the export of bananas from Jamaica alone without an undue commercial risk' (Third Report Fruit, 1926, p. 45). The Committee believed that a complementary source of bananas would be needed to make the shipping of fruit from Jamaica to the UK viable. The islands of St Lucia and Grenada were judged as possibilities (Third Report Fruit, 1926, p. 46). The Committee considered the option of starting an independent service relying on Jamaica alone, but believed that this was 'primarily a matter for Jamaica to consider' (Third Report Fruit, 1926, p. 255). The Committee also provided strong support for the concept of growers' organizations, both in terms of organizing production and marketing of their produce. The Committee suggested that grants of £1200 a year for a period of two years could be given to approved organizations of banana growers (Third Report Fruit, 1926, pp. 28 and 265).

However, the Imperial Economic Committee report was not uncontroversial. Arthur Stockley of Elders and Fyffes was strongly opposed to the Committee's suggestions, arguing that the geographical position of

Jamaica would prevent the island from supplying significant quantities of bananas to the UK market (Jamaican Banana Producers' Association Dossier, Chapter C, p. 25). Further, it was threatened that if the suggestions of the Committee were to be acted upon, the development of a banana export trade on the Gold Coast (Ghana) by the UFC, something that was considered desirable by the UK government would not be enacted (Jamaican Banana Producers' Association Dossier, Chapter D, p. 39). The tactic on the part of the UFC to threaten either to pull out of a country, or to develop a new source of supply elsewhere was something it used to resist changes that were perceived to go against its interests. In a time before 'globalization', companies like the UFC were able to shape the policy process by threatening to transfer their investments elsewhere, overriding any concerns states might have had over the companies' investment policies.

The Imperial Economic Committee report was the first official investigation into the interests involved in the Jamaica trade since its inception at the beginning of the century, and highlighted concerns both over the role of American interests dominating the banana industry in a British colony, and the nature of banana sourcing for the UK market. However, despite the Committee's comments and recommendations, together with those of the Empire Marketing Board, established to implement the recommendations of the Imperial Economic Committee, little immediate action was taken. The new Conservative government was divided over the merits of preferential trade, and was reluctant to commit itself to any major changes as suggested by the Imperial Economic Committee as they pertained to the banana trade. The government was more concerned that a banana trade in Jamaica was providing a living for a number of its citizens, than where the bananas were being shipped to, and by whom. However, notwithstanding the divisions within the UK government and the opposition of the UFC domestic pressures within Jamaica were once again to provide the impetus in challenging American corporate power on the island.

The establishment of the Jamaica Banana Producers' Association

While the Imperial Economic Committee was conducting its investigation, there was a growing level of support amongst all sections of Jamaican society for producer co-operatives in general, and for a banana co-operative in particular. This was reflected not only among farmers but also among professionals and traders. Even growers who remained loyal to the UFC wanted to see a co-operative in operation to give the buying market a competitive edge. In official circles as well, there was a strong demand that the Jamaican government should lend its help against the foreign banana firms. The Governor of Jamaica, Sir Edward Stubbs became an advocate of the new movement, and urged the Colonial Secretary, Arthur Jelf, to support the undertaking. A preliminary, unofficial visit to the UK in June 1926 by F.H. Robertson, General Manager of the Jamaica Producers' Association, was undertaken to investigate the market situation in the UK, and to make representations to the British government. Once Robertson had returned to Jamaica, W. Coke-Kerr, President of the Jamaica Producers' Association began a correspondence with the Colonial Secretary in the autumn of 1926, regarding the establishment of a 'Cooperative Marketing Organisation for the Producers of Jamaica Bananas' (Black, 1984, pp. 21–6). The Colonial Secretary, acknowledging the Governor of Jamaica's view and the commitment on the part of the growers, was generally in favour of such an undertaking, but demanded certain clarifications and reassurances, particularly over the contracting of growers and the provision of shipping.

Despite the fact that a number of problems still had to be overcome, the embryonic Jamaican Banana Producers' Association had done enough to persuade the authorities that it was serious about its undertaking to export bananas from the island. In a letter, dated the 26 August 1927, to the Manager of the Association, the Colonial Secretary, after consultations with the Governor of Jamaica and the Attorney General, gave the necessary clearance for the registering of the company, and confirmed that the Governor would be prepared to support the scheme if sufficient crop contracts were obtained to guarantee a viable freight operation (Jamaican Banana Producers' Association Dossier, Appendix E, p. 86). It was also decided that a second source of supply would not be necessary, despite the recommendations of the Imperial Economic Committee (Black, 1984, pp. 29 and 31 and Third Report Fruit, 1926, p. 46). The decision not to develop an additional source of supply is significant, as it suggests that there was confidence on the part of those involved in establishing the co-operative, that they could organize a sufficient supply of bananas from Jamaica to sustain their undertaking. This was despite the fact that the UFC still dominated the trade in Jamaica, and had used its position to undermine the viability of Elders and Fyffes at the turn of the century. In addition, it would seem that the colonial authorities were not too concerned about developing a banana export trade on St Lucia and Grenada, which may have provided the opportunity for economic improvement on the islands in question.

The primary concern now for the newly established Association was the organization of shipping. The estimated cost for the establishment of a direct shipping line between Jamaica and the UK was in the region of one million pounds. The UK government was asked to guarantee the repayment of the total amount, but this was rejected. This was a blow to the Association, as control of both shipping and marketing was an essential element in their independence (Black, 1984, pp. 24 and 44). In order to overcome the impasse, the Association was obliged to link up with the Di Giorgio Fruit Corporation, which had been involved in Jamaica for some time. However it was reported, 'His Excellency the Governor has taken such a strong line throughout on the matter that it seems fairly safe to say that the decision of the Association does not count unless it happens to agree with that of the Government' (West India Committee Circular, 9 February 1928). Such demands by the Governor were necessary for he had to convince his Privy Council and the Jamaican Legislative Council that government aid was necessary and that the venture would be successful. When a modified scheme was put forward which required less capital than the previous estimate, the Governor approved it. At a meeting of the Jamaica Banana Producers' Association explaining developments, Charles Johnston stated that the Governor 'had done yeoman service to the Association' (*Daily Gleaner*, 16 March 1929). The role of the Governor in this process was vitally important, in that he was able to bring together the different interests involved without compromising his own position. Without such coordination, the process of accommodation between the various actors would have been much more unwieldy, and the chances of failure that much higher.

With the amount of capital reduced from previous expectations it was necessary to cut costs to a minimum, so four old meat carriers were purchased and reconditioned for the carrying of bananas. These were controlled by the Jamaica Direct Fruit Line Limited, the shipping arm of Di Giorgio and the Association (West India Committee Circular, 29 November 1928). Further ships were added to the fleet in 1931, this time under direct control of the Association, after financing had been raised from a number of sources including the Colonial Development Fund (Jamaica Banana Commission, 1936, p. 31). In terms of the distribution of bananas, the Jamaica Producers' Marketing Company Limited arranged to sell both the Association's and Di Giorgio's fruit in Europe. The shipping of bananas to the US was provided under a separate agreement with the Di Giorgio Fruit Corporation, while the Canadian National Steamship Company (whose parent company was ironically the UFC) transported bananas to Canada under a reciprocal trade agreement Canada had signed with Jamaica. Once the scheme had been approved, two pieces of legislation were passed to give the Association an institutional and financial framework in which to operate. The Association had made representations to the Government of Jamaica that such legislation was necessary to make sure the contracts would be adhered to, and that those contracted bananas could not be purchased by the other banana companies (Jamaican Banana Producers' Association Dossier, Chapter C, pp. 27–8; Kepner and Soothill, 1963, pp. 296–7; *Daily Gleaner*, 16 March 1929; and West India Committee Circular, 10 January 1929). Although, there were strong hopes that the Association would be a success, the memories of past failures were not forgotten. The short-lived independence of Elders and Fyffes was due to the UFC being able to purchase the majority of the bananas grown on Jamaica, and it was thought legislation would help provide the Association with the necessary security of supply if any challenge from the UFC was forthcoming.

Elders and Fyffes was rather surprised by what had taken place, and A.R. Ackerley, then Managing Director stated, 'The scheme was never expected to materialise. We have always been assured by the Colonial Office that no financial support of the character asked for would be given' (Black, 1984, p. 41). It is important to highlight the fact, that even though the UFC was a powerful force in Jamaica, the colonial authorities were not beholden to it. When a viable scheme was formulated by an influential section of Jamaican society, the colonial authorities knew where their loyalties lay, and acted accordingly. Although, it can be said that the colonial authorities were careful not to provide the UFC with any hostages to fortune, so kept the negotiations with the Jamaica Banana Producers' Association relatively discreet.

Once an agreement had been finalized Di Giorgio, according to the *Gleaner* of the 7 February, when asked how the contract would affect the UFC, replied, 'We don't want to see everyone promptly signing up with the Association, and keeping away from the United Fruit Company. We want the United Fruit Company to take their share of the fruit and for a spirit of give and take to exist. If the United are forced to plant it might lead to over-production and that may mean suicide for all of us. I hope a sensible view will be taken on this matter' (West India Committee Circular, 8 March 1928). Di Giorgio was well aware of the power of the UFC, so cooperation, rather than competition seemed to be the best form of survival. The aim of the Association in partnership with Di Giorgio was to develop a viable interest in the banana export trade of Jamaica, not to usurp the position of the UFC.

It was feared that if the UFC was to react in a negative manner, the whole fabric of the industry might be put at risk, damaging the interests of both the growers and the marketing companies.

The first shipment of bananas to the UK by the Jamaica Banana Producers' Association came on 6 May 1929. In response to the Association's early shipments, Elders and Fyffes issued a letter to the trade which stated, 'It is hardly necessary for us to remind you that we have this week imported into England over 4 times more Empire bananas than all other Banana Importers combined. We think that it should be generally known that the importation of Empire bananas into England is nothing new. Empire bananas have been carried by us for years in British ships, and these bananas are handled by a British organisation' (West India Committee Circular, 16 May 1929). It seems apparent from this extract that Elders and Fyffes was somewhat exasperated by the publicity around the new company, and the fact that Elders and Fyffes' 'Britishness' was being questioned. It is interesting that Elders and Fyffes should be thinking in these terms, as it indicates that the nature of ownership was once more an important issue within the context of the Caribbean banana trade.

With the Jamaica Banana Producers' Association making regular shipments, growers that were not associated with the company became more interested in its operation. In the period from April to September 1929 nearly two thousand farmers were added to the membership roll, making the total number close to 11 000 members (West India Committee Circular, 3 October 1929). By the end of the year the Association had shipped 4 083 000 stems of bananas, equivalent to 21.7 per cent of Jamaica's output. In the 12 months of 1932 out of a total of 20 270 000 stems shipped from the Islands the Association supplied 6 351 000 stems (Jamaican Banana Producers' Association Dossier, Chapter C, p. 30 and Jamaica Banana Commission, 1936, p. 9).

The establishment of the Jamaica Banana Producers' Association can be seen within the context of previous developments in the Jamaica banana trade. Even though the UK government did provide some financial aid to the new organisation, its action could in no way be seen as benevolent. As in the past, the demand for help came from within the island itself, and only then did the government countenance assistance. However, it took the involvement of a well-established American company to safeguard the growers undertaking before UK government assistance was forthcoming. The UK government continued to be more concerned with the sustainability of the

Jamaica banana trade itself rather than the mechanics by which the trade was undertaken, although the government did respond to the political demands for action from the colony when the necessity arose. The establishment of the Jamaica Banana Producers' Association was important as it broadened the nature of the interest group dynamic within the Caribbean and UK banana trades, as there was now a company that was once again attempting to co-exist with the established American commercial interests on Jamaica. The fundamentals of the interest group relationship between the UK government, the companies, and the growers continued to be on an *ad hoc* basis, but there was now a new set of interests in the relationship with its own particular concerns and priorities which had to be accommodated within the pre-existing interest-group dynamic.

Economic difficulties for the UK and the introduction of preferential access for colonial banana producers

By the end of the 1920s, the UK economy was in a bad way; a worsening recession and high unemployment typified the extent to which the UK's world trading performance had declined. In addition the worsening balance of payments situation meant that the UK government was forced to institute a number of dramatic policy changes. These included the withdrawal from the 'Gold Standard' and changes to the long held 'Free Trade' policy that had underpinned British overseas trade for three generations. However, as Grove argues the changes made were not to protect domestic manufacturers against foreign competition, 'but because it was necessary to safeguard the balance of payments and teach Britain to "live within her means"' (Grove, 1962, p. 45). When Ramsay MacDonald's National Government was returned to office in August 1931, there was a large protectionist majority, and even some of the most prominent supporters of free trade were calling for a protective tariff (Grove, 1962, p. 45). As a consequence, in February 1932 the Import Duties Act was passed which imposed a general tariff of 10 per cent on virtually all foreign imports, although exemptions for goods from the British Empire were granted (see Law Reports 1932, the General Public Acts, pp. 21–43), exemptions that were consolidated at the Ottawa Conference later in the year, involving countries under or formerly under British rule.

Under the Import Duties Act an *ad valorem* duty of £2 10s a ton on foreign bananas was introduced. The banana duty was to prove highly significant in the context of the history of the Caribbean and UK banana trades, as bananas from Jamaica now had an advantage over imports from other countries. Bananas from the Canary Islands, Honduras, Brazil, Costa Rica, Panama, and Colombia were now subject to the duty, while Jamaica bananas were not. The effects of the duty were felt immediately, as in March 1932, compared to the same month a year earlier, banana imports into the UK from Jamaica increased from 364 000 bunches to 786 000 bunches. Conversely, imports from Costa Rica and Colombia fell from 163 000 bunches and 259 000 bunches respectively in March 1931 to virtually nothing in March 1932 (West India Committee Circular, 4 August 1932). This trend continued with bananas from Jamaica taking an increasing share of the market at the expense of supplies from Costa Rica and Colombia in particular, and by 1937 Jamaica was satisfying almost 90 per cent of Britain's requirements (Jamaica Banana Commission, 1936, p. 2 and Black, 1984, p. 107).

The imposition of preferential access under the aegis of Imperial Preference was to prove all-important in transforming the nature of the Caribbean and UK banana trades. Prior to the Import Duties Act the majority of bananas supplying the UK market came from Central and South America, a situation that the Imperial Economic Committee had been concerned about as far back as 1926. However, from March 1932 the banana-supplying companies, and Elders and Fyffes in particular, had no choice but to rearrange their services, and to increase the supply of Jamaica bananas that went to the UK market. More fundamentally, the concept of preferential access would underpin the structure of the UK banana market for the following seven decades. However, it is important to recognize that such a fundamental change in the structure of the trade had little to do with colonial responsibility and much more to do with safeguarding the rather narrow economic interests of the UK itself. Although it should be recognized that the move towards a more protectionist form of trade would not have occurred had the international trading environment been more secure. As Grove argues, 'the departure from free trade in 1932 has been called a stroke of fate rather than an act of policy' (1962, p. 45).

The government appreciated the potential of the situation when it came, but it can be argued that up to a few months before, such a restructuring of the UK banana market would not have been considered despite the benefits of such a change as highlighted by the Imperial Economic Committee. The Committee's suggestion, therefore, came into being more through eventuality than design. Nevertheless, notwithstanding the motivations, the UK banana market was by the end of the 1930s almost totally supplied from a colonial source. For the first time, UK demand and colonial supply were in concert with one another, a situation that was to continue for almost another 50 years. It is also interesting to note that despite the change in the banana sourcing for the UK, the nature of the interest group relationship that had developed prior to the imposition of Imperial Preference was not fundamentally altered, as the banana growing and shipping interests were able to adapt to the new circumstances and re-focus their commercial operations.

The threat to market competition and the need for UK government action

Despite the tariffication changes which in fact did not affect production totals, just the destination of them, the Jamaica Banana Producers' Association's position was becoming increasingly insecure by the early 1930s. There was a hurricane in Jamaica during November 1932, a drought in the spring of 1933 and floods and storms from August to October 1933. The situation was exacerbated by the existence of both Panama disease and leaf spot disease, which badly hit production, with the quantity and quality of the fruit suffering. The effect was that the freight rate per count bunch of bananas (a stem with nine or more marketable hands) for the Association was much higher than normal, and with banana prices generally lower than in the past because of the difficulties in the international economy, the Jamaica Banana Producers' Association's financial base was weakened. It was at this point that the UFC and the Standard Fruit Company (the successor of the Atlantic Fruit Company) made a determined attempt to put the Association out of business by offering higher prices to the growers than the co-operative could afford, and the world market price justified. The two American-based companies had the ability to do this because they sourced bananas from a range of countries and what they lost on the sale of Jamaican bananas could be clawed back by dealing in bananas from other sources. The Association, with its relatively small capital base, depending solely on Jamaican bananas was unable to follow suit (Black, 1984, p. 77 and *Daily Gleaner*, 18 July 1935). Further, the laws that had been introduced to help safeguard the market position of the Association were not rigorous enough to prevent the two American companies from undermining the Association's viability.

From 1933, large quantities of bananas grown by members of the Association, and which should have been delivered to the Association's agents, were instead diverted to the United Fruit and Standard Fruit companies. It was noted, 'disloyalty in this direction on the part of a member is a definite blow to the interests of every other member of the Association' (West India Committee Circular, 28 March 1935). The amount of bananas handled by the Association as a percentage of the total exports of Jamaica fell in the early to middle years of the 1930s. In 1931 the figure was 32 per cent, but by 1934, even though the Association had contracted additional land, the Association's percentage share of Jamaica's banana output had fallen to 19.6 per cent (Jamaican Banana Producers' Association Dossier, Chapter C, p. 30 and West India Committee Circular, 15 August 1935). Such a reduction prevented the Association from obtaining sufficiently large cargoes to allow for the efficient transportation and marketing of bananas.

The poor trading situation was exacerbated in March 1935, when the Jamaica Banana Producers' Association terminated the agreement with the Di Giorgio Fruit Corporation (now under the control of the rival Standard Fruit Company) (West India Committee Circular, 28 March 1935). Without Di Giorgio's contribution to the cargo the Association had to produce enough bananas to fill the ships completely. In addition, the Association had to make arrangements for the disposal of fruit independently from Di Giorgio. (The relationship with the Canadian National Steamship Company was also dissolved at this time.) In an attempt to mitigate the difficulties, the Association signed an agreement with the Afrikanische Fruit Company to market Cameroon bananas in the UK (Jamaica Banana Commission, 1936, p. 67). However, the union was unable to stop the rival banana companies from exploiting the Association's weakness.

The two American companies hoped that the Association would either be forced to arrange other costly shipping arrangements, or that it would have to reduce its involvement in its traditional markets. It can be argued that the motivations and conduct of the American commercial interests have parallels with the situation at the turn of the century with Elders and Fyffes, in that an attempt was made to undermine an independent competitor through the imposition of severe market pressures. However, on this occasion the colonial interests had learnt from past experience, and as a consequence acted more precipitously to defend their position against the powerful American-owned companies.

The Jamaica Banana Commission and the securing of market accommodation

With the situation as it was, the Association approached the Governor of Jamaica, Sir Edward Denham, for assistance, believing that it was in the government's interest to safeguard the Association from unfair competition (West India Committee Circular, 9 May 1935). As R.F. Williams, the Jamaican Banana Growers' Association's assistant manager argued, 'if conditions were permitted to continue as they were, it would have been merely a matter of time for the entire operations of the Association to have been crippled and the Association annihilated owing to bananas contracted to it having been disposed of otherwise' (West India Committee Circular, 4 July 1935). The demands for action strengthened after one of the largest ever meetings to be held in Kingston, on 18 July 1935, gave over-whelming support for the Jamaica Banana Producers' Association to continue operating. Those at the meeting also demanded that an investigation should be undertaken to assess the industry in all of its aspects. In late September, reacting to the ground-swell of opinion, the Governor of Jamaica persuaded the Colonial Secretary to estab-lish an enquiry to investigate the workings of the Jamaica Banana Producers' Association, and the question of co-operative marketing (*Daily Gleaner*, 19 July 1935; West India Committee Circulars, 15 August 1935, 10 October 1935, and 24 October 1935). It can be argued that the UK government did not want another attempt to challenge American corporate dominance on the island to be emas-culated, particularly within the new trading circumstances of Imperial Preference. The government had learnt its lesson with Elders and Fyffes, and now acted more forcibly to safeguard the Jamaica Banana Producers' Association's viability.

In response to these moves the UFC attempted to both reassure its existing banana growers and attract new converts. The general manager of the Jamaica division, J.G. Kieffer, stated

> During the last few months opinions have been freely expressed to the effect that, in certain eventualities, banana growers in Jamaica would in future years receive ridiculously low prices for their fruit. These expressions bear the impress of absurd propaganda, with which we are not concerned. We wish to assure our contractors that … we will continue to pay the highest possible price for their fruit. (West India Committee Circular, 7 November 1935)

Kieffer also made clear that the company would be prepared to con-sider entering into 10-year contracts with the growers. It is apparent that the UFC was making every attempt to pre-empt what any inquiry might have to say about them, by making great efforts to reassure the growers, and indirectly the colonial authorities, that future terms and conditions of producing bananas on Jamaica would not be detrimentally affected if the Jamaica Banana Producers' Association was to lose its place in the market.

The Banana Commission was established on 28 November 1935, with the terms of reference

> To undertake a general investigation into the banana industry in Jamaica and into the marketing of Jamaica bananas both in the Colony and elsewhere, taking special account of the position of the Jamaica Banana Producers' Association and the desirability of promoting cooperation in the industry; and to report to the Governor by what measures the interests of the industry as a whole can best be fostered in the future. (Jamaica Banana Commission, 1936, p. iii)

The Commission started preliminary work at the beginning of December 1935 in London, and left for Jamaica on 31 December (Jamaica Banana Commission, 1936, p. 42). Despite the background to the dispute the Commission believed that an agreement would benefit the UFC, in that the 'present condition of friction and enmity' would end; that the UFC would be seen by both Jamaica and the UK government as being responsive to their wishes; that the UFC would avoid the imposition of a solution; that the scope of the Association's operations would be limited; and more generally that the image of the UFC in other countries might be enhanced (Jamaica Banana Commission, 1936, pp. 47–8).

Indeed, even before the report was presented to the Governor of Jamaica on 23 May 1936, unofficial negotiations were under way between the Commission and the UFC in particular, attempting to find a solution to the problems, which in turn helped to shape the Commission's own proposals (Jamaica Annual Colonial Report, 1936, p. 15). As the Commission stated, 'it would be of little service to put forward recommendations dependent upon voluntary agreements without ascertaining in advance if these agreements were likely to be acceptable to the parties concerned' (Jamaica Banana Commission, 1936, p. 50). The Commissioners were reluctant for a solution to be imposed as they suggested that 'if ever there was a situation calling for a voluntary solution with reasonable participation by each party in the trade, and coordination instead of competition in the selling markets it is this one' (Jamaica Banana Commission, 1936, p. 54).

The Commission approached Sam Zemurray, President of the UFC to consider the provisional proposals, but Zemurray stated that no agreement could be made with a co-operative society, which the Jamaica Banana Producers' Association was at the time, which he thought was 'a form of trading that was opposed to their own interest' (Jamaica Banana Commission, 1936, p. 47). The UFC demanded that the Jamaica Banana Producers' Association should be reconstituted as a trading company, a change accepted by the Association, in the hope that a degree of stability would return to the trade (Jamaica Banana Commission, 1936, pp. 50–1). An agreement was then finalized during the summer of 1936, the provisions of which helped to stabilize the banana industry in Jamaica until the outbreak of the Second World War.

In the agreement, the Jamaica Banana Producers' Association undertook to stop exporting bananas to the US and Canada, and to restrict its marketing operations to the UK and Continental Europe. There was also an undertaking that every company with an interest in Jamaican bananas would pay growers the same price per count bunch. Further, the UFC agreed to sell bananas to the Association to make up for any shortfall in their supply, while during periods of high banana production the UFC agreed to purchase all the Association's excess bananas at dockside (Jamaica Banana Commission, 1936, pp. 47–54. See also CO 852/31/8 and CO 852/31/10). In a vivid metaphor, Zemurray stated, 'communists and capitalists were no longer sitting around the same table', the communists being the Association in its co-operative form (A. Hart, 1954, p. 222).

The dynamics of the Banana Commission was one of delicate positioning of interests, with the colonial authorities once again only acting when there was sufficient pressure to do so. The position of the Jamaica Banana Growers' Association was under serious threat, and there was a possibility that the Association would follow the path of Elders and Fyffes 30 years earlier, by being subsumed by more powerful American corporate interests. However, the attempts to safeguard the future of the Association proved to be more successful the second time around, both because of the aforementioned historical legacy, and the fact that as Jamaica was now the UK's main source of bananas the government was keen for a colonial interest to be retained in the endeavour. Despite the seriousness of the dispute, none of the actors involved took their positions beyond the point of no return. There was recognition that if the situation had escalated further all of the actors' interests may have been damaged. The eventual agreement between the UFC and the Jamaica Banana Producers' Association was fairly successful in providing an accommodation between the commercial priorities of the American-based interests, and the requirements for an adequate return on bananas grown in Jamaica on the part of the colonial interests.

Chapter conclusion

The issues of foreign dependency, monopoly power, and colonial responsibility underpinned the interest group dynamic at this time. There were two separate policy issues that were important, that of the control of banana exports from Jamaica, and their destination. With regard to the former, action was only taken to address the issue of American corporate control when there was significant colonial pressure on the UK authorities to do so, which meant that the issue was never dealt with in a coordinated manner, and so the UFC, in the guise of Elders and Fyffes, was able to retain its dominant position in supplying bananas to the UK. The interest-group dynamic at this time had certain characteristics of the group approach, such as the role of personal networks (Baggott, 1995); the need of groups to consult over specific, technical, complex, and managerial decisions (Richardson and Jordan, 1979); and the ability of groups to retain policies that are beneficial to them (Bachrach and Baratz, 1970; Crenson, 1971; Rose, 1976). However, the relationship between the actors was based on *ad hoc* arrangements. When problems within the banana sector came to the fore, attempts were made to address them, albeit with varying degrees of success. However, there was no desire at this time to 'regularise and routinise' the relationship in a policy community, as there was an underlying belief that in general the banana trade was operating successfully, and should be left to its own devices whenever possible.

The second policy strand was the origin of the UK's banana imports, and it is interesting to note that change was only forthcoming when the UK itself was experiencing acute economic problems, having little to do with colonial needs. The decision to introduce Imperial Preference meant that preferential access was now afforded to colonial, which meant at this time, Jamaican banana imports, and such a system of preferential access remained the central defining element of the UK banana trade until the end of the twentieth century. Although, there was a change in banana sourcing, the interest group dynamic remained fundamentally unaltered, as the com-

mercial interests were able to re-adjust their operations to accommodate the new market circumstances. However, throughout, this early
period there was a trade-off between colonial necessity and the need
for commercial freedom, in order that a viable large-scale banana
export trade could be established and sustained, even during the
period of the First World War.

3

The Second World War and its Aftermath: Political Control and Corporate Adjustment

The first year of war: government action and corporate sensitivity

Even before the outbreak of hostilities on 3 September 1939, the UK government set out clearly and forcibly how future-trading arrangements would be conducted. On 1 September 1939, the President of the Board of Trade, Oliver Stanley, introduced the Imports, Export and Customs Powers (Defence) Bill to the House of Commons. The Bill was to provide the Board of Trade with the power to regulate imports and exports. While introducing the Bill, the President of the Board of Trade made it clear why such a piece of legislation was necessary,

> No one, I think, can question the great necessity in war-time for the most rigid control of both exports and imports, of exports from the point of view of conserving our own resources, and imports from the point of view of seeing that only those goods which are vitally necessary for the national emergency should either occupy our shipping space or be a call on our foreign exchange. (Hansard, 1 September 1939, columns 171–5 and for Royal Assent see Hansard, 2 September 1939, column 220)

The provisions of the resulting Act, and the intentions of the President of the Board of Trade meant that the UK government was to have a much more interventionist role in the supply of bananas to the UK than it ever had in the past, including during the First World War.

However, the UK authorities were keen to reassure Jamaica in particular, that for the time being banana imports would continue as close to pre-war levels as possible (MAF 86/149). Even though organizing the war effort took precedence, the UK government had no choice but to recognize its colonial responsibilities. Since the imposition of Imperial Preference in 1932, the main market for Jamaican bananas had been the UK, and as the crop was so important to the colony, the authorities appreciated the need to sustain that form of economic activity for as long as possible. In addition, by maintaining such a trading link, the colonial authorities were giving themselves sufficient time to design contingency measures that would compensate Jamaica if the occasion arose when the importation of bananas was no longer feasible.

Despite the undertakings to sustain the trade, banana exports from Jamaica were in decline, with the growing threat to shipping from the German navy and the effect of hurricane damage on the island both taking their toll. Jamaican banana imports to the UK declined from 102 050 tons during the period September 1938 to February 1939 to 70 450 tons for the corresponding period ending February 1940. The Jamaican deficiency was largely made up with bananas from Cameroon, whose imports increased from 4 650 tons to 27 350 tons over the same period (MAF 86/149). Further, the UK received bananas from Brazil, the Canary Islands, and Colombia (MAF 86/149). As a consequence of the additional supplies 1939 was a near normal trading year, although the overall trading environment was becoming increasingly difficult.

A further reason why banana imports continued at relatively high levels in the first months of war was due to the belief on the part of the UK government that banana boats were too difficult to use for other purposes. In an internal Ministry of Food memorandum, it was suggested that the Ministry of Shipping only regarded banana boats, 'as a possible means of increasing refrigerated space for other commodities in extreme emergency, because before they could be used for other purposes the refrigerating plant of these boats would have to be supplemented' (MAF 86/149). Therefore, there was great reluctance on the part of the Ministry of Shipping to utilize the capacity on the banana ships for other produce, unless it became absolutely necessary to do so.

During the spring of 1940, the Ministry of Food began to assess the options available for future banana imports if the shipping situation worsened. In a briefing paper dated 8 May 1940, both a reduction in banana imports and the option of the Ministry of Food becoming the sole importer of bananas were considered. However, the Ministry was cautious in proposing either course of action, because as an internal memorandum stated, 'In Jamaica and Central America the very powerful position held by the United Fruit Company, will have to be given very special thought' (MAF 86/149). It seems that the Ministry of Food was influenced by the likely reaction of the UFC to the proposals at this time, as neither was taken any further. However, the proposals did give an indication of the thinking of the UK government, and were to provide the seeds for tougher action later that year.

The relationship between the UK government and the UFC became increasingly strained during 1940, and underlay many of the policy considerations at the time. The first issue of contention concerned the price of bananas, as during the spring of 1940, the price rose rapidly from £20 10s per ton to £30 per ton. A Ministry of Food minute stated

> [The Ministry] felt that some explanation of this increase was called for and invited the Managing Director, Mr Henry Stockley, to discuss the matter with them. The meeting appeared to be amicable but Mr Stockley subsequently made a general complaint as to his treatment in circles outside the Ministry. For this there was no justification, but it is possible that a firm, which throughout its existence had brooked no interference, may have found irksome even the mildest form of control. The mere fact that in the course of its duties [the Ministry] had to hold a watching brief over their activities, may have conveyed the erroneous impression to such a firm that it was antagonistic to them. (MAF 86/149)

There were suggestions that an investigation would have to be undertaken into 'the price margins of the shipping companies, particularly Elders and Fyffes' (CO 852/333/4). The Ministry of Food was concerned that if the price of bananas increased by too much, it would be impossible to defend the continued importation of bananas on the grounds that 'the fruit has a wide spread demand amongst the bulk of the population' (CO 852/333/4). It is clear that the value of personal networks that had been important in maintaining group-executive relations in the banana trade prior to the war, were now being put under severe pressure by the particular political and economic problems that existed. Indeed, it can be argued that during the early war period shared educational backgrounds, friendships and common personal interests did not contribute to effective communication between the banana companies and the executive.

Further tensions with regard to the banana issue came to the fore in July 1940, when the Economics Division of the Ministry of Food shared its concerns about the high banana imports from Central America, and whether anything could be done to restrict them.

However, it was recommended by the Fresh Fruit and Vegetables Branch that no action should be taken, 'there is going to be difficulty enough with Elders and Fyffes, and I would sooner that they were told the whole story at one time than to cut them a little here and a little there and so prolong the agony' (MAF 86/149). The extracts illustrate how UK civil servants looked upon the role of the UFC as being generally uncompromising in its commercial activities, resenting interference from any quarter. Further, the extracts would suggest that the UFC in the guise of Elders and Fyffes was still having difficulty in adjusting its corporate outlook to meet the new climate of cooperation, and in accepting the increased role of the UK government in the banana trade.

Notwithstanding the tensions with Elders and Fyffes, the increasing difficulties surrounding shipping in general led the Economics Division VIIa of the Ministry of Food to write to its sister Fresh Fruit and Vegetables Branch on 15 August 1940 explaining, 'War developments may necessitate the discontinuance of banana imports at any date and therefore your licences may be revocable on notice' (MAF 86/149). This was the clearest indication yet that a total ban on banana imports was likely, although for the next three months the Fresh Fruit and Vegetable Branch continued to organize banana shipments, albeit significantly only of British colonial origin. In addition, no licences were given for the importation of bananas in ships that had replaced those that had been lost (MAF 86/149). By the autumn of 1940, the shipping situation had worsened, with imports of apples and pears from the United States having ceased, while a significant reduction in the imported volumes of oranges, lemons and onions had also been seen (MAF 86/149). The banana, meanwhile, was given a certain latitude by the UK authorities, because of its significance as a fruit in the market (in normal times bananas accounted for more than one-fifth of total fruit consumption), the problems associated with converting the banana ships, an awareness of the UFC's position, and the importance of the banana to Jamaica in particular. With the continuation of banana imports, the interests of the UK government, the UK consumers, the banana companies, and the colonial banana growers were preserved, at least in the short-term.

The preparation for the cessation of the banana trade: the colonial dimension

In late October 1940, however, banana imports from Cameroon were halted due to the worsening shipping situation, and it seemed only a matter of time before banana shipments from Jamaica would suffer the same fate (CO 852/333/4). In order to prepare the island for the cessation of banana exports from Jamaica to the UK, the Colonial Office undertook a process of consultation in an attempt to formulate an arrangement, which would give the colony a degree of reassurance in the context of a worsening shipping situation. Four factors were given priority in the negotiations, namely, 'the availability of shipping, the priority of the needs of the UK for oranges and bitter oranges, the actual production of bananas in Jamaica, and the payment of a price to the banana grower which will allow him to subsist on the output of his cultivations' (*Daily Gleaner*, 11 November 1940 and CO 852/333/4).

In early November, the Governor of Jamaica, A.F. Richards, set out the government's plans for the future of the export trade, whereby the price at which bananas would be purchased by the fruit companies operating in Jamaica would be fixed. 'Such action becomes desirable because from time to time there will be surpluses beyond the capacity of available shipping. In these circumstances it is essential that all growers of good marketable fruit should be treated in the same way' (Governor's Statement, 1 November 1940 quoted in the *Daily Gleaner*, 2 November 1940). The solution was a pooling of all the banana returns from sales to Europe and North America, and from that a price could be calculated and be paid to all growers for the fruit that they produced, underwritten by the British Treasury. The price was three shillings per count bunch (*Daily Gleaner*, 11 November 1940). This meant that there would be no discrimination in price between those bananas that were shipped for export and those bananas that remained on Jamaica. In justifying the price controls the Governor stated

> It will be appreciated by every thinking person in the Colony that under conditions of war, Colonial Dependencies have to assist to carry the burden, which is principally shouldered by the mother country. One of the ways in which we in Jamaica are called upon to assist is by the reduction in the amount of shipping allotted for the transport of fruit to the United Kingdom. In taking this step, however, the United Kingdom authorities have given the most careful consideration to the effects which it will have on the banana planters and the Colony generally. (*Daily Gleaner*, 11 November 1940)

Perhaps most significantly in terms of providing an indication of what lay ahead the Governor said, 'there is no reason to believe that the present shipping position in so far as bananas are concerned will not suffer further deterioration' (*Daily Gleaner*, 11 November 1940). It is apparent that the UK government felt it necessary that the grower interests on Jamaica were given a degree of security, both to underpin the economic welfare of the island, and to safeguard the UK's main banana source in order that the trade could be resumed when trading conditions improved.

The end of banana imports into the UK

By early November 1940, the shipping situation was 'critical', with a large number of refrigerated vessels being taken by the Admiralty for other war purposes, particularly for the maintenance of forces stationed in the Near East. This action was taken unilaterally, without reference to the Minister of Food. As a consequence a general review was undertaken in early November of all import programmes to meet a reduced tanker tonnage of 35 million tons, of which only 15 million tons was allocated to the Ministry of Food (MAF 152/12 and MAF 286/3). Under such circumstances it was felt that it was better to have a good supply of one fruit, oranges, rather than small quantities of several fruits (MAF 152/12).

In terms of when the decision to end banana imports was actually made, there seems to be a degree of uncertainty. Davies (1990) states that the decision to ban banana imports came on the 9 November 1940 (p. 166). However, there is evidence to suggest that as late as 18 November 1940, the Ministry of Food was still organizing banana allocations with the importing companies, up to the period ending 30 June 1941 (MAF 86/149). Notwithstanding, the official announcement came on 25 November (MAF 86/149). The decision to end banana imports was at first to apply for a preliminary period of two months, but was subsequently extended indefinitely. Licences were given for all banana supplies that were afloat or about to be loaded at the time of the announcement. In peacetime 28 ships were employed in bringing bananas to the UK. When the ban on banana imports was announced only 13 were still in use for this purpose, the others having been withdrawn for other duties or had been sunk. In preference to bananas, the Ministry believed those 'high-energy' foods such as cereals, fats, meat and fish should be imported (MAF 86/149). The decision on the part of the UK government had not been taken lightly, but the increasingly dangerous shipping situation and the ever-growing demands of the war effort meant that the government could no longer accommodate the various commercial and growing interests within the banana trade. Thus, for the first time since bananas began to be imported into the UK, the government was forced to end all banana shipments.

Colonial considerations: provisions for the banana grower during the war

The situation in the UK may have been accepted, but the banana import ban was having wider ramifications, particularly for those banana-growing areas that had once supplied bananas to the UK. The purchasing of Jamaica bananas by the UK government continued throughout the war in order to keep a nucleus of the industry in existence, and by 1945 the Guaranteed Purchase Scheme had cost the government nearly £3.5 million (West India Committee Circular, April 1946). A price to growers was fixed by the Food Controller of Banana Accounts and paid by the UK government, which also paid subsidies for the control of leaf spot, wages, salaries and administration expenses, and an allowance to the companies then operating in Jamaica, for tasks such as providing cashiers to pay growers for bananas accepted, employing and paying labour, and supervising the handling and loading of whatever bananas it was possible to export (a small number to Canada and the US). In order to strengthen local food supplies, bananas bought by the Controller were sold locally at a price below that paid to the grower (CO 852/317/7). Similar schemes were also introduced in the Cameroon and the Windward Islands, the latter a group of British colonies that had exported small amounts of bananas to North America prior to the Second World War (Davies, 1990, p. 169; West India Committee Circular, November 1944; and CO 852/594/4).

With such support schemes 'outside' groups were involved in the administration of policies under government control rather than conducting their business in a relatively unhindered manner. The banana-growing organizations and particularly the banana companies became integral components of the government machinery, being responsible for overseeing wartime controls. Indeed, the close relationship that developed between the government and private banana interests during this time can be said to have laid the foundations for increased cooperation between the actors in the future.

In a relatively short period of time, from the beginning of the war in September 1939 to December 1940, a once large and profitable export industry had ended. The role of government was much more pro-active in the Second World War than the first, both because of the lessons learned from the previous war, and because of a more general willingness on the part of the authorities to impose control over all sectors of the economy. Under these circumstances the traditional actors involved in the banana trade had to readjust to the state having a greater role in setting the trading priorities. However, each actor did have some trouble in adjusting to the new roles. For the first time the UK government had to take the lead in organizing banana imports, and then had to make the decision to end them. It is clear that those within the government were not prepared for their new role, and as a consequence certain issues were not dealt with in the manner in which they should have been. Conversely, the banana companies, and particularly Elders and Fyffes were reluctant to defer to the government, and it took some time for the companies to accept their subservient role.

The resurrection of the UK banana trade

When hostilities came to an end in Europe in May 1945, there was a hope, but not an expectation on the part of the countries that had supplied bananas to the UK that the UK government would permit the importation of bananas once more. As early as July 1945, banana shipments from Jamaica to the US were being undertaken, but the prospects of an early resumption of banana exports to the UK from Jamaica were not good. However, the UK authorities were aware of the symbolic importance of the banana for the British public, and felt that if imports could be resumed, it would be an indication of new hope for the country more generally. In early August 1945, there were discussions between the Colonial Office and the Ministry of Food regarding the resumption of banana imports from the Canary Islands, as the lack of refrigerated shipping meant that neither Jamaica or the Cameroon were considered to be viable sources of supply at this time. There was, however, an acknowledgement that two refrigerated vessels, which were being used to carry bacon, might become available for the importation of bananas from Jamaica, but it was felt that 'it was still premature to say anything to Jamaica on the subject' (CO 852/593/1).

By the end of August, with the cessation of hostilities in the Pacific Theatre, it seemed likely that three vessels would be available for the Jamaica run. As a consequence, meetings were held between the Ministry of Food, Elders and Fyffes and the Jamaica Producers'

Marketing Company in late August and early September. Here the details regarding the resumption of the Jamaica banana trade were discussed (CO 852/593/1). As a result of the negotiations, the UK government partially lifted the banana import ban in September 1945 (*Fruit, Flower, and Vegetable Trades' Journal*, 22 December 1945). The plans for the resumption of Canary Islands bananas were thus superseded. It is interesting to note that the early discussions on resuming the UK banana trade involved the UK government and the two shipping companies with an interest in Jamaica. Although the banana growers on the island obviously had a strong interest in the trade's resumption, arranging a shipping service was the overriding concern at this time. Without a means of transport that utilized the expertise and resources of both companies, the re-establishment of the trade would have been impossible.

Despite the agreement to resume banana imports, there were tensions between the UFC (Elders and Fyffes), and the Jamaica Banana Producers' Association. The UFC had in the immediate pre-war period found that sourcing bananas from Jamaica was less profitable than sourcing from elsewhere. In an attempt to give itself more room for manoeuvre the company had cancelled the 1936 agreement with the Jamaica Banana Producers' Association, which had been designed to provide a degree of security for both the Association and the individual growers. The UFC was able to do this as the agreement contained a clause, which allowed the agreement to be suspended if war broke out (Jamaica Banana Producers' Association, Text of Agreement with the United Fruit Company, 31 December 1936, Clause 14 (b), CO 852/70/12). The effect of this was not immediately felt, as first the UK government took control of the shipping and purchasing of fruit, and then imports were banned altogether. However, it has been argued that, 'as the war drew to a close it became quite apparent that with the cessation of hostilities the Jamaican banana grower would again stand in grave peril. The whole protective structure that had been so painfully built up over the years since 1919 had been completely undermined by the United Fruit Company's cancellation of the 1936 contract' (H.T. Hart, 1968, p. 12). If, as banana imports resumed, the trading environment simply returned to its pre-1936 state, the UFC might have again attempted to take full control of Jamaica's banana industry by offering growers prices that the Jamaica Banana Producers' Association could not match. Under these circumstances the Association may not have survived, meaning that 'growers would have been right back where they were in 1919 before Jamaica Fruit and

Shipping Company came to the rescue' (H.T. Hart, 1968, p. 12). Such a state of affairs is interesting in terms of setting the scene for the subsequent post-war banana import system for the UK. As the UK government had in the past attempted to restrain American corporate power on Jamaica, it would seem likely that the government would not have wanted to provide the UFC with an opportunity to re-establish its predominance on the island.

The contract that was subsequently signed allowed the Jamaican government, which was given a licence by the UK government, to import bananas into the UK. This agreement provided for the introduction of a system under which the banana companies would act as 'selling agents' on behalf of the Ministry of Food. The original contract was for two years. The arrangement therefore continued the banana companies' involvement in the administration of the banana export industry under government supervision, the principles of which had been established during the Second World War. The share of bananas to be exported was divided 77.5 per cent to 22.5 per cent between Elders and Fyffes and the Jamaica Producers respectively. Half of the operation's profits were taken by the Treasury to set against the subsidies given by the UK government to the industry during the war years, while the remaining half was retained by the Jamaican government and formed the nucleus of a fund to provide hurricane insurance and other services to the growers. In 1947, the UK government was persuaded to extend the agreement until the end of 1952, with a further two-year continuation granted soon after. The actual organization of banana distribution in the UK was highly controlled, with only children and adolescents, and then expectant mothers and people over 70 receiving bananas.

The first ship to carry bananas to the UK was the SS *Tilapa*, an Elders and Fyffes steamship, which arrived in Jamaica on 4 December 1945, heralding the return of a number of Jamaican servicemen who had fought in Europe during the war. After loading its cargo the *Tilapa* departed Jamaica, arriving at Avonmouth on 30 December 1945. The vessel carried 94 800 bunches of bananas, along with 14 126 cases of oranges (*Daily Gleaner*, 5 December 1945, 14 December 1945, 15 December 1945, and West India Committee Circular, January 1946). The return of Jamaican servicemen from the front, and the resumption of banana exports to the UK, had symbolic importance for both Jamaica and the UK, as there was now hope that a gradual normalization of political and economic relations within the Empire would be possible.

However, as Jamaican banana exports were well below pre-war volumes, mainly because of the effects of war, and the damage caused by hurricanes and disease, even the UK's restricted consumption needs were not being satisfied. As a consequence, Elders and Fyffes successfully persuaded the British government in 1946 to widen the range of supplies, although bananas from Central and South America were not included because of the shortage of dollars at the time. The UK was desperately short of hard currency, and as the government wanted to conserve its reserves, it required that items paid in dollars should be kept to a minimum (Hansard, 30 June 1947, column 958).

Under these circumstances, Elders and Fyffes re-established its interests in the Canary Islands and Cameroon, the latter being a British Trustee territory and therefore benefiting from Imperial Preference. The nature of the immediate post-war UK banana trade was thus underpinned by two separate, but complementary policy measures. The Imperial Preference could be traced back to 1932, but the specific restrictions on dollar banana imports was a new measure to deal with the wider trading constraints experienced by the UK at the time. However, the import restrictions on dollar bananas were to become a permanent and highly significant measure in framing the dynamics of the UK banana trade over the next 50 years. Despite the fact that the problems of dollar shortages were to fade, the restrictions on dollar bananas were reconstituted as a measure to secure the position of colonial banana sources in the face of cheaper bananas from Latin America, where production techniques and economies of scale were drastically reducing costs of production.

The return of the banana trade to private hands

At the beginning of the 1950s, with the major banana-supplying countries of the UK market slowly recovering from the ravages of war, and banana imports from Dominica also beginning to be accepted, the UK government decided that the time was right to withdraw from the banana trade. This began on 2 April 1951 when an amendment to the Banana Order ended all restrictions on the distribution of bananas (West India Committee Circular, June 1951). Thus the arrangement by which bananas were reserved for children and young people under 18, expectant mothers and people over 70 years of age and over was terminated. However, it took the best part of two years for the government to finally end its involvement in the banana trade, because as a Ministry of Food memorandum, dated 14 April 1951, explains, 'We are precluded from taking immediate action to withdraw from this trade by the existence of our purchasing agreements with certain supplying countries' (MAF 86/151). The government had signed contracts with Jamaica until the end of 1954, the Cameroon Development Corporation and Elders and Fyffes for 1951, the Canary Islands until the autumn of 1951, and Dominica until the spring of 1952 (CO 852/1147/11). The memorandum continues, 'while we should have little, if any difficulty in arranging an earlier termination of the Agreement with the Cameroon Development Corporation and Elders and Fyffes, there is no prospect of our being able to reach a quick understanding with Jamaica' (MAF 86/151). The Ministry was certain that the government should withdraw from the trade in one go, believing that it would be unsatisfactory for the government to retain a role in the Jamaican industry, while bananas imported from elsewhere were back under private control.

Within this context, the primary task of the UK government was to persuade Jamaica that the return of the banana trade to private hands would be in the interests of the growers. While acknowledging Jamaica was the main stumbling block to agreement, the Ministry did appreciate the concerns that Jamaica had.

> Having recently secured our agreement to an extension of their contract with us for a further two years ... any direct approach by us for an earlier termination would, I feel sure, be misunderstood by the Colony. Growers are still very suspicious of the United Fruit Company, and despite all our expressions of sympathy with the growers and the help we have already given them in their struggles to put the industry back on its feet, we should be accused of abandoning them to their fate. We would not, therefore, recommend making any direct approach at the present time to secure an earlier termination of our contract. (MAF 86/151)

The government therefore attempted to engineer an agreement between the Jamaica growers' representatives and the banana companies whereby their respective interests would be safeguarded, which in turn would allow the government to withdraw from the trade. However, despite informal talks between the interested parties, little progress was made. This is perhaps not surprising given the long-standing antipathy between some sections of Jamaican society and the UFC, with the former being wary of returning to a privately run trade that had been the source of so many problems in the past. Further, as the

UK government contract with Jamaica was not to expire until the end of 1954, together with the fact that the UK government itself was reluctant to force an agreement, there was little impetus for an early settlement.

With regard to the banana companies, it is apparent that Elders and Fyffes viewed the ending of government involvement in the banana industry as something that would be beneficial to them, owing to the range of countries they exported bananas from, and the flexibility a return to private trading would give them. Conversely, the Jamaica Banana Producers' Association, which was in a weak position in regard to the lack of a second banana source, their poor shipping provisions and the absence of proper marketing arrangements in the UK, wanted the present situation not only to be maintained, but also to be continued beyond the existing contract. In a memorandum, relating to the proposal to end government involvement in the banana trade, the Association set out its main concerns. It feared that without governmental safeguards it would lose out to Elders and Fyffes, particularly if its guaranteed per cent share of the UK market did not continue. The Association was suspicious of Elders and Fyffes' intentions, drawing reference to the exploits of the UFC before the war. The memorandum suggested that Elders and Fyffes would try to discourage the marketing of a new variety of bananas in the UK, the Lacatan, which was being developed on Jamaica to replace the disease-ridden Gros Michel. The memorandum further intimated that the company would try to monopolize the marketing of bananas in the UK and that they would attempt to undermine the Association's shipping commitments (MAF 86/151).

The buying of Jamaica bananas by the UK government and the severe quantitative restrictions on dollar banana imports was considered by the Jamaica Banana Producers' Association to afford the Jamaica banana grower complete protection against domination by the UFC. It was argued that this protection rested on two facts.

> So long as the UK government was purchasing all of Jamaica's bananas it would not be possible for the UFC to have any say in the prices to be paid to growers. And so long as quantitative control of imports of Dollar bananas into the UK continued the UFC could not drive Jamaica out of the UK market with low priced bananas from Dollar sources.' (H.T. Hart, 1968, p. 14)

Such comments highlight the difficulties that had to be overcome if the trade was to return to private hands, as the Jamaica Banana Producers' Association itself an established private banana company was unsure of the merits of the resumption of private control. As a consequence, not only was there a need for an accommodation between the companies and the growers, there was a need for an understanding between the companies themselves.

However, there was a belief in the Ministry of Food that the Jamaica Banana Producers' Association's assessment took too hostile a view of Elders and Fyffes' intentions. The Ministry stated that

> On many of these points [made by the Association], [Elders and Fyffes] would not be unreasonable. They know that for years to come the UK will not be able to afford dollars for bananas; they know that if Jamaica is prevented from sending Lacatan bananas to the UK they will have hardly any bananas to send at all. As distributing agents to the Ministry of Food they do not attempt to discourage the sale of Lacatan bananas and there is no reason to think that they would not undertake to give them a fair position in the UK market. They would, we are told, probably give an undertaking not to try to take away the Jamaica Banana Producers' Association's customers and not to manipulate the wholesale trade to the disadvantage of the Jamaica Banana Producers' Association. They would also probably be ready to come to agreement about the coordination of shipping and freight rates. (MAF 86/151)

From these extracts it seems that the UFC in the guise of Elders and Fyffes was aware of the concerns of the Jamaica Banana Producers' Association and was prepared to accommodate them, realizing that by doing so the return of the trade to private hands would happen more rapidly. Further, the extracts suggest that the Ministry of Food was cognizant of the issues at stake, and would have been prepared to act as they had in the past to secure the position of the Jamaica Banana Producers' Association if any challenge from the UFC was forthcoming. Indeed it could be argued that from past experience each actor had a good idea of what would be acceptable to the others, and therefore a common approach began to develop.

While admitting that the Jamaica Banana Producers' Association was in a difficult situation, the Ministry of Food stated, 'we cannot let the interests of this Association be put forward as a reason for our staying in the business' (MAF 86/151). The Ministry made it clear to the Jamaican government that the Jamaica Banana Producers' Association should not influence them. 'If the representatives of the Jamaican Government can put aside the interests of the Association in our negotiations we can convince them it is in the long term interests of Jamaica to reach an early agreement with Elders and Fyffes' (MAF 86/151). The Colonial Office, in general, supported the Ministry of Food's desire to withdraw from the trade, but it believed that a more immediate official announcement should be made stating the government's intention to leave the business, in order that the colonial governments would have time to make alternative arrangements. The Ministry of Food accepted this advice, and on 20 June 1952 a statement was made about the government's intentions in answer to an inspired parliamentary question. The colonies were given advanced warning of the announcement, and were advised that the date of government withdrawal from the banana industry was likely to be 30 September 1953 (MAF 86/151 and Hansard, 20 June 1952, column 129). The UK government's official announcement to return the trade to private hands was made to focus attention on a specific deadline, hoping that this would provide the necessary impetus for agreement. Indeed, even in Jamaica where opposition was still strong to the trade returning to private control, there was a dawning realization that the UK government was determined to remove itself from the trade, and that such a change would have to be prepared for even though the exact details of the process were not yet known.

Government impatience, corporate willingness and grower reluctance

The substantive negotiations began in early September 1952. A delegation from Jamaica, headed by First Chief Minister Alexander Bustamante, and including representatives from the All Island Banana Growers' Association, the Jamaica Agricultural Society and the Agricultural Development Corporation visited the UK to discuss matters with the Ministry of Food and the Colonial Office, as well as the two marketing companies. The negotiations made some progress but no final agreement was possible. In an account of the negotiations, a Ministry of Food representative was highly critical of the Jamaican delegation.

In my view the Companies have dealt most generously with the Delegation on all matters. In addition Elders and Fyffes have done far more to safeguard the interests of Jamaica Producers ... than we ever anticipated. The Delegation are apparently prepared to sacrifice all the goodwill that has been created amongst all the parties and all the concessions that they have secured from the Companies, and that Jamaica Producers had secured from Elders and Fyffes, because of their determination to persist in demanding from the Companies at the last moment a guaranteed price until the end of 1954. (MAF 86/151)

The main item at issue was the demand by the Jamaican delegation that any new contract signed with the companies should provide a similar return on their bananas as under the existing government contract. The delegation wanted £35 per ton from the companies; a figure the UK government thought was both 'unreasonable and unrealistic'. The government believed that as part of the £35 per ton consisted of a special provision to help the banana industry overcome its difficulties caused by the August 1951 hurricane, such a figure could not be expected under normal trading conditions. As a consequence of the disagreements, the Ministry of Food negotiator became rather exasperated with the Jamaican delegation:

> I formed a very poor opinion of the Delegation. They were quite unable to present the facts in any convincing manner and had little ability to argue them; their documentation was brief in the extreme. The impression I got was that the Delegation was afraid to reach any agreement with the companies and was determined to go back to Jamaica without committing themselves to anything. We can only hope that better counsels will prevail in Jamaica but unfortunately the growers are mainly ignorant men and the full facts may not be properly presented to them. (MAF 86/151)

It can be argued that the Ministry of Food's criticism of the Jamaican delegation's demand for a high banana price was legitimate, but in the circumstances it is understandable that the delegation would have been concerned about the level of return, in order to properly safeguard the interests that they represented. Notwithstanding the debate over price, the theme that comes out most strongly is the desire on the part of the Ministry to complete the negotiations as quickly as possible, and a feeling of being inconvenienced when the Jamaican delegation wanted further time to consider its options. Much of the pressure for a rapid conclusion to the talks came from the Treasury, as the government was incurring a loss of about £1 per ton on all bananas imported (MAF 86/151). In addition, it seems that a part of the problem was the Ministry of Food's relative impotence. The Ministry officials were present at the negotiations, but the discussions were out of their hands. The UK representatives had made clear their decision on the future of the government banana contract, but beyond that it was dependent on the marketing companies and the Jamaica delegation to arrive at an agreement.

After the negotiations closed, the Jamaican delegation returned to Jamaica to discuss their position, while the Ministry of Food began to assess the options available to it if the Jamaican growers continued to reject the companies' offer. However, by mid-November, the Ministry of Food had received a telegram from the Governor of Jamaica putting forward a compromise arrangement for the decontrol of Jamaican bananas, 'that all existing arrangements should continue until the end of March 1953 including the existing price of £35 4s or that instead a guarantee should be given to make good any short fall in realisation back to Jamaica below the price of £35 4s until March next' (MAF 86/151). The Governor also hoped that the government would be able to give some price guarantee until the end of 1954. The Ministry assumed that if the two points were met, the Jamaican representatives would then proceed to complete negotiations with the marketing companies, and relieve the UK government of all its obligations by March 1953 at the latest. The Ministry, therefore, agreed to extend the existing arrangements until March if private contract agreements were signed, although it was not prepared to give any guarantees after private control resumed.

There was considerable relief within government circles that a compromise seemed likely. As a Ministry of Food memo states, 'if we can put an end to all obligations to Jamaica at the cost of maintaining the present contract at the present price up to 31 March next, I should feel we were well out of our troubles' (MAF 86/151). Elders and Fyffes agreed that the government contract for Jamaican bananas could continue until the end of March, provided a free market for the sale of Cameroon bananas was instituted from 1 January 1953. The relief on the part of the UK government was illustrative that after seven years of overseeing the banana trade, it was eager to unburden itself of a highly demanding role. The government believed that its job had been done in terms of overseeing the trade through the difficult post-war period, and felt that it was now right to relinquish its control of a trade which was recovering its pre-war strength. Further, it is important to recognize the role of the Governor of Jamaica once again in helping to bring about a likely accommodation between the disparate parties involved in the Jamaica banana trade, being able to use his good offices to bridge the divide between the growers, the companies, and the UK government.

However, it is also important to acknowledge that Jamaica was undergoing a number of political changes that would in time lead to the island gaining its independence in 1962. In 1944, a new constitution was established which provided for an elected government on the basis of universal suffrage. As a consequence, there was a general move towards greater self-government, which meant that local politicians were having a greater role in the affairs of the island, with a slow diminution in colonial power. In terms of the banana trade, however, the interest-group dynamic did not undergo fundamental change as the banana growers and the banana companies on Jamaica still underpinned the relationship with the UK government. In addition, the concerns of the local politicians were not dramatically different from those of the colonial authorities, as each group had to respond to the banana interests based on the island.

An agreement for the decontrol of Jamaican banana exports now seemed likely, but the final decision still had to be made. The pressure on the Jamaican side increased when the UK government made clear that it would probably not renew its contract for Jamaican bananas beyond 1954, and that any price negotiations for 1953 would be on a purely commercial basis, with no continuation of the hurricane supplement. In addition, on 28 November 1952 the Ministry of Food officially announced that the importation and marketing of Cameroon bananas would return to private account on 1 January 1953 (MAF 86/151). Under these circumstances, the Jamaican delegation returned to the UK, and negotiations were resumed with the marketing companies on 8 December 1952. The delegation's membership was slightly altered, with Mr Bustamante and the representative from the Agricultural Development Corporation no longer involved. Whether, this was to prove significant is open to debate, but the fact that there was a change in the leadership of the delegation would seem to indicate that a new approach was sought. The delegation was already under considerable pressure to come to an accommodation with the banana companies, and this increased when the Ministry of Food undertook to end its arrangements with Jamaica from April 1953 (MAF 86/151). After further negotiations, and despite the fact that no price guarantee was given, the delegation accepted the terms of an agreement. The delegation feared that any later arrangement would be less favourable, depending as it would on the benevolence of the companies alone. The negotiations had been long and arduous, weighed down by the legacies of the past. Indeed, it can be argued that without the historical baggage the other banana suppliers with which the UK government had a contract were able to readjust to the trade's return to private control with much less foreboding and anxiety.

Once a provisional agreement had been reached a joint communiqué was released on 17 December, which announced the acceptance (subject to ratification by the Jamaica government and the shipping companies) of agreements providing for Elders and Fyffes Ltd and the Jamaica Banana Producers' Association Ltd, to act as selling agents and provide ocean transport for Jamaica bananas until the end of 1964, while releasing the Ministry of Food from its contract as from 31 March 1953 (West India Committee Circular, May 1953). The 'Ocean Transport Agreement' and the 'Marketing Agreement' were ratified in January 1953. Under the marketing agreement both companies undertook to market all the exportable surplus of Jamaica bananas in the UK. It was agreed that Elders and Fyffes would receive 77.5 per cent of Jamaican bananas imported into the UK, while the Association would receive 22.5 per cent. As the Association had no other sources of bananas to ship at its disposal, the agreement stipulated that if production in Jamaica fell, as a result of drought or hurricane, Elders and Fyffes would make available to the Association bananas from other sources to make up 22.5 per cent of the total quantity of bananas marketed in the UK. This was done to allow the Association to sustain its interest in the business until production in Jamaica recovered. Further, the agreement stated that neither company should discriminate against Jamaica in favour of bananas from other sources of supply (*Daily Gleaner*, 22 January 1953 and West India Committee Circular, February 1953).

To support the 'Ocean Transport Agreement' and the 'Marketing Agreement', the Jamaica Banana Board was established in 1953, which had the sole right of purchase for all Jamaican bananas of exportable quality, with the task of selling the fruit on to the companies. It was hoped that the Banana Board would provide a degree of stability in the purchasing of bananas on Jamaica. The creation of the Jamaica Banana Board together with the two agreements were designed to reassure both the Jamaica Banana Producers' Association and the banana growers on the island, that the UFC would be locked into a structure that would make it very difficult for the company to undermine the stability of the trade.

While the 'Ocean Transport Agreement' and the 'Marketing Agreement' were awaiting ratification, the Board of Trade and the Ministry of Food announced on 18 December 1952 that from the end of the year bananas consigned from and originating in the sterling area, except Jamaica and British Honduras, would be admitted to the UK under General Open Licence. The Fruit and Vegetables (Returnable Containers) and Bananas (Revocation) Order, 1952 came into operation on 29 December 1952. The General Open Licence came into force on that day (Statutory Instruments, 1952, No. 2204, MAF 86/151). While on 17 March 1953, the Ministry of Food announced that imports of bananas from other non-dollar areas, which were subject to import duty, were to be returned to private hands (West India Committee Circular, May 1953). Therefore, by the end of March 1953 the importation of bananas from non-dollar sources had been returned to private hands, a process which had taken two years to complete. The build-up to the decontrol of the trade was undertaken in an atmosphere steeped in historical symbolism, but in the end the political and economic needs of the time were strong enough to precipitate the creation of a banana-trading structure which was to prove extremely resilient in the years to come.

Chapter conclusion

The period from the onset of the Second World War to 1953 was one of great challenges and new undertakings, with the interest-group dynamic undergoing fundamental change. In the immediate aftermath of war being declared the government was obliged to take a much more active role in the banana trade, and continued to support the banana growers during the period when banana imports into the UK were banned in November 1940. When banana imports were resumed in December 1945 the government continued to exert control, but improving market conditions in the early 1950s provided the grounds for the trade to be returned to private hands. The government needed the companies to re-establish their day-to-day running of the trade, which led to the government being obliged to repair its relationship with the companies that had developed in the build-up to the banana import ban. However, as the growers had benefited from government control of the trade, they were reluctant to have it returned to private hands, which strained their relationship with the UK government and the marketing companies. Despite these tensions, once the banana trade had returned to private hands the pre-war interest group dynamic resumed. Further, owing to the exceptional nature of the relationships that existed from the beginning of the Second World War to the time when the trade reverted to private control, a greater awareness of the respective roles of the actors developed, and as Grove suggests such understanding can result in a closer working relationship between the actors in question (1962, p. 61). Indeed, it can be argued that the dynamic that Grove recognizes set the parameters for a formalized interest-group relationship that was to develop within the UK banana trade, and which is best interpreted by Richardson and Jordan's (1979) group approach.

4

Competition and Accommodation: the Development of the Windward Islands Banana Export Trade and the Problems of Caribbean Rivalry

The establishment of a Windward Islands banana export trade to the UK

Prior to the outbreak of the Second World War, the Windward Islands had exported bananas to Canada, although not to the UK. After the defeat of the Axis Powers in the summer of 1945, despite the Windward Islands not having an established shipping service attempts were made, particularly on Dominica, to resume banana exports. A number of small-scale shipments were made between 1945 and 1948, involving companies such as A.C. Shillingford, the Grayson Shipping Line, and the Alcoa Shipping Line (author's interview; *Dominica Tribune*, 11 September 1948 and 18 June 1949; West India Committee Circular, July 1948; and CO 852/902/2). However, it was not until 1949, that a regular banana shipping service was established, again solely on the initiative of private interests, which in time led to the establishment of a new source of bananas for the UK.

The Tropical Fruit Company, which had imported bananas from the Canary Islands into Ireland prior to the Second World War, found that post-war, because of high demand for the islands' bananas from Spain and the increasing costs of production, it could no longer access bananas from that source. As a consequence, the Managing Director of the company, Ernest Foley, attempted to find an alternative banana source, and his brother who was working in Trinidad suggested there were islands in the West Indies that were eager to get a contract to export bananas. In consequence, towards the end of 1947 Foley visited the Eastern Caribbean in search of a new banana source. One of the islands he visited was Dominica, and Foley decided that a banana business could be developed there. Foley, who had good contacts with a number of shipping companies, believed that organizing shipping to collect the fruit from Dominica would not be a problem (author's interview). In association with Geoffrey Band who had a fruit import business in Liverpool, measures were undertaken to establish a viable export industry on the island, under the auspices of Antilles Products Limited. As with the origins of the banana export trade in Jamaica, the role of private endeavour in appreciating an opportunity for commercial advancement should be recognized. The whole basis of what was to prove an important trade for the Windward Islands had little to do with government action, and much to do with individual risk-taking.

In early October 1948, it was announced, 'Antilles Products Limited to purchase Lacatan bananas for the next 15 years' (*Dominica Tribune*, 9 October 1948). Once provisional agreement had been reached, Foley and Band approached the Colonial Office in an attempt to persuade them to convince the Crown Agents Shipping Department to allow UK government cargo to be shipped to Dominica and other West Indian Islands on the vessels chartered by the company. Antilles Products hoped that with such an agreement the viability of their undertaking would be enhanced, with an assured two-way trading link. However, the Crown Agents Shipping Department turned down the request, believing that the existing arrangements with the West Indies Transatlantic Freight Conference were in the best interests of the colonies. The shipping conference consisted of a number of companies including Elders and Fyffes and the Jamaica Banana Producers' Steamship Company, which restricted and regulated competition in the carrying of goods between the Caribbean and the UK. Under such conditions where there was a degree of cooperation between the shipping companies, the West Indies Transatlantic Freight Conference was able to provide a regular service with rebates on its freight charges which saved the West Indian islands around £6000 a year (CO 852/902/3). In general there was little enthusiasm for Antilles Products' undertaking within government circles. In one Colonial Office communication in March 1949, it was stated, 'we were glad to hear that there is little likelihood of any large areas of new land being put into banana cultivation, which would be embarrassing later if the scheme did not go ahead as well as its promoters hope it will ... We are not too happy about the long term prospects for the export of bananas' (CO 852/902/3).

It is also interesting to note that a number of white expatriate residents were not keen that a banana export industry was to be developed on the island. These residents feared that if the endeavour proved successful, their way of life, their idyll in the sun, would be changed for the worse. As a consequence a number of white residents did their upmost to persuade Patrick Foley (son of Ernest) and Geoffrey Band, who oversaw operations on Dominica, not to develop their business interests on the island (author's interview). The doubt and opposition of the Colonial Office and the expatriate residents to the banana endeavour illustrates the natural conservatism of those actors who had an historical interest in Dominica. In addition, it can be argued that there was a degree of resentment on the part of the colonial interests, that an Irish-based company who had no previous ties with the region should be developing a business there. Such attitudes further reinforce the image of a private company establishing an enterprise despite the opposition of colonial forces.

Despite such opposition a draft contract was agreed in June 1949, and finalized in December, 'for the purpose of export during a period of fifteen years ... subject to the terms and conditions hereinafter contained and the Company agrees to purchase from the Association all the said Puerto Rique (Lacatan) bananas grown in Dominica and accepted at the Company's Receiving Stations' (Contract signed between the Dominica Banana Association and Antilles Products Limited, 30 December 1949, p. 2, paragraph 2, see CO 852/1148/3 and Antilles General Minute Book, pp. 5 and 10). The first shipment of nearly 9000 stems of bananas departed for Dublin and Antwerp on 18 July 1949, on the MV *Brarena* of the Belgian Fruit Line. The *Branita* undertook the second shipment at the end of July. The majority of the fruit was distributed in Ireland, while some was sold in Belgium. A number of future shipments were sent to Sweden and Holland (*Dominica Tribune*, 8 April 1950 and CO 852/1148/3). Antilles Products did not ship bananas to the UK, as they had no contract with the Ministry of Food to do so.

The first Windward Islands banana shipments to the UK

Despite the expectations, Antilles Products had problems in chartering vessels for the trans-Atlantic voyage, and occasionally was unable to export any bananas at all. The Belgian Fruit Line Service then ceased altogether because of increasing freight rate costs, and as a short-term measure arrangements were made in November 1949 to load two Ministry of Food ships from Jamaica. Such shipments were possible as Jamaican banana volumes were below historic levels, which meant spare shipping capacity was available. In addition, the vessels were fast enough to pick up bananas from Dominica without endangering the supplies loaded in Jamaica (CO 852/1148/3). The origins of a

Windward Islands banana export trade to the UK was thus based on a fortunate combination of factors, rather than on a long-term assessment of the needs of Dominica and St Lucia (from which a small volume of bananas was now being shipped to Dominica for export) by the UK government. In addition, it is ironic that weakness in Jamaican production allowed bananas from the Windward Islands to first enter the UK, a banana source which in time was to cause a dramatic change in the balance of supply, challenging the primacy of Jamaican bananas in its traditional market.

With the Ministry of Food providing such a service, Antilles Products made every effort to persuade the Ministry to buy the whole exportable banana surplus from Dominica and St Lucia on the same terms as the Ministry's contract with Jamaica. As a way of trying to convince the authorities to agree a contract, Ernest Foley and Band gave the Colonial Office the impression that Antilles Products would develop a banana business to rival that of the United Fruit Company. The Colonial Office, in turn, doubted whether Antilles Products could do what it said, and in such a situation, 'the argument for substituting a British controlled organisation for the United Fruit Company would not appear to be sufficiently strong to counteract the disadvantages of losing the latter's goodwill' (CO 852/1148/3). It is significant, however, that the Colonial Office should think in terms of corporate ownership, and the respective benefits of domestic and foreign control in this context.

The Ministry of Food was not prepared to agree a long-term contract as it felt that Dominican and St Lucian production at the time was insufficient to warrant the shipment of supplies to the UK. Such an outcome was not welcomed by the Governor of the Windward Islands who wrote, 'The vague hope that, when ships can be filled and cost of freight reduced the Ministry of Food is likely to be interested, takes no account of the present situation and the future of a vitally important pioneer industry in two Treasury controlled Colonies is in jeopardy ... I do not think the local difficulties or the issues at stake have been fully appreciated' (CO 852/1148/3). Again, the comments highlight that the UK government seemed to be less than fully committed in supporting the development of a banana industry on the Windward Islands, despite the fact that a number of the islands' traditional industries were in decline, including those of sugar, nutmeg, limes, arrowroot and cotton.

However, by the beginning of 1951 with banana production and exports from Dominica and St Lucia increasing, 3000 tons had been shipped in Antilles Products' first year of operation, the Ministry of

Food agreed to purchase Windward Islands bananas for shipment to Northern Ireland, and then more widely in the UK as volumes increased. Although significantly the contract did not extend to the provision of a regular shipping service. The first shipment under the Ministry of Food's contract came in April 1951 on the SS *Genale* (Antilles Products Ltd. General Minute Book, AGM 29/6/50 and the *Dominica Tribune*, 28 April 1951). In addition, the British government began to develop schemes in Dominica in an attempt to encourage a greater number of peasant farmers to grow bananas. In July 1952, a scheme jointly financed by the government, Antilles Products and the Dominica Banana Association to develop banana demonstration plots for peasant farmers was established (Annual Report on Agricultural Development, 1952, p. 8). While in St Lucia over 120 000 banana plants were imported in 1949 and 1950 (Colonial Report, 1949–50, p. 26 and Windward Island Annual 1955, p. 34). Nevertheless, the development of the industry was disappointing. Antilles Products was still having difficulty in chartering regular shipping, there remained reluctance on the part of farmers, particularly larger ones, to grow bananas in greater volumes, and the UK government was still uncertain over the potential of a banana industry in the Windward Islands.

The impetus for expansion: a change in the ownership of Antilles Products

When Geoffrey Band resigned from Antilles Products Limited in 1952, the company had to find a new UK distributor. As a consequence, Ernest Foley who had long-standing ties with Elders and Fyffes asked whether the company would be interested in handling the distribution of Windward Islands bananas in the UK. However, Elders and Fyffes was not interested, believing that the islands were ill-suited to producing bananas on a large scale. It has been argued that underpinning this view was a more general disenchantment with the Caribbean banana industry on the part of Elders and Fyffes at this time (author's interview). With Elders and Fyffes not wanting to become involved, John van Geest, a Dutch businessman who was developing a fruit and vegetable business in the UK, took shares in Antilles Products in December 1952, becoming a director of the company in July 1953 (Antilles Products Ltd. General Minute Book, pp. 90 and 98). In addition, a new company was created in January 1953 called Antilles Imports Limited, based in Liverpool, which oversaw the distribution of Windward Islands bananas once they had arrived in the UK (Companies House, 00515647).

By the spring of 1954, the issues of double taxation, the continuing shipping problems, and the poor levels of banana production led the shareholders based in Ireland, who constituted the majority interest in Antilles Products, to consider their position. There was a general view that there was no real future in the Windward Islands, and so preparations were made to sell the company to Lord Vestey, head of the Blue Star Line (Antilles Products Ltd. General Minute Book, p. 110, and author's interviews). On hearing this at a specially convened shareholder meeting, John van Geest made an offer to purchase the company, although not before confirming his intention by telephone with contacts in Holland. John van Geest took control of the Antilles companies in late June 1954 (Companies House, 00515647). The name of the Antilles Products company was changed to Geest Industries (B.W.I.) Limited in September 1954 (Antilles Products Ltd. General Minute Book, p. 116).

By September, John van Geest had also finalized negotiations with the respective banana associations of the four Windward Islands for exclusive rights to ship and market all the bananas that the islands could produce. Both Dominica and St Lucia were established banana exporters, while Grenada and St Vincent had only started exporting bananas to the UK in late 1953 (Colonial Reports: Grenada, 1953 and St Vincent, 1953). Underpinning John van Geest's involvement was the belief that the banana industry in the Windward Islands could develop further. Although Geest Industries at the time did not have the infrastructure in the UK to handle a large volume of bananas, John van Geest had a feeling that despite Elders and Fyffes' apparent domination there was a gap in the market, which could be exploited (author's interview). The commitment on the part of van Geest to ship and market all the bananas that the Windward Islands could produce was really the turning point in providing the necessary impetus for expansion. Once again, it was the role of private initiative in the banana export trade, rather than government action, which led to its further development. Indeed, it was only after van Geest had committed himself to the banana industry of the Windward Islands, that the UK government began to take an active interest.

In the folklore surrounding John van Geest's involvement in the Windward Islands it is suggested that the UK government actively encouraged his participation, both financially and diplomatically. However, I have found no evidence to support such a contention. The chronology of van Geest's purchase of the Antilles companies seems to indicate that it was a decision made quickly, with little forward planning. Further, the telephone call to the Netherlands perhaps reveals the true source of any financial support that was forthcoming. It is unclear whom John van Geest spoke to in Holland, but it is likely that he contacted his family, his city financiers, or perhaps even the Dutch Royal Family. The Dutch Royal Family is mentioned in this context because they saw John van Geest as a favourite son (author's interview). It is said that during the Second World War, the Dutch Royal Family, to prevent their financial assets from falling into the hands of the Nazis, gave John van Geest the role of overseeing them. Apparently, as van Geest did such a good job in this regard, the Dutch Royal Family was pleased to support his ventures whenever assistance was asked for (author's interview). Despite these high level connections, it cannot be said with certainty that van Geest's purchase of the Antilles companies was as a result of such contacts. Nevertheless, the telephone call is important, as it seems to indicate that John van Geest did not receive any special assistance from the UK government in the build up to the acquisition.

In addition, it has been argued that the role of the West India Committee was essential for van Geest's smooth entry into the banana industry. Thomson states that, 'according to George Miller, who worked for the Committee for many years, John and Leonard van Geest, the controlling forces within Geest Industries, only joined just before they took over Antilles Products Ltd. and 'from nowhere' were soon elected onto the Executive Committee' (Thomson, 1987, p. 5). It would seem likely that the West India Committee would have supported Geest Industries, given that its purpose was to champion British interests in the West Indies. However, the quote attributed to George Miller, seems to overstate the case. It is true that Antilles Products Limited became a member of the West India Committee on 17 February 1953, just over a month after John van Geest took a stake in the company. However, it was not until 19 May 1959 that John van Geest, along with Geest Industries, gained membership to the Committee, and van Geest did not join the Executive until September 1962. The dates of membership seem to indicate that the West India Committee was not as influential as Thomson suggests (West India Committee Circulars, March 1953, June 1959 and October 1962).

Developing colonial commitments: financial assistance for Windward Islands banana production

Once John van Geest had committed himself to purchase all bananas of exportable quality, and to sustain a regular shipping service to the

UK, the colonial authorities became much more inclined to support the venture. As the Governor of the Windward Islands stated, 'I consider it important as a matter of economic and general policy that the banana industry of St Vincent should be rapidly expanded. It appears that the signing of the contract between Geest Industries Limited and the St Vincent Banana Growers' Association Limited, has provided the necessary impetus for expansion' (letter to Colonial Secretary, 11 February 1955, CO 1031/1559). The economic benefits of such an expansion were also recognized, as the Governor's Deputy wrote in early 1954, 'Rapid expansion is most desirable as a measure of economic development as a means of reducing the present dependence of St Vincent on grant-in-aid assistance from HMG' (letter to Colonial Secretary, 24 February 1954, CO 1031/1559). As a consequence, tens of thousands of pounds in financial assistance was provided by the UK government in the form of grants and loans for items such as the importation of banana suckers, the creation of nurseries, disease control, fertilizers, and for the training of agricultural officers in methods of banana cultivation (Colonial Reports (St Lucia), 1953–54 and 1959–60; CO 1031/1558; CO 1031/1559; and CO 1031/1563). In addition, a Price Adjustment Scheme was established to ensure that banana prices were relatively stable and high enough to encourage farmers, in the Windward Islands, as well as in Jamaica, to expand their production to satisfy growing consumer demand in the UK. It is palpable that once John van Geest had committed himself to ship and market all the bananas that the islands could produce, the UK government's whole approach changed. The government began to realize that the banana export trade could provide the means for economic development in the Windward Islands, thus reducing the amount of direct government financial assistance given to the region, while providing the UK with a valuable source of bananas.

The combination of private enterprise and government assistance led to a substantial increase in banana exports from the Windward Islands during the latter part of the 1950s. In 1954, total exports from the Windward Islands amounted to 19 700 tons, while by 1959 exports had reached 88 500 tons. As a consequence of the increase in exports a more integrated system of cooperation was needed between the islands to deal with all aspects of the trade, thus in 1958 the Windward Islands Banana Growers' Association (WINBAN) was established. The development of the Windward Islands banana export trade first by Antilles Products Limited, and then extended by John van Geest, was to prove a defining moment in the history of the UK banana trade, as it ended Elders and Fyffes' and

Jamaica's dominance of the UK banana market. In Jamaica, production was affected by a number of production and administrative difficulties (leading to a Commission of Enquiry in 1959), which meant that exports to the UK fell from 138 600 tons in 1954, to 133 200 tons in 1959. In percentage terms, Jamaica's share of the market fell from 76.3 per cent in 1938 to 39.9 per cent in 1959 (Tripartite Banana Talks Report, July 1966, Annex One and West India Committee Chronicle, May 1960). Despite such a transformation, the UK government, and to some extent the colonial authorities were slow to appreciate the possibilities of a banana export trade in the Windward Islands. Indeed, if the private interests had not been so persistent in their undertakings, the important role these islands' bananas have since played in the international economy may never have been realized.

The establishment of the General Agreement on Tariffs and Trade and the issue of market liberalization

A part of the post-war economic settlement was the creation of the General Agreement on Tariffs and Trade (GATT) in 1948, an agreement setting out the rules for the liberalization of international trade, with an associated *ad hoc* body to support the agreement. By the mid-1950s the 'contracting parties' of the agreement were pressurizing the UK government to reduce tariff barriers that favoured colonial trade. One consequence of any reduction in tariffs would have been a restriction in the freedom of choice to determine what action should be taken to provide assured markets for the various branches of the West Indian fruit industry. There was considerable disquiet amongst those involved in the West Indian fruit trade that any reduction in tariff protection would undermine the viability of colonial imports. Discussions took place in London, during the summer and autumn of 1954, between representatives of the UK and other Commonwealth governments in preparation for a planned meeting to review the GATT arrangements later that year. It is interesting to note that some of the arguments used to defend colonial interests in 1954 would be used again some 40 years on. There were demands that the GATT system should be made more compatible to the United Nations Charter, in as far as recognizing 'the principle that the interests of the inhabitants of these territories are paramount, and to promote the well-being of these territories to ensure with due respect for the culture of the peoples concerned, their political, economic, social and educational advancement, their just treatment, and their protection against abuses' (Article 73a, quoted in the West India Committee Circular, December 1954). There was a belief that GATT should meet the specialized needs of the colonies.

Under pressure from its colonial interests, the UK government agreed to safeguard market access for West Indian agriculture, and after lengthy discussions, the UK was given permission to waive its obligations under GATT enabling the government to extend to an industry or branch of agriculture in the dependent overseas territories assistance similar to that permissible in the case of domestic industry or agriculture (West India Committee Circulars, May and June 1955). The waiver had an almost immediate effect in that the UK government increased the general rate of duty for bananas from £2 10s to £7s 10s per ton in April 1956, which restored the preference to its former level (West India Committee Circular, April 1956). The colonial interests had been concerned over subsidized bananas from Brazil, and the effects of import licensing changes in 1955, which had allowed a greater range of non-colonial banana sources to enter the UK. Indeed, after the import duty was increased, bananas from Spanish West Africa, Brazil and the Canary Islands all lost their place in the UK market (Tripartite Banana Talks, July 1966, Annex one). The importance of the increase in the import duty for non-colonial bananas, and the associated GATT waiver cannot be overstated. Despite pressures to liberalize the UK banana trade, those actors with an interest in sustaining colonial banana exports were strong enough to resist any liberalization. Indeed, the UK government was persuaded of the need to increase the preference for colonial bananas, which was used as a specific act of policy to secure colonial supplies in the face of particular market pressures. Thus, despite the international calls for market liberalization, colonial interests were sufficiently influential to successfully counteract calls for change. The tensions between market liberalization and the legacy of preferential access within a complex political environment were to define the nature of the UK banana trade for the next five decades.

Despite the increase in the banana import duty the UK balance of payment situation had significantly improved over the 1950s and the UK now had considerable dollar reserves that led the government to ease restrictions on the importation of dollar bananas in 1959. This was highly significant, as it was the first time since the Second World War that dollar bananas had been granted access to the UK market. However, if anything this slight liberalization of the market reignited the opposition to the UK's banana import restrictions, as the dollar quota had been set at 4000 tons, equivalent to only around one per cent of the UK's total banana imports. As the original reason for the quantitative restrictions on dollar bananas no longer existed, the UK government felt vulnerable to the calls for change, particularly as the government in general believed in the liberalization of international trade and an adherence to its obligations as a member of GATT.

There was a debate within the government over whether the existing policy on dollar imports should be sustained. As the Board of Trade noted:

> It is recognised that we cannot justify maintaining the present very severe quantitative restrictions on dollar bananas and we are under increasing pressure to relax them. We tend to have a favourable trade balance with most of the banana exporting countries in the dollar area. While we would not claim that an increase in the dollar quota would necessarily have the effect of increasing our exports to these countries, it would remove the risk of outright tariff or other discrimination against our goods. (DO 200/21)

In order to address the international criticism, the UK government in 1961 attempted to increase the dollar quota by seeking to get GATT agreement for an increase in the tariff (and thereby the preference) in return for the West Indian governments agreeing to a programme of liberalization. The UK government hoped to obtain an increase in the tariff from £7 10s a ton to £10 0s a ton, and in return it would have increased the dollar quota over three years from 4000 tons to 20 000 tons with the hope of liberalizing completely thereafter subject to a further review of the position with the West Indian governments. However, the UK government was unable to get GATT agreement, and as a consequence no increase in the dollar quota was forthcoming.

Although, there was no official undertaking that liberalization was solely conditional on an increase in the tariff, the Colonial Office was vehemently opposed to any changes without such conditionality. It is apparent that the historically close relationship between the Colonial Office and the governments and banana growers of the West Indies had an effect. However, unlike the Colonial Office, the Board of Trade continued to believe that the dollar quota for bananas should be increased and 'there would never be a better opportunity of getting the West Indian producers to acquiesce than at the time at which the preferential status of West Cameroon was withdrawn' (DO 200/21). The withdrawal of the West Cameroon preference was to have fundamental consequences for the future structure of the UK banana trade, but not in the manner the Board of Trade had expected.

Changing market circumstances and increasing competition between Jamaican and Windward Islands banana supplies

The withdrawal of preference was precipitated by the decision of the Trustees of the United Nations to hold a referendum to allow the population of British administered North and South Cameroon to determine whether to become a part of Nigeria or to join the French Cameroon. The outcome was that the North joined Nigeria, while the South became the Western part of an enlarged French Cameroon. The amalgamation between the former British-controlled South (now West) Cameroon and French Cameroon on 1 October 1961 had important ramifications for the balance of the UK banana trade. The decision to leave the Commonwealth and join the French Cameroon ended the West Cameroon's membership of the Commonwealth preference area, which sustained banana imports of 80 000 tons annually to the UK. Although the UK government allowed West Cameroon two years' grace to adjust to the new trading conditions, the effect of finally losing its special status at the end of September 1963 was dramatic. In 1962, 74 900 tons of bananas were shipped to the UK, but by 1965 that figure had fallen to below 10 000 tons (Tripartite Banana Talks, July 1966, Annex One).

With the collapse of Cameroon exports and with diminishing options for the accessing of banana supplies for the UK market, Elders and Fyffes concentrated its efforts on expanding production in Jamaica. The result was that by 1964 banana exports from Jamaica to the UK had reached 157 700 tons, up from 135 900 tons in 1961 (Tripartite Banana Talks, July 1966, Annex One). However, the continuing growth of Windward Islands' production meant that when Jamaican output rose to replace the supply shortfall in the UK market caused by the decline in Cameroon banana imports, no shortfall existed. By 1964, the combined total of Jamaica and the Windward Islands exceeded the amount the market could absorb. It was estimated that shipments to the UK in December 1964 were 25 per cent above average (FAO, 1966, p. 8). As a consequence, prices fell sharply to levels lower than at any time during the post-war period and fluctuated considerably. The situation was at its worse during the winter of 1964-65, when retail prices dropped by some 30 per cent (Tripartite Banana Talks, July 1966, Annex Six; WINBAN News, September/December 1969, p. 4; and Beckford, 1967, p. 30). At the heart of the problem was that once the Cameroon preference ended Geest Industries through the Windward Islands was able to increase its market share at the expense of Elders and Fyffes. Geest was not constrained by history, and did not feel that Elders and Fyffes should have a pre-ordained right to market the majority of bananas in the UK. Conversely, Elders and Fyffes, under the auspices of the UFC, who had dominated the UK market for 50 years, felt both threatened and aggrieved that a relative newcomer exporting fruit from the Windward Islands, a set of islands that the company itself had dismissed as being unsuitable for large-scale banana production, was now challenging its predominance in the UK market.

The nature of the 'banana war', as it has been referred to, had serious consequences for all those involved. For the governments of the Windward Islands and Jamaica the dispute severely strained their relationship, and undermined their credibility, being seen as passing the initiative for decision-making to the banana companies. This was a particularly unwelcome accusation, as Jamaica had just gained its independence, while the Windward Islands were preparing for Associated Statehood, which in essence meant almost complete self-government. However, as has been seen before the power and influence of commercial banana interests should not be underestimated, and it can be argued that even under colonial rule the 'banana war' may well have taken place. The banana growers meanwhile suffered from low prices, being under pressure from the marketing companies to do their bidding. As the *New World Fortnightly* argued, the banana war was 'essentially a struggle for control of the British market between the two private interests that are contracted to market fruit, Van Geest for the Windward Islands, and Elders and Fyffes for Jamaica, has been transformed into a struggle between Windward Islands' and Jamaica's growers' (Issue No. 4. 15 December 1964, p. 20, quoted in Beckford, 1971, p. 84). Even the London *Times* commented that, 'the glut has now produced an all-in fight with Fyffes and Jamaica against Geest and the Windward Islands. While the Jamaican producer faces ruin, Jamaica itself would suffer only a minor cut in its exports, if the Windward Islands won. Is the fight necessary?' (Quoted in the *Daily Gleaner*, 4 February 1965).

The UK market had not witnessed such competition in the past, and after more than a year of high volumes and low prices, those with an interest in the trade were suffering, including the marketing companies who were facing financial losses. As a consequence there was a growing feeling that some form of accommodation between the actors was necessary. Indeed, it was recognized that even though preferential access was sufficient to safeguard colonial banana imports ahead of other imports, it was not able to deal with the instability caused as a consequence of competition between colonial sources. It was the first occasion when there were two large-scale colonial banana sources competing for a share of the UK market. As on previous occasions when colonial banana interests were in a fractious state, government involvement was necessary, even though on this occasion Jamaica was independent and the Windward Islands were preparing for a high degree of autonomy. Further, it is important to highlight the nature of the conflict. Previously, problems had arisen because of divisions within Jamaica, now divisions were apparent between Jamaica and the Windward Islands, although the destabilizing influence of the UFC remained a constant.

The need for conciliation: the Tripartite Talks and the subsequent agreement

In July 1966, the 'Tripartite Conference' was held with representatives from the UK government, the Jamaican government and from Dominica, Grenada, St Lucia, and St Vincent, making up the Windward Islands delegation. The conference was held in London, under the Chairmanship of Lord Beswick, Parliamentary Under-Secretary for Commonwealth Relations and the Colonies. The involvement of the UK government was crucial, as there was a feeling that without it no agreement would be forthcoming. In order to provide the conditions for an agreement the UK Minister of Agriculture, Fred Peart, announced that the government would for the first time accept a sharing of the UK market by Jamaica and the Windward Islands (West India Committee Chronicle, September 1966). Prior to this announcement the UK government had always been reluctant to countenance such a sharing of the market as being too restrictive, but came to realize that if there were no mechanism to accommodate the competing interests, instability would continue.

However, the government was careful to frame its undertaking within strict parameters: that the UK market price should not be maintained unreasonably above comparable 'free-market' prices; that other Commonwealth suppliers should not be excluded from the UK market against their wishes; that any such agreements (including subsidiary agreements with importers) should not compromise the government's position in regard to the Restrictive Trade Practices Act; and that the government's obligations to GATT should be observed. The UK authorities were aware that existing restrictions on imports from non-Commonwealth sources were contrary to GATT obligations, and that any further market restrictions would exacerbate the situation. Nevertheless, the government undertook that if a market share arrangement was agreed, it would not increase the dollar quota before the end of 1967 (FCO 23/334; First Plenary Session, Tripartite Banana Talks, 18 July 1966; and the *Daily Gleaner*, 19 July 1966). The UK government was in a difficult position in terms of balancing its commitments between its colonies and former colonies, and the GATT. However, by sanctioning a market-sharing arrangement, the UK government paved the way for a period which can be seen as the high-point of peace-time market intervention, as never before had the UK banana market been apportioned between its major suppliers.

Although no agreement was reached at the Tripartite Talks, further discussions produced 'the Banana Marketing Agreement', between the banana growers' associations. The purpose of the agreement, signed on 2 November 1966 in Grenada, was to regulate supplies for the UK market to correspond with seasonal price fluctuations, and to regulate the overall maximum quantities of fruit to be supplied to the market by each territory (WINBAN News, Vol. 2 No. 4, 1966, p. 2). The growers' associations agreed to split the UK market on a 52 per cent and 48 per cent basis, with Jamaica taking the largest share, a formula later accepted by Elders and Fyffes, Geest and the Jamaica Producers' Marketing Company. The companies were not party to the original arrangement, an exclusion born of past difficulties in finding an agreement. An essential element of what became known as the WINBAN Agreement was the 'principle of exclusivity', which committed Elders and Fyffes and Geest not to ship bananas from other sources unless, between them, Jamaica and the Windward Islands could not meet consumer demand (*Daily Gleaner*, 15 December 1966 and Hansard, 26 February 1971, p. 1186). Within the Jamaican part of the agreement, the share for Elders and Fyffes was 77.5 per cent, while that of the Jamaica Banana Producers' Association was 22.5 per cent. The agreement was finalized with the sanction and approval of the UK government with the proviso that no artificial increase in prices would result and that supplies would be adequate for trade turnover (FCO 23/334). The WINBAN Agreement put an end to the worst excesses of the competition between the marketing companies, and the respective banana-producing countries. The role of the UK government in setting the framework for an agreement was important, although in reality all those involved in the trade had little option but to accept some market accommodation. The agreement provided a degree of market stability, but as on many occasions it was to be superseded by events. A developing malaise within the banana industries of Jamaica and the Windward Islands would weaken their respective positions in the market, and create tensions between Elders and Fyffes and the Jamaica Banana Board.

The beginnings of Caribbean decline and a reassessment of market needs

It is ironic that by the time the WINBAN Agreement had been signed, the height of West Indian banana production had passed. Despite all the anguish and upheaval that had occurred through the middle part of the decade, the Caribbean banana industry was now finding it difficult to meet consumer demand in the UK, which in time forced a reassessment of the agreement. Underpinning the decline were economic difficulties in the UK, particularly the 1967 devaluation of sterling. Following sterling's devaluation, it became necessary to devalue both the Eastern Caribbean dollar and the Jamaican pound, which increased the cost of imported banana inputs such as fertilizers, herbicides, pesticides and related agricultural materials and machinery. The overall costs of banana production rose, which in turn damaged the industry's profitability, and the farmers' interest in the crop. As a consequence, Jamaican banana exports in particular, began to decline. Indeed by 1968, the UK market was being supplied with greater volumes of bananas from the Windward Islands than from Jamaica for the first time. However, the situation in the Windward Islands was also proving difficult, with quality in decline, and production stagnant. Therefore, a temporary increase in the dollar quota was sanctioned by the UK government in the spring of 1968, despite opposition from the West Indian grower interests. The Foreign Office argued that the increase 'would be in the interests of consumers and would be helpful in our relations with producing countries in the dollar area ... Such a relaxation is defensible to our preferential suppliers given their inability at present to keep our market fully supplied ...' (FCO 23/335, FCO 23/336 and FCO 23/338). Such a move was important, as it was the first time since the dollar quota was introduced in 1959 that the UK government deemed it necessary to increase the imported volume of dollar bananas above the level of the quota. Despite the fact that it was only a temporary increase it signalled the beginning of a decline in the importance of Commonwealth Caribbean banana imports into the UK. However, the increase in dollar bananas had more to do with the decline in banana production in the Caribbean, than any dramatic change in the UK government's import policy. Indeed, the bottom line was that if Caribbean production could not meet demand, the UK had little choice but to accept bananas from other sources.

Despite the short-term increase in the dollar quota, Fyffes Group Limited (as Elders and Fyffes was now called) wanted a more fundamental reform of the UK's banana import system, in order that it could access a wider range of banana sourcing. The company was keen to change the nature of the relationship with Jamaica, claiming that the quality of Jamaican bananas supplied to the UK was below an acceptable standard, and that this had been a source of loss and market embarrassment (*Daily Gleaner*, 31 January 1971). The problems over quality, together with the shortage of bananas led Fyffes to inform the Jamaican Banana Board that it would begin to acquire bananas from other sources, something that was prohibited under the WINBAN Agreement. However, this mattered little as Fyffes, who had always been a reluctant signatory, terminated the agreement with the Banana Board at the end of January 1970. The parties continued an *ad hoc* arrangement, but Fyffes used its new-found freedom to purchase bananas from the Ivory Coast and Suriname (*Daily Gleaner*, 16 May 1970 and the Denning Report, November 1970, pp. 7 and 8).

The termination of the WINBAN Agreement led to a further period of market unrest, with relations between Fyffes and the Jamaica Banana Board coming under severe pressure. The fear of the Banana Board was that if Fyffes freely imported bananas into Britain from other non-dollar sources, the company could lower or manipulate the prices on the market. There was also a concern over the dominant position Fyffes had with regard to the selling of Jamaican fruit in the UK, and whether the growers might be beholden to Fyffes in getting bananas to their traditional market. In an attempt to reduce this dependency the Jamaica Banana Board in January 1970 established the Jamaica Marketing Company (JAMCO) to develop and monitor Jamaica's banana trade in the UK (JAMCO, 1991, p. 1). Previously the Jamaica Banana Board after having bought bananas from the growers, employed Fyffes and Jamaica Producers as their agents to transport the bananas to the UK, to discharge them at dockside, to distribute them, and to sell them to ripeners based in the UK. However, the agents not only sold the fruit, but they also bought fruit on their own account, as each had their own ripening facilities. So the companies were in essence selling bananas to themselves, and there was disquiet that the growers in Jamaica were not getting the return they deserved (author's interviews). As a consequence, JAMCO was formed to sell bananas to ripeners in the UK in an attempt to increase the returns for growers.

Despite the organizational change, the relationship between Fyffes and the Jamaica Banana Board remained fractious. However, after lobbying on the part of the governments of Jamaica, and the Windward Islands who were also concerned about the future of banana sourcing, the Labour government appointed Lord Denning, Master of the Rolls, to conciliate between Fyffes and the Banana Board. Despite attempts to bring the two parties together during 1970, Denning's efforts proved to be unsuccessful. In the report he subsequently submitted to the new Conservative government, Denning put forward a number of recommendations to provide a degree of stability within the trade. The most significant was the proposed establishment of an advisory committee to oversee the trade for the benefit of Jamaica and Windward Islands supplies. Denning suggested that the committee should be based on the French system, where growers, shippers, importers, ripeners and retailers all played their part in advising the government on managing the market (Denning Report, November 1970, pp. 18–20 and 23). However, as both Fyffes and the Conservative government were against such market intervention, no action was taken.

The Jamaican representatives were very critical of the decision not to act on Denning's recommendations, and in an internal memorandum it was stated, 'The Tories are totally mesmerized by the Common Market. They have no sympathy for the Commonwealth ... they are particularly disenchanted with the "black" Commonwealth where they see nothing but problems and little gratitude for helping to solve them' (internal memorandum, JAMCO, 16 October 1970, in Denning File). Whether these comments truly reflect the Conservative position at the time is less important than the impression they convey of the Jamaican perception of the changing priorities that the UK had at the beginning of the 1970s. The comments are instructive in that they identify an important geo-political change that was taking place. The era of colonial rule was coming to an end, while membership of the European Economic Community was seen as a means by which the UK could re-establish a strategic interest in world affairs, although in reality neither agenda proved to be mutually exclusive.

The continuing poor relationship between Fyffes and the Jamaica Banana Board was exacerbated in early 1971, when Fyffes began negotiations to take bananas from British Honduras (Belize), a Commonwealth Caribbean source (the exclusive marketing rights were secured in 1973).

The action taken by Fyffes was indicative of an under-performing banana industry in Jamaica, and a very disenchanted marketing company. Such disenchantment even led Fyffes to withdraw its shipping from Jamaica for a time in February 1970 (author's interviews and *Daily Gleaner*, 17 December 1970). This was to prove the beginning of the end for the UFC's involvement in Jamaica, as JAMCO exercised its new powers over banana exports and renegotiated the shipping contracts giving Jamaica Producers the larger share of the shipping, and thus relegating Fyffes to a supporting role (author's interviews). By the early 1980s, the UFC (then known as United Brands) had become a marginal player in Jamaica having given up most of its banana interests on the island (author's interview). The scaling back of the UFC's involvement in Jamaica symbolized the island's decline as a major banana producer and exporter. The UFC had always been able to move its investments to more profitable sources of production, and in the early 1970s it was able to reduce its dependence on Jamaica by investing in Belize and Suriname. Indeed with the new sources of supply the UFC led the way in diversifying banana sourcing for the UK market in general.

Despite the problems Fyffes was still an important player in the Jamaican industry in the early 1970s, and as a consequence an accommodation was reached between the company and the Jamaica Banana Board in March 1971 to stabilize their relationship, albeit only after UK government intervention. The Banana Board undertook to improve the quality and quantity of bananas supplied to the UK, while Fyffes committed itself to only import non-Commonwealth Caribbean bananas when a shortfall developed, but in practice this meant that about 20 per cent of the market was being regularly supplied from other sources. Owing to the continuing decline in both Jamaican and Windward Islands exports the British market could only be maintained with the aid of non-Caribbean fruit (Hansard, 9 March 1971, column 85; *Daily Gleaner*, 5 and 6 March 1971; *West Indies Chronicle*, April 1971; Price Commission, 1975a, p. 7; and the Denning Report and Discussions, Denning File). The problems within the Jamaican banana industry were indicative of the general malaise of the traditional banana supplying interests. Over a relatively short period of time, exports to the UK from Jamaica and the Windward Islands had gone from a position of unrivalled strength to one of relative weakness. Indeed it was only the involvement of the UK authorities, which helped to calm the fractious nature of the banana trade at this time. However, further problems were on the horizon that led to a more fundamental reform of trading relations.

An institutionalization of the interests within the UK banana trade

As a consequence of the upheavals between the interests involved in supplying bananas to the UK, there were moves, at least on the growers' side, to rationalize and institutionalize their existing relationship. On 31 August 1972, the Commonwealth Banana Growers Association (CBEA) was established, which at its inception had Jamaica and the Windward Islands as members, although it was later to include Belize. The aim of the Association was 'to increase the profitability of banana growing for thousands of small plantation owners in the West Indies ... [through the rationalization of] certain areas of its industry such as research and the bulk purchase of materials and services needed by the growers' (*Daily Gleaner*, 1 September 1972). The CBEA received the full support of the respective governments, who believed that the association could play an important role in overseeing the European Economic Community (EEC) negotiations (*Daily Gleaner*, 2 September 1972).

However, despite the creation of the CBEA, the situation in the UK banana market was still one of instability, particularly towards the end of 1972. At this time around a thousand tons of bananas a week were entering the UK from the Ivory Coast, Suriname, and Martinique, all of which had duty-free access to EEC markets. As a consequence, there was a fear that such imports as they stood, were just the prelude to larger volumes entering the UK once Community membership became a reality on 1 January 1973. It was also alleged 'this market situation has been brought about by Fyffes flooding the market with foreign fruit' (Etienne, 1973). The consequence was an oversupply of bananas, causing prices to fall, and a fear that banana supply conditions could worsen further (*Daily Gleaner*, 23 December 1972 and 11 January 1973). However, there was an expectation that the UK government would intervene if banana oversupply became a serious issue (Etienne, 1973). The problem of traditional EEC banana sources entering the UK was thus seen for the first time, foreshadowing the likely pressure Commonwealth Caribbean banana sources would come under once the UK joined the EEC. Further, the role of Fyffes in recognizing the potential to increase its market power through a wider range of banana sourcing should also be acknowledged. Under such circumstances, the traditional banana suppliers of Jamaica and the Windward Islands wanted guarantees from the UK government that their market access would be sustained. At the request of the governments of the Caribbean talks were convened at the beginning of January 1973, with the British Ministry of Agriculture. The Prime Minister of St Lucia, John Compton, who led the Windward Islands delegation set the scene for the negotiations by stating, 'prices are now getting way below production costs and the economies of St Lucia, Grenada and Dominica are on the verge of collapse'. In response it was reported that

> The British Government confirmed its full appreciation of the vital importance of the banana industry to the economies of the Windward Islands and Jamaica, recognised the need for growers to enjoy a reasonable rate of return, and undertook to use its best endeavours to secure this objective. In this connection recent price fluctuations have underlined the importance of greater stability in the United Kingdom market. The British government will hold immediate discussions on this with interested parties. (*Daily Gleaner*, 11 January 1973)

After lengthy negotiations, the UK government stated that it would be prepared to involve itself in consultations with those with an interest in the UK banana trade (*Daily Gleaner*, 17 January 1973). This did not go as far as the Caribbean delegation had hoped, as they had asked for more concrete and specific measures (*Daily Gleaner*, 19 May 1973). However, the UK government, aware of its international obligations believed it had gone as far as it could to safeguard Caribbean banana exports. In an effort to mitigate any disappointment, the government also promised to focus its aid programme more specifically in an attempt 'to improve the viability and competitive position of the industry' (*Daily Gleaner*, 11 January 1973). After further consultations between the interested parties, the UK government on 18 May 1973 appointed an advisory committee on bananas for the UK market (*Daily Gleaner*, 19 May 1973). Once again the UK government was called upon to balance the interests of its traditional Caribbean suppliers with those of the wider international trading community, and once again the government did enough to secure the interests of the Caribbean. Despite the fact that by this time the UK had become a member of the EEC, the government recognized the need to safeguard the banana industries of Jamaica and the Windward Islands. The historical ties that underpinned the UK banana trade were sufficient to frame the government's banana policy in a new era of political and economic relations.

The Banana Advisory Committee (later called the Banana Trade Advisory Committee) contained representatives from the Ministry of

Agriculture, Fisheries, and Food, the Department of Trade and Industry, the three major importers, Geest, Fyffes, and Jamaica Producers, and the Windward Islands and Jamaican trade organizations (WINBAN and JAMCO). Its terms of reference were to provide a forum for exchange of statistics and information, including the volume and quality of bananas on the UK market, to consider the state of the banana industries in the Commonwealth Caribbean and to study the long-term future of the industry (Price Commission, 1975, p. 15). The committee, which was purely advisory and operated until the middle of 1993, usually met monthly and was chaired by the Ministry of Agriculture, Fisheries, and Food. The committee's most important role was to advise on the supply situation, and to recommend the quantity of dollar banana imports needed to meet consumer demand (Price Commission, 1975, p. 15). In many ways the Banana Advisory Committee followed the model suggested by Lord Denning three years before (Denning Report, November 1970, pp. 18–20). To complement the Banana Advisory Committee, a Banana Market Consultative Committee was established which had a wider range of participants, including shippers, ripeners, independent companies, retailers, and some wholesalers. This committee met four times a year to consider the general state of the market, and to provide a wider perspective than could be sought from the Banana Advisory Committee. As Smith (1992) has highlighted, an agricultural policy community has an inner and outer circle of members. The actors within the inner circle 'are intimately involved in policy making on a day-to-day basis, whereas the secondary community includes groups which have access to the department only when an issue which specifically affects them is being considered' (p. 31). In general, the committee system was seen as an effective tool in providing a degree of stability for the UK banana market, and security for Jamaica and Windward Islands supplies. The counterpoint to the Banana Advisory Committee was a requirement on the part of the Caribbean to improve the quality of their bananas. The view of the Ministry of Agriculture was that if the Caribbean was going to have a guaranteed market, they had to make sure they were supplying bananas of good quality.

The eventual development of a formalized interest-group relationship within the UK banana trade, as encapsulated by the Banana Advisory Committee in particular, is best interpreted in terms of Richardson and Jordan's group approach. Specifically, their contention that the nature of interest-group behaviour regarding a particular policy area is one of a regularised, routinised relationship, which appears to be the normal response to problems that automatically reappear on the agenda ... that over time any governmental/interest group relationship on a matter of substance will evolve a special machinery. (1979, p. 98)

After a decade of market instability, which had badly damaged the fabric of the UK banana trade, the traditional banana interests had little room for manoeuvre, and few other avenues to explore. The establishment of a policy community was important for the interest-group dynamic of the trade, as it provided a structure for discussing issues of mutual interest. Indeed, the suggestion of Richardson and Jordan that the 'consultation phenomenon' in British government is due to a number of factors is pertinent. There was a realization within the trade that the implementation of policies had been affected by a lack of cooperation among the actors involved. In addition, it is clear that there was recognition within the Ministry of Agriculture that the banana companies and banana growers' organizations would be helpful in assisting policy implementation and the provision of detailed information regarding the trade, and that the department's legitimacy would be increased as a consequence. Further, after the upheavals within the banana trade there was a desire to maintain professional relations with the representatives of the various banana interests.

As Richardson and Jordan argue:

For these and other reasons consultation takes place, and of course the development of committees is the extension of this consultative tide. By the use of committees with some continuity of existence there is administrative convenience – a process is established that obviates the need for decisions on procedure and protocol on each issue. But the formalisation of consultation has a greater importance. With a longer-term perspective, the possibility of a gradualist solution becomes more likely. (1979, p. 98)

However, although Richardson and Jordan's group approach is important in interpreting the development of the UK banana trade at this time, the concept needs to be supplemented in order that its use as an interpretive paradigm can be secured. John (1998) argues that a serious drawback with the approach is that there is little consideration of why decisions emerge when they do, and thus it is descriptive rather than explanatory (p. 71). It can be argued that Richardson and Jordan's model in itself does not provide adequate explanation of why a 'regularized, routinized relationship' developed when it did. However, within the context of the study there is a clear explanation of why the

Banana Advisory Committee was created in 1973, and not before. The influence of a new source of colonial banana supply in the Windward Islands, and the resulting market instability that was precipitated over the course of a decade, provided the rationale for the establishment of a policy community. Previously, competition between two colonial sources of supply had not been a problem, and as a consequence a more *ad hoc* approach had been taken whenever the issue of market instability had arisen, using the mechanisms of Commonwealth Preference and dollar quota restriction.

In addition, the approach of Richardson and Jordan has been criticized for being too broad, with little difference between a policy community and a close relationship between officials and outside actors. However, an attempt has been made to highlight the difference between the relationship of the actors in the Banana Advisory Committee, and the nature of the interactions before the committee's establishment. The Banana Advisory Committee was underpinned by a formal relationship between the UK government, the banana companies, and the banana growers, involving a series of regular contacts. While the nature of the interactions in the past had been based on a much looser association, with little contact between the three different groups of actors unless a particular problem had to be overcome.

Further, Richardson and Jordan's approach has been criticized for under-emphasizing the role of institutions and the state in the group approach. John (1998) argues that powerful groups can use the institutions of the state to safeguard their own priorities, while institutions of the state can have an important bearing on the interest-group dynamic within a particular area of policy, in that institutions can shape group interactions. In short, the government is involved in the policy process, but it has a special status. In Richardson and Jordan's study there is recognition of the problem, and they look to Lijphart's (1968) concept of the government's right to govern, in order to emphasize the privileged role government has in interest-group relations. Indeed, the UK government has been an important participant in the banana trade, acting as a catalyst to reduce tensions between the 'outside' actors, as can be seen with the establishment of the Banana Advisory Committee. Conversely, it is important to recognize the influence of the 'outside' banana interests on the institutions of the state, as the Banana Advisory Committee was only established when the banana companies and the banana growers were sure that their interests would be safeguarded in such a committee.

Chapter conclusion

Although the colonial authorities had at first been sceptical of the merits of developing a banana export trade on the Windward Islands, once significant banana volumes began to be exported, the government could not discriminate between two colonial supplying areas. Despite the fact that Jamaica had gained its independence in 1962, and the Windward Islands had achieved Associated Statehood by the end of the 1960s, together with the external influences of the European Economic Community and the General Agreement on Tariffs and Trade, the commitment on the part of the UK government to retain preferential access for banana supplies from its former colonies did not weaken. It is true that the nature of the interest-group relationship between the islands and the UK altered, as there was no longer the direct link between the colonial administration on the islands and the Colonial Office in London, but the legacy of these relationships meant that in reality a close bond between the islands and the UK government continued to exist.

With the government unable to discriminate between bananas from Jamaica and the Windward Islands, competition within the Commonwealth Preference area seriously compromised the stability of the UK market. The resultant decline in banana exports on the part of the traditional Caribbean producers from the late 1960s, and the particular problems in Jamaica, meant that the UK government was forced to widen the supply base of the market beyond Jamaica and the Windward Islands, to include an increasing amount of dollar bananas. Although it is important to stress that despite the divisions, both Jamaica and the Windward Islands themselves were united in successfully resisting fundamental market liberalization in the UK. The necessary easing of restrictions on dollar bananas was strongly supported by Fyffes, who wanted to diversify its sourcing away from Jamaica because of problems of quality and volume. The resistance of the Jamaica Banana Board to this led to the UK government appointing Lord Denning to conciliate between the parties, and when this proved unsuccessful Denning suggested the establishment of a committee to oversee the operation of the UK banana market. However, because of the reluctance of Fyffes to accept such a recommendation, it took a further three years for the Banana Advisory Committee to be established. By this time Fyffes was now able to access bananas from other sources, and as a result was less concerned with the effect a committee might have on dictating its banana sourcing, while the Windward

Islands and Jamaica were still being adversely affected by market instability in the early 1970s. As a consequence, the UK government established the Banana Advisory Committee to oversee the banana trade
involving all the traditional interests, which in turn changed the way
in which the actors related to one another in a policy community.

5
The EEC and the Lomé Convention: a Weakening of the National Approach

The Treaty of Rome and the different national import policies

The basis of the UK's membership of the EEC and the provisions surrounding the safeguarding of certain banana producers can be traced back to the Treaty of Rome of 1957. The negotiations leading to the signing of the Treaty were influenced by disagreements over the banana issue, an illustration of how important the issue has been in shaping international political outcomes. There was a fundamental divergence of approach between those member states, such as West Germany, who intended to maintain their imports of bananas from Latin American sources, and those such as France, who demanded preferential access for their dependent territories, and traditional suppliers. A solution was only found after discussions between West German Chancellor Konrad Adenauer and French President Charles de Gaulle, whereby national controls were retained.

In West Germany, there were no quantitative restrictions on imports. Imports from Member and Associated States of the EEC entered duty free. Further, although imports from third countries were officially subject to the EEC's common external tariff of 20 per cent, a special protocol attached to the Treaty of Rome allowed West Germany a duty-free, third-country quota which, together with negotiated additional quota allocations, were sufficient to cover all import requirements (Treaty establishing the European Economic Community, 1957, pp. 142–3). Imports into West Germany mainly came from Ecuador, Honduras, and Costa Rica, with smaller amounts originating from Colombia and Guatemala. The import policy of West Germany was particularly important for the future debates within the European context, as there was a powerful member state defending the concept of dollar banana imports, while resisting the arguments of other member states for continued preferential access for their colonial banana sources.

In France, the importation of bananas was controlled by a licensing and quota system. The market was reserved predominately for supplies from the Overseas Departments (Guadeloupe and Martinique) and the African countries belonging to the franc zone (Cameroon, Ivory Coast and Madagascar). Some small quantities of bananas also entered France from the Canary Islands, Somalia, Suriname and Zaire. If there was a shortage in traditional supplies, bananas from Central and South America were accepted. Bananas from the Overseas Departments, franc zone countries, and those associated with the EEC entered France free from duty, while other sources were subject to the 20 per cent external tariff. The French banana import system thus had a number of similarities with the UK arrangements, which meant that when the UK finally joined the EEC, there was already a powerful set of interests within the Community determined to safeguard preferential access for its traditional banana suppliers. In other words the UK had a precedent to follow when EEC membership was being negotiated.

In the Benelux countries there were no quantitative restrictions on imports. Imports from associated and member countries of the EEC entered free from duty, while those from third countries, which contributed the great majority of banana imports into the Benelux, were subject to the EEC's common external tariff. The bulk of supplies came from Colombia, Ecuador and Central America. In Italy, meanwhile, imports were regulated by an overall global quota system under which quotas were allocated between countries. Among the EEC Associates, Somalia was the most important banana supplier to Italy, with Suriname, the Ivory Coast, and Martinique also providing bananas. From the third countries, Italy's major banana suppliers were Honduras, Costa Rica, Ecuador and Guatemala. A consumption tax was levied on bananas, with Somalia getting a partial exemption. Thus within the EEC there was no consistent banana market regime. However, this did not prevent the traditional UK banana suppliers from the Commonwealth Caribbean fearing that the privileged access that they had had for 40 years would be undermined if the UK became a member of the Community. It is important to recognize that even though membership of the EEC was designed to usher in a new era of cooperation, the historical baggage of each state continued to be important in shaping their actions.

The prelude to EEC membership and the concerns of the traditional suppliers

When Harold Wilson's Labour government applied for EEC membership in 1967, the concerns of the traditional Commonwealth Caribbean banana producers came to the fore, despite the fact that the original six members had all retained distinctive national banana markets. There was uncertainty on the part of the Commonwealth Caribbean regarding EEC membership, and what measures could be undertaken under EEC law to secure continued preferential access for their bananas. It was clear, however, that the Commonwealth Caribbean would need to agree some form of agreement with the EEC, based on the provision in the Treaty of Rome (Part IV) that had institutionalized a formal association between the EEC and the member states' former and existing overseas territories. Without that, bananas from the Commonwealth Caribbean would have been subject to the EEC's common external tariff, while bananas from Cameroon, Ivory Coast and Somalia would continue to have been exempt. In addition, there was a belief that bananas from the Commonwealth Caribbean would need added protection from other associated states and dollar bananas, in order to retain their position in the UK market (see Spector, *West Indies Chronicle*, October 1967 and The United Kingdom and the European Communities, Command Paper 4715, p. 29). The Labour government understood the concerns of the Caribbean, and tried to reassure the region's producers. Lord Beswick, a member of the government, who had held preliminary negotiations with the EEC, argued 'Her Majesty's Government, if it accedes to the EEC, will seek for the banana producers treatment no less favourable than that extended by Europe to its traditional suppliers' (Select Committee on Overseas Development, 1973, p. 127). As with the existing member states of the EEC, it is clear from these early exchanges that the UK was prepared to maintain preferential access for its traditional suppliers. Therefore, the divisions over the banana issue, which had existed within the EEC since its inception, were likely to be reinforced with the UK's accession.

The surprising defeat of the Labour government at the 1970 General Election meant that the concerns of the Commonwealth Caribbean regarding the EEC had to be re-emphasized. In turn, the incoming Conservative government attempted to reassure the Commonwealth Caribbean of its good intentions (Minutes of the Meeting of the Management, West India Committee, 26 March 1971 p. 5 and

Hansard, 8 March 1971, column 3). The reassurance the Caribbean sought came when the UK government won a commitment from the Community to safeguard the interests of those countries that were dependent on the export of primary products (Part III of Protocol 22, Treaty concerning the Accession, 1972). Such a commitment was important in paving the way for UK membership of the EEC, which was achieved on 22 January 1972.

With this provision in the Treaty of Rome allowing member states to retain their national banana regimes, the main consequence of EEC membership for the UK was that the Commonwealth Preference of £7.50 per ton was gradually replaced by the EEC's common external tariff of 20 per cent *ad valorem*. This meant those EEC banana suppliers such as Guadeloupe and Martinique could enter the UK market duty free. Although, this exemption was not immediate, as the duty on bananas was phased out until it became zero on 1 July 1977. Despite the French Overseas Departments gaining duty-free access to the UK market, the UK's traditional banana suppliers hoped that with the tariff rate now at 20 per cent *ad valorem*, some of the protective value of the Commonwealth Preference that had been lost over the years would be regained. The UK tariff of £7.50 on non-Commonwealth banana imports had been fixed in 1956, and by the early 1970s had eroded in value, because of inflation and more specifically due to the devaluation of the pound in 1967. As a consequence of the deep to divisions between the member states, the UK was able to retain control over its banana trade. Although the entry of bananas from EEC sources was important, in that it signified that there was now a new set of actors with an interest in the UK market deriving its influence from the regulatory power of the EEC.

The Lomé construct: developing a new institutional relationship

With the UK now a member of the EEC, the issue of what kind of relationship the Commonwealth Caribbean should have with the Community had to be decided. Prior to the UK's accession, the Yaoundé Convention had been agreed between the EEC and the associated states of the Six, which extended Part IV of the Treaty of Rome in response to the new political and legal situation in the newly independent countries. Having been signed in 1963, and renewed in 1969, the Convention was due to expire on 31 January 1975 and, as a consequence, there seemed to be an opportunity to integrate the Commonwealth and Francophone countries into one agreement.

Notwithstanding the possibility of a post-Yaoundé arrangement, the dependent territories of Britain were offered association under Part IV of the Treaty of Rome, which provided for the allocation of Community aid and trade preferences. Such provisions applied to Belize and the four Windward Islands, although Grenada was to gain independence in 1974, which meant it then became involved in the post-Yaoundé negotiations. The situation for the independent Commonwealth Caribbean states was more uncertain, as there was a choice over which form of association they could collectively, or individually take. The preliminary conference at which the enlarged EEC had their first discussions with the independent Commonwealth countries, as well as the African Yaoundé signatories, took place in Brussels in July 1973. The Commonwealth Caribbean countries, in order to benefit from the expertise of the African countries in dealing with the EEC, initiated regular contacts and consultations with the region. This led in time to the creation of an African, Caribbean and Pacific grouping (the ACP), which the participants hoped would maximize the strength of their negotiating position. Indeed, the ACP felt that a fundamentally new 'association' with the EEC could be negotiated.

The Commonwealth Caribbean wanted a form of relationship with the EEC that was *sui generis* (Gonzales, 1997, p. 72). It called for non-reciprocity, protection of traditional arrangements, and no difference in treatment between independent Caribbean countries and the self-governing territories of EEC member states in the region. In many respects, the First Lomé Convention met the objectives that the Caribbean had set itself. The aim of the Convention was 'to establish a new model for relations between developed and developing states compatible with the aspirations of the international community towards a more just and more balanced economic order' (*The Courier*, March 1975, p. 3).

In more specific terms, there was an undertaking by the EEC to design special arrangements to give legal force to the protection afforded to the ACP producers by the Community. The ACP wanted legal commitments in order to safeguard, over the long term, a number of their primary exports to the EEC, including bananas, sugar and rum. The negotiations surrounding these products were highly contentious and the interest-group dynamic during this period of negotiation was highly complex, with a large number of actors discussing a wide range of interrelated issues. The scale of negotiations was therefore quite different from the rather limited discussions that had occurred within the context of the UK banana trade, prior to the UK's accession. The openness of decision-making at the European level, its multinational character, and the important role of national political-administrative elites in the process, meant that interests groups had to contend with an unstable and complex environment, which had important ramifications for interest-group strategies. As Streeck and Schmitter argue, the European policy process is characterized by 'a profound absence of hierarchy and monopoly among a wide variety of players of different but uncertain status' (1991, p. 159). The traditional Caribbean banana interests, therefore, had to adjust and adapt their diplomatic approach in order to maximize their influence in a more complex decision-making environment.

The Banana Protocol negotiations and the new paradigm of influence

The substantial negotiations on the Banana Protocol took place at the end of 1974 and into January 1975. However, the talks were not undertaken in a very positive atmosphere. The basis for such disharmony was the fact that the negotiators representing the EEC, primarily from the Development Directorate (DG VIII), were determined not to produce another Sugar Protocol, which was highly prescriptive. As a consequence the EEC representatives in the negotiations were extremely reluctant to give much ground to the ACP delegation. Further, the relationship between the African states and the Caribbean representatives involved in the negotiations was also strained. The African states that produced bananas (Cameroon, Ivory Coast and Somalia) were Francophone in allegiance and had been part of the Yaoundé Agreement. While the Caribbean banana producers (Jamaica and Grenada) were part of the Commonwealth, and had never before undertaken such important discussions with the EEC. The African representatives had felt rather hard done by in the Lomé negotiations up to this point. Francophone interests had dominated the Yaoundé Agreement, but with the Sugar Protocol finally nearing agreement, Anglophile countries such as Swaziland and to a lesser extent Mauritius and the Commonwealth Caribbean seemed to be benefiting the most.

Thus the African banana-producing countries felt it necessary to redress the balance, and pressed for the creation of a Banana Protocol to match the provisions in the Sugar Protocol. The Africans were determined to take a leading role in both designing the protocol and in discussions with the EEC. The Caribbean representatives meanwhile, being significant banana producers themselves, felt disinclined to allow the African representatives to have it all their own way, and preferred to have a joint ACP approach. As a consequence of the various tensions and split loyalties, the negotiations surrounding the Banana Protocol were riven with hostility and suspicion (author's interview). The effect of such disunity illustrates the problems that occur during negotiations of any kind, when the issue under consideration can be superseded by other unrelated matters. For example, despite the fact that the whole rationale for the negotiations was to sustain former colonial ties, the distinctive colonial histories of Africa and the Caribbean proved to be a source of division, which in turn shaped the discussions to come.

During the negotiations it became clear that despite Caribbean hopes, their interests were being marginalized to a degree. With Dominica, St Lucia, St Vincent, and Belize still British dependencies, and therefore unable to take part in the negotiations, the remaining independent Caribbean banana-producing states of Jamaica and Grenada did not have the political influence or the geographical size and population to push the negotiations forward. Conversely, Cameroon, the Ivory Coast and Somalia did have the standing to conclude an agreement. Such a situation in some ways suited the balance of interests within the EEC. Among the EEC member states, the French took the greatest interest in the banana issue, because of Francophone African production and their own production. If provision were made in the Lomé Convention for banana imports from the ACP states, then French imports of bananas from Martinique and Guadeloupe would hopefully be more secure within the EEC market. Such an accommodation of interests is interesting in that France was able to exploit the Banana Protocol negotiations in order to benefit both its former colonies and its domestic producers. This cross-fertilization of agendas well illustrates the complexity of the policy-making process at the European level.

Within the negotiations two particular policy issues dominated proceedings; first, what undertaking should there be within the Banana Protocol regarding market access for ACP bananas; and, secondly, what if any special assistance should be given to Somalia whose banana trade was in difficulty? As has been explained the EEC negotiators were reluctant to agree to comprehensive and prescriptive provisions as existed in the Sugar Protocol, while the African banana-producing countries in particular were determined to secure some safeguards for their banana sector. As a consequence, negotiations were very slow, and there were days on end when no progress was made (author's interview). However, despite the difficult negotiating conditions agreement was eventually reached on the wording of the protocol. The articles that were to constitute the Banana Protocol were shaped in part by the representatives of the respective banana associations in the individual countries of the ACP. So for example both the Windward Islands Banana Growers' Association (WINBAN) and the Jamaica Banana Board lent their expertise and knowledge in constructing the best form of wording, which it was hoped would secure EEC market access for their exports in the future (author's interviews). By co-opting those interests with a particular grounding in the subject, politicians and officials were able to secure the greatest level of support for any decisions made. Further, the overall credibility of the process was enhanced with the involvement of those actors with a particular expertise in the industry. Indeed, the cooperation between the European Commission and banana-growing interests was to become a strong feature of European policy-making over the coming years.

Perhaps the most important decision concerned the particular wording of Article One of the Banana Protocol: 'As regards its exports of bananas to the markets of the Community, no ACP state will be placed, as regards access to its traditional markets and its advantages on those markets, in a less favourable situation than in the past or at present' (*The Courier*, March 1975, p. 77). With such wording, those countries whose banana exports to the EEC were low by historic levels, including Cameroon and Jamaica, would not be prevented from exporting their normal volumes of bananas to the EEC in the future, once production had recovered.

However, the wording of the Banana Protocol was very much more indefinite than that of the Sugar Protocol. When comparing Article One of the Banana Protocol, with the same article of the Sugar Protocol, the nature of each can be seen quite clearly. Article one, paragraph one, of the Sugar Protocol states, 'The Community undertakes for an indefinite period to purchase and import, at guaranteed prices, specific quantities of cane sugar, raw or white, which originate in the ACP States and which these States undertake to deliver to it' (*The Courier*, March 1975, p. 73). The difference in content and detail of the two articles illustrates the difference in approach that the EEC took for the two commodities. The Lomé Convention did not contain anything as contractual as the provisions within the Sugar Protocol. A minimum price for a stated amount of ACP sugar was fixed after negotiations between the EEC and the ACP sugar producers. The price was calculated with reference to the price European producers received, which meant that ACP producers benefited from price increases decided by the Community. Owing to the disparity between the Banana and Sugar Protocols, those involved in the Lomé negotiations knew that the Banana Protocol would be the first to be undermined if pressure from any quarter was exerted upon them (author's interview).

With regard to Somalia, Italy was pushing for special provision to be made for its main ACP banana supplier within the protocol. There was a belief that Somalia should be specifically mentioned, in order to highlight and address certain unique problems that were present in its banana sector. About 20 per cent of the banana output in Somalia was not exported, partly because of poor quality and partly because the seasonal peak of production coincided with the period of lowest demand in Italy. Further, the country had poor inland and harbour facilities, which were holding back the expansion of the industry (FAO, 1972, p. 40 and the *Courier*, March–April 1983, pp. 71–2). Thus there was pressure to institute special measures for Somalia to promote banana production, improve the quality of the fruit through technical assistance, and to reduce the high operating costs of the industry. However, some countries involved in the protocol negotiations, such as Grenada and Jamaica, were against such special treatment for Somalia believing that Somalia's problems were little different to their own. Both Caribbean islands were suffering from volume and quality problems at the time. However, after further discussions it was agreed that Somalia should be specifically mentioned in Article Two of the protocol, and this was one of the last items to be finalized in the Lomé negotiations (*West Indies Chronicle*, February/March 1975 and the *Courier*, March 1975, p. 77). The importance of the reference to Somalia was significant, in that since the Banana Protocol's inception Somalia has claimed that the Protocol was in fact created especially for them.

The subsequent signing of the Lomé Convention, in February 1975, meant that the structure of the UK banana market was altered slightly. The preferential access that the UK had previously given to banana supplies from Belize, Jamaica, the Windward Islands, and EEC sources was sustained, while all ACP banana producers, such as Cameroon, the Ivory Coast and Suriname were now able to enter the UK market free from duty. The new arrangements also permitted those countries that supplied bananas to the UK to export to the other EEC states on a duty-free basis, although the traditional shipping and distribution networks greatly constrained the possibility of exploiting new markets. The signing of the Lomé Convention thus further undermined the special position of Commonwealth Caribbean supplies in the UK market, with African bananas now being able to enter free from duty.

However, the greatest significance of the change can be seen in the fact that there was now a common commitment throughout the EEC for the importation of ACP bananas. Despite the fact that non-ACP sources continued to be treated differently by member states, the Lomé Convention set a precedent for future attempts to unify the disparate national banana markets. Further, it is important to recognize the role of traditional shipping and distribution networks in sustaining the pattern of banana imports over the last quarter of a century, despite the changes that have been made to the banana import policies of the EEC during that time.

The importance of Article 115 in sustaining national markets

The imposition of restrictions on the importation of dollar bananas was an important part of the UK's banana import policy to prevent dollar bananas being transported directly into the UK, and thus under-mining the commitments given in the Lomé Convention. However, the EEC's common external tariff would not have been sufficient to check the circulation of bananas from one member state to another. Therefore member states had to be able to control the importation of dollar bananas from other member states, and this was possible under Article 115 of the Treaty of Rome. This article allowed for derogations from the requirement that states should be part of a common market, in this case for bananas. The Article allowed the European Commission to grant a member state the power to impose controls on those goods which originated in a 'third country' (that is, a non-EEC member), and whose trans-shipment would have circumvented national quotas. As Francis has argued, 'this measure gave authority to the relevant member state to apply surveillance (i.e. monitor imports by licensing, but with no specific authority to refuse licences) and when necessary, to apply protection (i.e. be authorized to refuse to issue import licences)' (1989, p. 9). The use of Article 115 thus allowed the UK, and other member states to continue with their existing national banana regimes, underpinning the safeguards in the Banana Protocol, despite the fact that the article was only meant to be used as a transitional measure before a common market was introduced (Article 115, in Rudden and Wyatt, 1980, pp. 61–2). The accommodation between legal obligations and political expediency was important in signifying the complex nature of the political system within the EEC, and the flexibility of the decision-making structure when there is a strong commitment on the part of the member states and the European

Commission to settle for a political compromise, even though its legality might be questionable. Indeed, throughout the Lomé Convention's existence, the banana issue was underpinned by an uneasy compromise between the need for political agreement, and an adherence to Community law.

The Banana Protocol and the issue of interpretation

A divergent interpretation of the imprecisely worded Banana Protocol was one of the main areas of tension between the Community and the ACP in the years immediately after the implementation of the Convention. According to the ACP, whose interpretation of the protocol has been described as 'creative' (Ravenhill, 1985, p. 246), the first article implied the Community would create a regime for bananas similar to that for sugar. As a consequence, the ACP producers attempted to clarify the scope of the article by suggesting that there should be an undertaking to guarantee markets and fixed prices, believing that only with these provisions would the EEC fulfil its legal commitments to sustain traditional market access for ACP bananas. Further, the ACP argued that the protocol obliged the Community to reserve a minimum part of each national market for ACP imports on terms which provided an adequate return, believing that the existing measures to implement the protocol were 'unsatisfactory, negative, and absolutely insufficient' (ACP-CEE/96/77, in Ravenhill, 1985, p. 248).

From the Community's perspective, the protocol merely helped to reinforce each member state's own market policy, as it existed prior to the signing of the Lomé Convention, and made clear that the EEC would not accede to ACP demands for the guaranteeing of prices and quantities in the market. While West Germany rejected out of hand any part of new Community markets being reserved for ACP bananas, a view the Commission sympathized with. The EEC argued that the problems of the ACP arose from their lack of competitiveness, as it related to price and fruit quality, a view supported by British politicians at the time (Select Committee on Overseas Development, 1978, p. 36). Overall, the European Commission felt rather aggrieved at the ACP's attitude, believing that it was down to the states party to the agreement to decide on the scope of the protocol, and not the Commission. As it was argued, 'Only the signatory Governments can finally establish what they meant by the Protocol and the sooner they are able to do so the less the atmosphere will be poisoned by the current sharp contention' (Select Committee on Overseas Development, 1978, p. 36).

The disagreements over the interpretation of the Banana Protocol once again highlight the weakness of the protocol when compared to the one for sugar. Indeed, the lack of precise undertakings in the Banana Protocol meant that when pressure was subsequently exerted on Europe's banana import regulations, there was scope for a gradual weakening of the commitment on the part of Europe to sustain preferential access for ACP banana producers. However, notwithstanding slight revisions to the protocol in the subsequent two Lomé negotiations, it remained fundamentally unchanged over the subsequent 25 years. This is not surprising considering the fact that any significant renegotiation would have been highly problematic. The ACP would probably not have got anything better, and would have feared diluting the existing provisions of the protocol if a fundamental renegotiation had taken place. The EEC meanwhile did want to threaten the stability of the whole Convention by demanding reform of the protocol.

The re-emergence of multinational corporate influence

The Treaty of Rome and the Lomé Convention were now centrally important in sustaining preferential access for ACP banana imports into the EEC. However, the ACP were becoming increasingly concerned over the influence of the multinational banana companies within Community markets. It was felt that these companies were able to use their powerful position within the EEC's distribution and retail networks to restrict the penetration of ACP bananas in their non-traditional markets. In 1974, for example, United Brands (formerly the United Fruit Company) had a 40 per cent share of the EEC banana market, while Castle and Cooke (Dole) and Del Monte made up another 15 per cent. The remaining part of the market was spread between a number of European companies. In the case of United Brands, not only did the company have a dominant market position, it also owned and/or controlled the most geographically widespread and largest ripening facilities in the EEC, which constrained other companies' room for manoeuvre. Indeed, the European Commission found that United Brands had unlawfully attempted to control the ripening, distribution, price, sales and promotion of its bananas, a ruling that was substantively upheld by the European Court of Justice in 1978 (Official Journal of the European Communities, 1976 and European Court of Justice, 1978).

Despite United Brands being forced to reform some of its operating practices, the ACP producers were in no position to compete with the might of an American multinational company, and so persisted in their demands that the protocol should provide greater market safeguards for their banana exports. The re-emergence of American corporate influence as an issue within the European context had important ramifications. Prior to the UK's accession to the EEC, a degree of stability had been achieved within the UK banana trade with an accommodation between the traditional actors, including Fyffes, which at that time was owned by United Brands. However, with the UK trade now being directly influenced by developments on a European level, American corporate interests had a new avenue of influence to challenge the preferential access that had been afforded to traditional ACP banana producers, including those of the Commonwealth Caribbean. Although, it should be acknowledged that as United Brands, through its ownership of Fyffes, had an interest in preferential sources of supply, its corporate agenda at this time discriminated between the different national markets of the Community. Indeed, it was not until later when United Brands made a strategic market error by selling its interest in Fyffes, did the company's policy against the Community's banana import regime become one of outright hostility.

Indeed, despite the fact that a new institutional framework had developed overseeing the UK banana trade when EEC membership was achieved, the effect of these changes was not obviously apparent. It is true that the mechanisms by which the UK government controlled its banana market now originated in Brussels, but the effect of these changes was negligible. The UK's national banana market remained intact, and the UK's particular preference for certain banana supplies continued. However, what is more significant is that the politics of the UK banana trade was now on a much wider canvass. As Marsh and Smith (2000) contend 'the context within which networks operate is composed, in part, of other networks and this aspect of the context has a clear impact on the operation of the network, upon change in the network and upon policy outcomes' (p. 8). Prior to EEC membership, there was a small number of groups with a direct interest in the UK's banana trade, and these groups had developed an understanding when dealing with particular problems. However, as EEC membership had become a reality, there was a new and potentially more important set of discernible relationships. There were now eight other member states who all had their particular banana interests, there were the European institutions that all had a role to play and there was a greater range of banana-supplying nations impinging on the UK market, from Africa, from the Community itself, and most importantly from Latin America, all of whom were now competing with the Commonwealth Caribbean for influence. Whereas before, the Commonwealth Caribbean banana-producing countries were large players in a small market, they were now small players in a much larger market. As a consequence, the Commonwealth Caribbean had to adapt their focus to include issues at the European level, which in time were to become much more significant.

In order to assess the changing interest group dynamic at the national and European level, an additional theoretical perspective is needed to supplement the group approach. Within this context the network approach to public policy proved valuable, suggesting as it does that 'the different types of relationships between group representatives, bureaucrats, politicians and other participants in decision-making account for the various ways in which political systems process policy' (John, 1998, p. 78). More particularly, the account of Marsh and Rhodes (1992a) can be adopted. They argue in *Policy Networks in British Government* that with an emphasis on the nature of policy networks, namely policy communities and issue networks, particular interest-group relationships can be determined, with consequent implications for the policy process, policy outcomes and policy change.

Marsh and Rhodes in their study identify a policy community as having an exclusive membership, stable relations between members, close relationships between groups and government, frequent contact, a high degree of consensus and interdependence between groups and governments. Whereas, in an issue network, there is a large number of participants, unstable relations between members, weaker and less regular contacts between groups and governments, much conflict, and little interdependence between groups and governments (1992a, p. 251). It can be argued that the traditional interest groups involved in the UK banana trade were now experiencing a gradual shift in the decision-making environment from a policy community to an issue network with a consequent effect on policy outcomes. However, it is important to recognize that during the 1970s and early 1980s the balance of influence remained within the sphere of the national policy community, which was able to mitigate the effects of the issue network at the European level.

Challenges to the balance of UK banana-market interests and the growing significance of dollar imports

The continuing role that national governments had in overseeing banana policy was seen clearly in the UK when a gradual liberalization of the banana market was instituted, leading to an import policy, which had not been so open since the early 1930s. The development that began this liberalization was the Price Commission Report of 1975. With the Banana Advisory Committee recently established to oversee the UK banana market, there was an awareness that the preferential access given to Caribbean producers, whose bananas were handled by Fyffes, Geest and the Jamaica Banana Producers Association, might provide grounds for disquiet among those excluded from the trade and from those consumers concerned about the cost of their produce. An awareness that the UK banana trade could be a source of monopoly profits led the Secretary of State for Prices and Consumer Protection, and the Minister of Agriculture, Fisheries and Food to ask the Price Commission in May 1974 to investigate the distributive margin on bananas (Price Commission, 1975, p. 1).

The report published in June 1975 argued that while Jamaica and the Windward Islands enjoyed a protected position in the UK market, there was adequate competition between the three major importers, and that their forward selling prices to other wholesalers and retailers were sufficiently competitive (Price Commission, 1975, p. 2). However, the report did note the variable quality of the fruit, drawing unfavourable comparisons with the quality of dollar bananas that were entering the UK in increasing amounts. Thus dollar bananas were beginning to set the standard that banana imports from other sources, including the Commonwealth Caribbean, had to match. Further, the Commission believed that there was a general malaise in the market with consumption static or falling, stemming from the issue of quality, which led many distributors to discount the positive marketing of bananas. It was argued 'that the trade and probably the consumer is suffering from this undercurrent of dissatisfaction and that there seems to be scope, and certainly the need for a more vigorous marketing policy on the part of the producers, importers and those involved in the distribution chain including retailers' (Price Commission, 1975, p. 4).

By the time the Price Commission reported, the volume of bananas coming into the UK from the traditional suppliers of Jamaica and the Windward Islands had declined significantly. Imports had fallen from 310 000 tons in 1969 to 190 000 tons in

1974. As a percentage share of the UK market traditional imports fell from 95 per cent in 1969, to around 58 per cent in 1974 (Price Commission, 1975, p. 9). The underlying causes of the banana export industry's decline in Jamaica was the impact of an over-valued exchange rate, and the inefficiencies in the government dominated structure of the trade. While in the Windward Islands, severe drought conditions in five of the first six years of the 1970s, a decrease in real banana prices for farmers, and increasing costs of labour and imported agrichemical inputs partly caused by the decision to tie the Eastern Caribbean currency to the US dollar rather than the pound sterling, all hit production. Despite a number of reforms that were undertaken in both the Windward Islands and Jamaica, the production situation in the five islands needed time to recover, and because of the long downward trend in production that had been seen, things got worse before they got better. Indeed, the nadir for Jamaican production came in 1984, when banana exports to the UK amounted to only 11 600 tons, while for the Windward Islands, their lowest point came in 1980 when 69 900 tons of bananas were exported to the UK (FAO, 1988, p, 16). At their peak, Jamaica and Windward Islands banana exports had been 360 000 tons and 180 000 tons respectively (Black, 1984, p. 107 and Davies, 1990, p. 264).

With banana production suffering in Jamaica and the Windward Islands, the shortfall in supplies had to be covered from other sources. The main supplementary source was from the dollar area, and exports from Latin America increased steadily during the 1970s, reaching a peak of 156 800 tonnes in 1981, constituting just under half of all supplies entering the UK at this time (Davies, 1990, p. 264). However, despite the importance of dollar bananas, those within the Banana Advisory Committee did not want to see dollar supplies overrunning the UK market. There was a fear that when banana exports from Jamaica and the Windward Islands recovered, their traditional market might be inaccessible to them if dollar bananas were allowed to establish themselves. As a consequence, other ACP banana imports were encouraged to counter the influence of dollar bananas. The two main supplementary non-dollar sources were Suriname and Belize, both under the auspices of Fyffes, contributing a total of around 30 000 tonnes a year during the late 1970s and early 1980s (FAO, 1983, p. 12 and 1988, p. 16). Small amounts of bananas were also forthcoming from the Ivory Coast, the Canary Islands and Cameroon. Fyffes was the principal importer of bananas from the dollar and non-traditional ACP sources, although Geest did obtain some dollar fruit from Colombia. Small quantities of bananas were also brought in by a number of independent importers.

It is important to acknowledge that despite the pressures at the European level, and the weakness of Jamaican and Windward Islands bananas exports to the UK, the Banana Advisory Committee upheld the commitment to support the UK's traditional suppliers even at a time of poor performance. The central interest-group dynamic that had been institutionalized within the committee, that of the Ministry of Agriculture, the Department of Trade and Industry, the three major importers, Geest, Fyffes, and Jamaica Producers, and the Windward Islands and Jamaican trade organizations (WINBAN and JAMCO), thus remained pivotal in determining the import structure of the UK banana market. The importance of Jamaican and Windward Islands banana exports in the UK market may have declined, but that was due to poor production levels, rather than any weakening of support for continued preferential access.

Despite the increasing amounts of dollar bananas entering the UK market, there was some dissatisfaction over the manner in which imports were being authorized. An illustration of this came in 1983 when a small fruit-importing company, Chris International Foods Limited, sued the Department for Trade and Industry (DTI) over the procedures for the issuing of dollar banana licences, after the DTI had refused the company such a licence. The majority of the bananas imported into the UK at that time were through Fyffes, Geest and Jamaica Producers, which Chris International believed was a constraint of trade. The company argued that the relevant Minister did not have the power under the Import, Export and Customs Powers (Defence) Act 1939 to protect Caribbean producers and exporters of bananas from the Commonwealth. Chris International also took the case to the European Court of Justice, and challenged the European Commission's acceptance of the UK's licence allocation system. It was suggested that the American Del Monte Corporation had backed the action, although Chris International denied this. Both the ACP Secretariat, and those countries, which had preferential access to the UK market, were concerned over the possible ramifications if any ruling went against the UK (Current Law Year Book, 1983, Ruling 3756; *The Times*, 1983; European Court of Justice, 1983, pp. 417–29; and author's interview).

Although Chris International did not succeed in its litigation, the UK government reviewed the import licensing system. Many companies, not just Chris International, became interested in securing a share of what they saw as an increasingly lucrative market in dollar bananas. However, the changes made by the government were limited, with small traders given only an additional 10 per cent of the dollar licence allocation, which made up any shortfall in Commonwealth Caribbean supplies. The dollar fruit trade continued to be dominated by the three traditional companies, with their dollar licence allocation standing at 80 per cent (*Financial Times*, 1984). The legal challenge by Chris International was significant in that it highlighted the growing eagerness of independent companies to become involved in the dollar banana trade. Indeed, it can be argued that the weakness of the traditional Commonwealth Caribbean suppliers meant that there was a gradual liberalization of the UK banana market, which involved a wider set of commercial interests.

A more fundamental change to the structure of the UK banana market came in 1988 after a review of banana policy, which considered the various market trends that had developed over the previous decade. The Ministry of Agriculture within the context of the Banana Advisory Committee pushed for greater competition within the market, in an attempt to overcome stagnating demand. There was now a greater emphasis on encouraging banana consumption, rather than deciding the market requirement as it related to the availability of Commonwealth Caribbean fruit. The effect of this change in policy, together with the promotional work of the 'The Banana Group' established in 1984, and representing the major banana importers and distributors in the UK, saw UK banana supplies increase from 388 154 tonnes in 1988 to 545 198 tonnes in 1992 (MAFF Statistics). Such an increase in overall banana volumes undermined the central position of Commonwealth Caribbean supplies (the Windward Islands, Jamaica and Belize), even though preferential access was being maintained and Windward Islands exports had recovered and were at record levels. In 1988, the Commonwealth Caribbean's share of the UK banana market was 75 per cent, while by 1992 that figure had fallen to 59 per cent (MAFF Statistics).

The changing nature of the UK trade increased the role of independent banana importers and distributors such as Bristol Fruit Sales, Del Monte, Keelings (UK) (in which Chiquita (United Brands) now has an interest), and Mack and S.H. Pratt and Company (Bananas) Limited. The increasing volumes of bananas entering the UK, both reduced the centrality of Commonwealth Caribbean bananas in the market, and further broadened the range of commercial interests and banana exporting countries with a stake in the UK. Although, it is important to highlight that in

1986, United Brands sold Fyffes Group Limited to the Fruit Importers of Ireland (FII). FII was and remains the leading Irish importer and distributor of fresh fruits and vegetables. Owing to the sale, the United Fruit/United Brand's involvement in the UK banana market ended after eight decades. The change of ownership did not lead to any dramatic change of direction for Fyffes, but there was a slow resumption of interest in exporting Jamaica bananas to the UK. In addition, FII who had a long-standing interest in dollar bananas was able to supply the UK market with bananas from that source when required.

Chapter conclusion

After the UK's entry into the EEC the underlying nature of the UK's banana regime remained fundamentally unchanged. Preferential access was incorporated within the Banana Protocol of the Lomé Convention, and underpinned by provisions in the Treaty of Rome, which allowed the Commonwealth Caribbean producers to retain their advantage over dollar banana imports; although bananas from EEC and non-Caribbean ACP sources could now enter the UK market free from duty. However, overall the interest-group relationship that had been institutionalized within the Banana Advisory Committee was still able to oversee the UK banana trade, although the tools for doing so were different than before. None the less, the broader interest-group dynamic at the European level, involving the institutions of the EEC, the member states, and their related banana interests was beginning to impinge on the national banana market of the UK. In particular, even though American corporate interests in the guise of United Fruit/United Brands Company no longer had a direct interest in the UK market, the trans-European position of the company meant that it still had a powerful indirect influence. Despite the fact that the UK's membership of the EEC did not intrinsically affect the nature of the UK banana market, change was enacted at the domestic level. With production difficulties continuing for Jamaica and the Windward Islands, and increasing volumes of dollar bananas in the market, there was now a greater acceptance of the latter source among the trade and consumers. The decision to encourage the expansion of consumer demand for bananas meant that the position of Jamaica and the Windward Islands banana supplies in the UK market was weakened. The overall climate for the traditional banana suppliers of the UK market had therefore become less secure than in the past.

6
The Creation of a Single European Market in Bananas and the Exploiting of Networks of Influence

The rationale for a European single market

In the early 1980s, there was a belief among those in the European cor-
ridors of power that inefficiencies resulting from trade barriers between
member states were causing the Community to lose ground with the
competing economies of Japan and the United States. As a consequence, the European Commission published a White Paper in 1985
laying out the basis for a more integrated trading structure, which
underpinned the subsequent negotiations between the member states
of the Community. Through the efforts of all those involved, the
Single European Act (SEA) was signed in February 1986, and enacted in
July 1987. The objective of the SEA was to achieve a single market by
31 December 1992.

One of the tasks committed to under the SEA was the elimination of
internal frontier controls, which required the introduction of common
rules to govern trading relations with third countries. In essence,
member states would no longer be able unilaterally to decide whether
to place restrictions on or provide preferential treatment for goods that
originated outside of the Community. Thus in order for individual
member states to continue their particular trade policies they had to
persuade fellow member states and the Commission to adopt
European-wide measures that satisfied their trading requirements. The
importation of bananas was one area of trade policy where the member
states were completely at variance with the ideals of the single market.
Bananas was one of the few agricultural products not yet covered by
Community rules, neither being subject to the Common Agricultural
Policy, or in reality the Common Commercial Policy with the 20 per
cent tariff only being effective in certain member states. The chapter

therefore provides an excellent example of an issue, which had to be made compliant with the requirements of the single market, highlighting the attendant political and economic concerns that defined the nature of the policy formulation process within the Community, and the interest-group dynamic that underpinned it.

When the Single European Act was passed there were three distinct banana regimes:

- a preferential market for EC/ACP produced bananas in Britain, France, Greece, Italy, Portugal and Spain;
- a duty-free market in Germany; and
- a market subject to a 20 per cent tariff in Belgium, Denmark, Ireland, Luxembourg and the Netherlands.

Within the context of a single market the continuation of national regimes was unsustainable, but because of the respective obligations on the part of member states to their banana suppliers, and the difference in production costs between Latin American banana imports (0.200 ECU/kg), and ACP/EC banana imports (0.500 ECU/kg), there was no single market arrangement that was readily acceptable to every member state (Pedler, 1995, p. 72). Any free-market solution would have undoubtedly been to the benefit of the US multinational companies, dealing in dollar bananas, while those companies dealing in ACP and EC fruit would have suffered. However, a too restrictive European banana regime would not have encouraged greater competitiveness and efficiency in the market, a fundamental aim of the single market. Thus the problem came down to finding a market mechanism, which safeguarded the position of the ACP/EC suppliers, while encouraging some degree of competition within the market.

The process of policy formulation and the construction of coalitions of interest

Despite the important ramifications of a single market for the preferred banana producers, particularly those of the Commonwealth Caribbean, the governments and grower organizations of these countries were rather complacent about its possible effects. Indeed, it took the banana-marketing companies, the West India Committee, and certain interested individuals within the UK to alert the Caribbean to the possible consequences of a single European banana market. By 1988, however, there was a general appreciation of the important developments within the EC, and as a result the Commonwealth Banana

Exporters Association was reconstituted as the Caribbean Banana Exporters Association (CBEA) to act as a political lobbying entity to influence the developing debate on the future European banana regime. The Association had as its members seven independent Caribbean banana-producing countries, with their respective banana-marketing companies having associate status, supported by a public relations agency recruited to coordinate the lobbying effort.

There was close cooperation between the banana growers and the marketing companies, as each group had an interest in sustaining preferential access in any future regime. Despite the historical differences between and within the various interests involved in the Caribbean banana trade, there was a realization that if a united effort was not undertaken to safeguard the concept of preferential access in the forthcoming single market, their mutually respective interests could be damaged.

However, some members of the CBEA took a greater role in the lobbying process than others. In order to build the strongest argument for continued preferential access it was decided that the Windward Islands should take centre stage. This was because the Windward Islands were the most dependent of all the Caribbean producers on banana exports for their economic welfare, and the islands had the greatest predominance of small banana farmers, a situation that could be favourably compared with the large-scale Latin American production. If Jamaica or Belize had been used to promote the case for Caribbean banana exports, then the arguments for retaining preferential access would have had less weight (author's interview). Both countries have larger estate systems based on the Latin American model, and their overall dependency on the banana crop is less than that for the Windward Islands. Owing to the emphasis on the Windward Islands, the Geest company, in classical lobby terms was in a strong position, and played a crucial role in arguing for the retention of preferential access in the new regime. Conversely, Fyffes was not at the forefront of the lobbying process as it was felt that because United Brands had just sold the company, the company's historical legacy would likely hinder the lobbying effort. Also, Fyffes was the major importer of dollar bananas into the UK, and it was thought unwise for such a company to be centrally involved in defending continued preferential access for Caribbean bananas (author's interview). In addition, there was some suspicion on the part of the ACP over Fyffes' intentions because of its involvement in shipping bananas from the Dominican Republic to Europe after the Republic became party to the Fourth Lomé Convention, which was seen by the Commonwealth Caribbean as a threat to its own bananas exports.

There was also cooperation in the lobbying effort between the Caribbean, African and European Community banana producers. In the early stages of the process, the Association of European Banana Producers (APEB) made overtures to the Caribbean, in an astute political move led by the French. The French producers believed that it made sense to associate themselves with the Windward Islands, as the political case for continued preferential access was the Windward Islands case. The French hoped that as the Windward Islands, Martinique and Guadeloupe were geographical neighbours; comparisons would be made between them in terms of their dependency on banana exports, even though in reality their economic circumstances were quite different. However, it has to be stressed that despite this cooperation, the EC producers were ultimately only concerned with their own welfare. The African countries, meanwhile, were also quite willing to let the Caribbean take the lead, while providing support when necessary. Again this was because the arguments that were to be used for continued preferential access were based on the methods of production in the Windward Islands; banana production in West Africa was conducted on a much larger scale. In addition, the Caribbean and African producers were represented on the ACP's banana group, which being based in Brussels, was able to keep in close contact with the European Commission, the Council of Ministers and the member states to make sure that any proposal suggested for the single market reflected the ACP's position. However, there were criticisms that as the ACP Secretariat was understaffed, those in the Caribbean lobby had to provide the impetus for ACP involvement in the process (author's interviews). Nevertheless, the establishment of a lobbying framework meant that those forces defending the concept of preferential access were well placed to oversee the formulation of policy.

The complexity of designing suitable proposals for a single market in bananas, and the fact that the issue interested a number of Directorates-General of the Commission, including Agriculture (DGVI), Development (DGVIII) and External Relations (DGI), meant that an *ad hoc* Inter-Services Group was established in 1988 to oversee the discussions. Owing to its central role in the policy process, the ACP lobby considered the group to be immensely important and closely followed its progress. In addition, the CBEA attempted to ensure that the Commission took account of political opinion within the Community more generally. In 1990, for example, the CBEA lobbied for and achieved an 'own initiative' opinion in the European Parliament, which supported continued preferential access for ACP/EC producers.

The Parliament took the subject up long before the Commission had formulated a proposal, and in doing so meant that the Commission would be obliged to accommodate the Parliament's view in some form. In a similar vein the Economic and Social Committee's (ECOSOC) Section for Agriculture and Fisheries produced an Information Report in 1991, which generally shared the European Parliament's view (author's interview). ECOSOC consists of employers, employees, and consumer representatives appointed by the member states. The CBEA recognized from an early stage the importance of the different institutions of the EC, and that each institution had a crucial role in the policy formulation process. The initiation of investigations by both the European Parliament and ECOSOC provided the lobby in favour of retaining preferential access for certain banana producers, a strong base of support which the Commission was obliged to recognize.

The importance of the banana protocol in the Fourth Lomé Convention

As the details of the single market in bananas had yet to be formulated the ACP and the CBEA knew it was crucial that the Banana Protocol of the Lomé Convention should continue in its existing form. The undertaking in Article One of the protocol, 'As regards its exports of bananas to the markets of the Community, no ACP state will be placed, as regards access to its traditional markets and its advantages on those markets, in a less favourable situation than in the past or at present', was seen as vital in committing the EC to uphold the interests of the ACP banana producers in any single market proposal.

The negotiations for renewing the Lomé Convention began at the ACP/EC Council of Ministers meeting held in Brussels during October 1988. It was here that the first official Caribbean initiative on the banana issue was taken. The Prime Minister of Dominica, Dame Eugenia Charles, made representations to the Council seeking to have the Banana Protocol maintained in Lomé IV without adjustments. Further, at an ACP–EEC Joint Assembly meeting in Bridgetown in January 1989, a resolution was passed re-emphasizing the special position of ACP banana exports, and the importance of the Banana Protocol in the Lomé Convention (Official Journal of the European Communities, 1989). A number of EC member states also recognized the importance of the Lomé Convention in setting the framework for future discussions on the banana issue, with the UK and France being particularly supportive of the ACP position. The German government, meanwhile, with some support from the Benelux countries, attempted to dilute the commitment of Article One of the protocol, believing that the ACP were not viable producers, and that they should instead receive compensation payments for diversification. The importance of the Banana Protocol lay in the fact that it was a legally binding commitment on the part of the EC to help safeguard market access for ACP banana producers, and thus the outcome of the renegotiation discussions would help determine the nature of the single market regime when it came.

Despite the opposition from some member states there was a critical mass of support for the protocol to be retained in its existing form. The Fourth Lomé Convention was subsequently signed in December 1989, and took effect the following March. The importance for the ACP of an unchanged Banana Protocol cannot be overstated. The various groups with an interest in sustaining the protocol had invested a great deal of time and energy in persuading member states and the European Commission to its point of view. The ACP/CBEA believed that no matter what kind of single market proposal on bananas was finally arrived at, the EC was bound by its legal commitments under the protocol. The securing of an unchanged Banana Protocol was important as it illustrated the ACP/CBEA's recognition of the inter-linked nature of the policy-making process of the EC. Further, there was an appreciation that a long-term approach was needed when attempting to influence policy, as the deadline for the introduction of a single market regime was still three years away.

A comparison of lobbying approaches: complacency versus active engagement

Although the commitment on the part of the EC to sustain ACP banana supplies in a single market was apparent, the exact method by which this would be done was still unclear. Therefore, all those actors with an interest in the banana trade still had an opportunity to shape the precise nature of the proposals. Within this context a number of member states undertook studies setting out their preferred single market options. The UK and France, for example, consistently supported proposals that would give clear guarantees to their preferential sources of supply, although they disagreed over the extent of market intervention that would be required to safeguard their traditional suppliers' place in the market. While the Benelux countries produced a document, which strongly supported a liberalized banana market regime (Caribbean Banana Exporters Association, 1990; ACP Secretariat, 1991; Benelux Economic Union, 1991).

The principles of the UK position were set very early on when, in July 1987, the then Prime Minister Margaret Thatcher, on a visit to Jamaica stated that, 'We shall continue to fight hard in the European Community, and we have quite a bit of experience of fighting in that organisation, to make sure that Jamaica and other Caribbean countries go on enjoying the preferential arrangements for bananas under the Lomé Convention' (Select Committee on Agriculture, 1992, p. 141). The Prime Minister was generally supportive because of her close relationship with the Dominica Prime Minister Dame Eugenia Charles, and because she was persuaded that the interests of the small island states should not be neglected by her government. In addition, it was clear that there was some residual guilt within government circles that the legacy of colonial rule had led to the existing difficult set of circumstances for the Caribbean, and that the government had some responsibility to assist the islands during this period of uncertainty. It is important to recognize that despite the fact that Margaret Thatcher's economic beliefs were firmly based on market liberalization, wider political and personal commitments were strong enough to override the Prime Minister's natural predilections.

Although, the UK government's position seemed to be generally supportive of the ACP, the Caribbean lobby was determined to keep the pressure on, believing that the UK would be its strongest advocate in the Council of Ministers. An extensive lobbying campaign was undertaken both within government and parliamentary circles by the CBEA, with the assistance of its Parliamentary adviser, Bowen Wells, Conservative MP for Hertford and Stortford. Those interests within the UK banana trade that were in favour of a more 'liberal' single market solution, including the supermarkets and many of the independent banana-importing and distributing companies, also undertook a lobby campaign represented in parliament by Michael Jopling, former Conservative MP for Westmoreland and Lonsdale (author's interview). However, those interests in favour of a more 'liberal' approach found only limited support within government and parliament, as there was an underlying sympathy for the Caribbean banana exporters in the UK. Despite the fact that there was a large Conservative majority in the House of Commons that supported an agenda that called for greater trade liberalization, the particular circumstances of the banana issue transcended such considerations. The historical ties between the UK and the Caribbean, and the fact that the UK authorities had assisted the banana industry in the Caribbean over many years, were important considerations in determining the extent of support for the Caribbean banana producers within the UK body politic. It can also be argued that the extent of support for the Caribbean was underpinned by a paternalistic attitude on the part of some within the Conservative Party in particular, who felt that the UK should still have a role in overseeing the welfare of its former colonies.

Elsewhere in Europe the Caribbean lobby attempted to influence opinion in any way it could. The Prime Ministers of the Caribbean islands visited various member states, supported in their efforts by those at lower ministerial level. Attempts were also made to sensitize political opinion in the European Parliament, as it was hoped that an awareness of the ACP position would filter back to the member states. Further, a lobbying mission was undertaken by a Surinamese delegation to the Netherlands, while the existing links Geest had in Italy were utilized. There was also a public relations campaign focusing on a number of publications, particularly those of the *Financial Times* and the *Economist*, which were perceived to be the most influential across Europe (author's interviews). In addition, the ACP Working Group on bananas published a memorandum, in November 1990, on its preferred option for a single market in bananas, and the West India Committee also published proposals and organized conferences to acquaint opinion formers of the issues involved in the single market. All these activities on the part of the ACP lobby were intended to increase awareness of the arguments in defence of preferential access at all levels of society within the EC.

The interests in favour of sustaining preferential access of ACP/EC bananas recognized that the process of EC lobbying was complex, and therefore attempted to coordinate their efforts both at the national and European levels. As Mazey and Richardson (1993b) suggest an exclusive reliance on a national level strategy is important but not sufficient to influence the policy process, and as a consequence the ACP/EC interests used a combination of a national strategy and a 'Euro-strategy' to influence European decision-making. The national strategy, where the ACP/EC interests maintained close links with national politicians and bureaucracies, was important. As Baggott argues, 'the relationships which exist between pressure groups and national governments are stable, well-developed and reliable channels of representation ... [and that] most pressure groups carry more weight with their own government than with European institutions ...' (1995, p. 212). Nevertheless, there was also a need for a 'Euro-strategy' that meant that the ACP/EC interests undertook representations at the European level. As Baggott further argues, '[Groups] need to adopt a much broader strategy which enables them to influence European institutions such as the Commission and the Parliament when necessary' (1995, p. 218). The institutions of the European Commission, the European Parliament and the Economic and Social Committee all played a significant role in designing a single market proposal for bananas, with the European Commission being the most important because of its central position in all stages of policy formulation through to implementation (Mazey and Richardson, 1993c and Nugent, 1994). The interests that depended solely on their established relations with national governments were to regret not accessing the other avenues of influence.

The forces supporting the ACP/EC banana producers had been active since 1988 both at the national and European levels. However, those interests that were in favour of a more liberal approach had in comparison badly misjudged the dynamics of the policy-making process believing that the influences of GATT and the SEA would deliver a 'liberal' regime. Although the American-owned multinationals of United Brands and Dole hired leading lobbyists and trade lawyers in Washington and Brussels, and the Latin American producing countries organized visits to Europe, their campaigns came too late for them to have a significant effect in the policy formulation process. This was compounded by the fact that the European companies that imported and distributed dollar bananas were also late in realizing the mood within the European institutions (author's interviews). In Germany, for example, the banana traders depended on the German government to represent their views, and did not lobby Brussels directly. Such an approach was relatively ineffective, particularly as the German government was criticized for its complacency. Indeed, despite the fact that there was a potentially strong lobby of liberal free traders in northern Europe, including Germany, Holland and Denmark, their attempts to shape the single market proposals were ineffective when compared with the efforts of those interests supporting preferential trading arrangements.

It can be argued that for the liberal interests the banana issue was not a matter of faith as it was for the ACP/EC, and as a result did not have the same commitment as those groups supporting a preferential solution. The ACP/EC interests had much more to lose than the liberal interests had to gain from a single market, and so were absolutely determined to make sure all aspects of the policy-making process were covered. Further, the liberal interests never took the trouble to understand the approach taken by the Caribbean, and their rationale for doing so, while the Caribbean could not believe that the Latin American and US interests were being so complacent.

As the liberal interests were at first expecting a relatively free trading regime for bananas, the major US multinationals, as well as the European importers and distributors of dollar fruit prepared for an increase in overall demand for bananas in the EC. The result of this was a rapid increase in the volumes of dollar bananas entering the Community, and even when it became clear in 1992 that a preferential regime might be introduced, the level of banana imports did not fall back, but continued to rise. In 1989, the volume of dollar bananas entering the EC was 1 716 056 tonnes, but by 1992 this figure had increased to 2 336 680 tonnes (Comtext data). There were indications that imports under the new regime would depend on who imported what prior to its establishment, and as a consequence the dollar importers and distributors hoped that by increasing banana imports to the EC, their position in a future unified banana market both in terms of absolute volumes and market share would be maximized. The consequence was a dramatic collapse in the price of bananas in certain European markets, particularly in Germany, although the safeguards in the preferential markets, underpinned by Article 115, protected them from the worst effects of increasing banana import volumes.

The issue of tariffication: the Dunkel Compromise and the shadow of GATT

After almost three years of discussion, the Inter-Services Group had formed a degree of consensus regarding proposals for a single market regime for bananas. In the autumn of 1991, the group circulated proposals that indicated support for a quota system for dollar banana imports and a requirement to encourage the marketing companies to deal in Community and ACP bananas. The European Commissioners were then preparing to put forward their proposals when the GATT Secretary-General Arthur Dunkel introduced a new factor into the discussions in December 1991, by suggesting that bananas be included under the provisions of GATT (author's interviews). Some measure of agreement had been reached in the Uruguay Round on market access for tropical products in late 1988, but bananas had been explicitly excluded at the behest of the EC. Dunkel produced his compromise in an attempt to solve the wider problems surrounding agriculture in the

Uruguay Round negotiations. He proposed that any restrictions on agricultural trade that had been underpinned by quotas should be replaced by tariffs, which could then be progressively reduced over time. The GATT Secretary-General's intervention went against what had been suggested by the Inter-Services Group, and as a consequence the European Commission felt it necessary to reassess its proposal. The intervention of the Secretary-General of GATT was important as for the first time it linked the development of a single market in bananas to the wider Uruguay Round trade negotiations that were entering their final phase. Although the GATT had shown an interest in the banana issue in the past, the intervention by Dunkel was significant in that it initiated the beginning of a period in which the body for world trade was to have a more influential role in determining the nature of the EC's banana import policy, and which in time was to supersede the traditional policy-making arenas.

After an intensive period of lobbying, during which time the ACP interests argued for the removal of bananas from the Dunkel compromise, a position supported by the ACP–EEC Joint Assembly and the European Parliament, the Commissioners agreed the approach by which a draft regulation would be constructed. They endorsed in principle the quota option with a complementary customs duty, ruled out Dunkel's proposal as a way forward, and decided to support the removal of bananas from negotiations on the GATT (*Caribbean Insight*, May 1992).

Despite the pressures on the European Commissioners to accept a form of tariffication, there was a general appreciation that such a system would not adequately safeguard the position of ACP/EC banana producers in the EC market. Within this context it is important to recognize that the undertaking of the EC to protect its own producers helped to safeguard ACP production. There was a realization that if the position of ACP bananas in the EC market were undermined in anyway, the arguments for continued support for EC production would be weakened. Indeed, such a rationale continued throughout the 1990s, with those member states having domestic banana producers seeing support for the ACP as a bulwark against any challenges to their own production.

In May 1992 the European Commission produced a more substantive and detailed report. This suggested that the quota for dollar bananas should be 1.4 million tonnes, subject to a bound customs rate of 20 per cent, and the introduction of an autonomous quota in association with a partnership scheme to encourage all importers to become involved in the marketing of ACP/EC bananas (Commission of the European Communities, 1992a). It is interesting that the concept of partnership was suggested by Del Monte, then owned by Polly Peck International, and taken up by the Competition Directorate. It is important to recognize the distinctive approaches of the multinational companies to the lobbying process, with Del Monte being a more constructive player in the negotiations than its competitors. Del Monte was less concerned with the fundamental preferential/liberal trade dichotomy, and more concerned with the fact that any new EC banana regime would provide them with a reasonable rate of return, a position supported by the fact that the company had an interest in ACP sourcing (author's interviews).

Following the report, the Commission consulted representatives of the member states, producers and traders in the Community, and the banana exporting countries in the ACP and in Latin America. Perhaps the most significant source of opposition came from the Latin American banana-producing countries, which were strongly critical of the proposals. As a consequence in June 1992, Costa Rica, Colombia, Guatemala, Nicaragua and Venezuela opened consultations with the EC on whether the existing national banana regimes within the Community were GATT compatible. Other Latin American producers, such as Ecuador, were also against the EC's proposals but as they were not members of GATT could not participate in the action. The move to begin consultations at GATT was highly significant, as it was the first indication that the Latin American countries had realized that their lobbying efforts had been unsuccessful, and alternative means to challenge the EC over bananas were needed. By challenging the existing national regimes of the Community, the Latin American countries hoped that this would set the scene for a challenge to the forthcoming single market regime, if it proved unacceptable to them.

The US tacitly supported the action of the five Latin American countries, but it was wary of provoking a direct confrontation with the EC at this time because of the wider Uruguay Round negotiations. In addition, the US Presidential election campaign was serving as a distraction. The US multinational banana companies, meanwhile, only had a marginal influence on the Latin American complainants, as they were beginning to concentrate their lobbying efforts on their own government in the US. Further, Chiquita who would become the multinational most opposed to the EC's banana regime did not have strong commercial links in four of the five countries that undertook the action, the exception being Guatemala, and therefore the company's influence was limited. There is a tendency for generalizations to be made about those actors involved in the dollar trade that opposed the EC's banana regime, and it is therefore important to stress the distinctions of approach between the different 'dollar' interests, in order to properly understand their particular motivations and actions.

The formal single market proposal and the return of tariffication

The assumption of the Presidency of the Council of Ministers by the UK in July 1992 meant that it had the responsibility of finding a solution to the banana issue that would be acceptable to the Council. Although agreement within six months, the length of each EC presidency, was not going to be easy, the Ministry of Agriculture was determined to find a settlement within that time. It was concerned that the two countries to follow the UK as President, Denmark and Belgium, would be less inclined to uphold the EC's obligations under the Lomé Convention. The Ministry of Agriculture believed that the UK had a responsibility to its traditional suppliers, a commitment shared by John Gummer, the Minister of Agriculture, who believed the issues at stake went far wider than purely economic considerations. The Minister believed that the EC had a moral obligation to protect ACP, and particularly Caribbean banana growers, against the powerful US multinationals. Support was also forthcoming from the Prime Minister, John Major, who had a close friendship with Sir James Mitchell, Prime Minister of St Vincent (author's interview). It is important to recognize in this context the role of individuals in the process of policy formulation, with both John Gummer and John Major being influenced by their own personal circumstances. The efforts of the London-based politicians and officials were supported by the UK Permanent Representation to the EC (UKREP) that acted as a contact point between Whitehall and the institutions of the EC. UKREP, which had within it a number of officials dealing with agricultural matters, was vital in coordinating attempts to find an acceptable solution to the banana issue.

Despite the deep divisions within the Council of Ministers, the European Commission published a 'Proposal for a EEC Council Regulation on the common organization of the market in bananas', on 7 August. The formula proposed by the Commission was a compromise between Commissioners aimed at meeting some of the concerns expressed by Latin American banana-exporting countries that the proposed regime was too restrictive. Nevertheless, the draft proposal issued leaned in favour of the ACP and EC producers, as had previous discussion documents, with no concessions on tariffication. The European Commission proposed a common regime for bananas that undertook to give free entry to ACP and EC bananas, to place an absolute limit on the entry of Latin American bananas via a quota of 2 million tonnes (20 per cent customs duty), with an additional quota if EC consumption increased, and to encourage all banana importers to trade in ACP/EC bananas through a 'partnership' scheme involving 30 per cent of the dollar quota (Commission of the European Communities, 1992b). Although, the Commission proposal was generally favourable to the ACP/EC position, it is important to recognize that the proposal was altered from its previous draft, adopting some of the recommendations suggested by the Latin American banana-exporting interests. Therefore, even though it seemed that the ACP/EC interests were in the ascendancy, there was still a degree of fluidity in the policy-making process.

After the Commission published its draft document, the issue was considered in the Committee of Permanent Representatives (COREPER), a body consisting of civil servants from all member states that are mandated to consider the political and technical aspects of policy prior to ministerial involvement, and the Special Committee for Agriculture, which has a more specific remit than COREPER. Although attempts were made to narrow the differences between the member states, the entrenched positions on all sides remained and little progress was made. When the issue was sent to the November Agriculture Council meeting for further discussion, the divisions between the member states came to a head when those countries opposed to the Commission's proposal used their blocking majority and refused to even open negotiations on it. As a consequence, the UK Presidency was convinced that to break the deadlock a new approach was needed. The Minister of State at the Ministry of Agriculture, David Curry explained the situation, 'the UK presidency has done everything that it can to give that [Commission] proposal a fair wind. We have promoted it and given it wide debate'. Curry continued, 'The proposal is deadlocked in Brussels and does not have majority support. We have done the best that we can, but a group of member states forming more than a blocking minority simply will not have it. We must therefore find a way out, and that falls to the Presidency' (European Standing Committee, 1992, p. 3).

The Ministry of Agriculture in association with the UKREP, therefore, began work with the European Commission to amend the proposal. It was hoped that the changes would provide the basis for an agreement at the December Council meeting. An indication of the way forward can be seen when David Curry argued, 'the Dunkel text (tariffication) provides richer opportunities than we thought for effective protection for ACP and Community fruit' (European Standing Committee, 1992, p. 4). The work to amend the Commission proposal was therefore to be based on tariffication, despite the fact that the concept had been rejected earlier in the year. As the deadline for agreement was approaching, a solution had to be found, and the idea of tariffication was widely known. Therefore, there was a pre-existing base of knowledge regarding the concept, which it was hoped would allow a solution to be found in the time available. In addition, work was undertaken by the Ministry and the Commission to formulate interim measures for the operation of the EC banana market beyond the end of December, if the details of a hoped for agreement were not in place by 1 January 1993. Such measures were designed to safeguard the ACP/EC banana suppliers place in the market, between the end of the old national regimes on 1 January and the introduction of the new regime whenever that came (Official Journal of the European Communities, 1993a).

While work was being undertaken on the amended proposal and the interim measures, John Gummer visited Jamaica and St Lucia at the beginning of December 1992 to meet with Caribbean leaders, and the representatives of the respective banana industries. Publicly, his trip was seen as an opportunity to inform those in the Caribbean about the framework of the new strategy and to reassure the islands that the new proposals would safeguard Caribbean banana-producing interests. In private, the suggestion was that the visit was an attempt to fend off more lobbying missions to Europe from Caribbean leaders, the cause of some embarrassment to the UK (*Caribbean Insight*, January 1993). However, it was apparent that the Caribbean countries were working closely with the Ministry on suitable amendments, despite the fact that tariffication was not their preferred option. On the size of the dollar quota, Curry stated that, 'the Caribbean countries have given us some parameters of what would be acceptable and what would be bearable, and clearly that will inform us in the discussions' (European Standing Committee, 1992, p. 10). In addition, consultations were undertaken with the French government, who significantly gave their support for what the UK was attempting to do. It is important to appreciate the close working relationship between the Caribbean banana interests and the UK government in designing a new proposal, illustrating the nature of the relationship that existed between them at this time. Further, if tariffication was to be the solution, it had to be remembered that agreement in itself was not enough. The new proposal had to sustain the necessary safeguards for ACP/EC producers, which meant consultations were necessary between the UK government and the ACP/EC.

Further, owing to the particular EC policy-making procedures, both the European Parliament and the Economic and Social Committee (ECOSOC) were involved in the consultation process. Although their remit was to consider the original Commission proposal, the Parliament and ECOSOC also took an interest in the process of amendment that was being undertaken by the UK government and the Commission. Once again the importance of the other institutions of the EC in helping to shape ideas that could be adopted by the member states should be recognized. Both the Parliament and ECOSOC acted as arenas of discussion, which helped to determine the nature of the new proposals, and it is significant that both institutions reaffirmed their support for the ACP/EC position (Official Journal of the European Communities, 1993b and 1993c).

A meeting of the Council of Agriculture Ministers was convened on the 14 December, at which John Gummer presented an outline compromise. Although the details of the amended proposal were significantly different to those of the Commission's original proposal, the underlying commitment remained the same, to preserve market access for EC and ACP bananas. There were three main elements to the amended proposal. There was an undertaking to provide tariff-free entry for traditional quantities of ACP bananas on a country-specific basis, in any year up to and including 1990, instead of just 1990 (a change suggested by the European Parliament). For the EC producers, there was provision for financial support and restructuring schemes, although banana production for the region was effectively capped at 854 000 tonnes. The proposal also called for the introduction of a fixed quota of 2 million tonnes for non-ACP/EC bananas at a tariff rate of ECU100 per tonne (approximately 20 per cent), and the imposition of an ECU 850 (170 per cent) per tonne tariff on imports above that level. This was a change from the original Commission proposal, which had purely quantitative restrictions on dollar bananas (*Caribbean Insight*, January 1993).

Further, there was a commitment to introduce a system for the allocation of the dollar quota so that 30 per cent of the licences went to importers of ACP/EC bananas, allowing them to cross-subsidize their operations with more profitable dollar fruit. This was a change from the draft proposal, since instead of 30 per cent being reserved for partnership arrangements, as was originally proposed, the percentage was to be given in its entirety and unconditionally to traditional importers of ACP and EC bananas. The amended proposal thus went some way towards meeting what had been set out in the Dunkel Compromise the previous year, in that quotas should be replaced by tariffs. Indeed the principles of the new regime were incorporated into the agreement on agriculture between the EC and the US within the context of the GATT Uruguay Round negotiations. When the amended proposal was presented the Commission and the UK government hoped that it would both be acceptable to enough member states for it to be adopted in Council, and would satisfy those interests outside the EC that had been critical of the original proposal.

The final negotiations

The December Council meeting

When the amended proposal was put to the Council in mid-December, it was positively received by most member states, although Germany, Belgium, the Netherlands, and Denmark remained opposed to its restrictive nature, and would have had sufficient votes to form a blocking minority. However, in an attempt to weaken the resistance to the banana proposal, the UK Presidency decided to present the banana compromise as part of a wider package of measures to be voted on at this, the final Agriculture Council meeting of its Presidency. The package included a number of different measures, such as agrimoney reform that was beneficial to Germany, Belgium and Denmark, measures regarding Spanish and Portuguese accession and measures to harmonize veterinary and plant health, which would assist Dutch exports. It was hoped that as the package had to be accepted or rejected in its entirety, each member state would have a reason to vote for it, even though they might disagree with the banana part of the package. Further, the UK Presidency had to take into consideration the voting power of each member state. Within the Council, France, Germany, Italy, and the UK each had 10 votes; Spain had 8 votes; Belgium, Greece, Netherlands, Portugal all had 5 votes; Ireland, Denmark had 3 votes each, while Luxembourg had 2 votes. The UK government hoped that the required qualified majority of 54 votes could be achieved with the package proposed, although only 23 votes were needed to form a blocking minority.

A qualified majority finally passed the package of measures costing ECU 2.5 billion with Spain, France, UK, Ireland, Italy, Netherlands,

Belgium, Greece, and Luxembourg, constituting 58 votes voting in favour, while Denmark, Germany and Portugal voted against (author's interviews). The decision to place the banana proposal within a broader package of measures assisted considerably in reaching an agreement. The way the package was constructed meant that the other measures within it were sufficiently attractive to overcome most opposition within the Council to the banana proposal. Curiously, one European banana-producing country, Portugal, voted against the package for reasons unconnected with bananas. Portugal voted against because it was unhappy with the transition arrangements dealing with its accession.

Although the compromise on bananas was substantially different from the Commission proposal, the European Commissioner for Agriculture, Ray McSharry, chose to accept it. The President of the Council, John Gummer, claimed that the proposal was 'wholly acceptable to all as it would safeguard the interests of ACP producers and protect the interests of EC banana producers, whilst being compatible with the Uruguay Round of free trade talks in the GATT'. He added, 'Small, vulnerable democratic nations like Jamaica and St Lucia will have access to their traditional EC market whilst having a real opportunity to grow and compete (Europe/Caribbean Confidential, 17 December 1992). Some in the European Parliament meanwhile were angered that the amended proposal had not been scrutinized by the Parliament, although there was recognition by MEPs that the timing was against such scrutiny, and backed away from a confrontation with the Council.

Usually with a compromise package at the end of a Presidency, all the legal texts are signed and sealed on the day of their agreement. However, for the banana issue, because of its controversial nature, there was no legal text. There was a Commission proposal, and a four-page compromise on what was planned, but there was no legal form to the commitments. As a consequence between December and February, there was a debate regarding what the legal text should have in it. In essence, December's vote had only established the principle of the regime, agreement over its detailed application still had to be decided. As it was the end of the UK's Presidency of the Council, the responsibility of securing a vote on the detailed application of the banana proposal passed to Denmark, who had in fact voted against the package in December. After five years of hard negotiations, compromises, and lobbying the banana issue had still to be finalized. The determination to secure the interests of the ACP/EC banana producers on the part of the

UK government had been crucial in getting agreement in principle on a single market regime. However, there was a degree of uncertainty over how Denmark, as President of the Council would settle the issue, as it had opposed the proposal in December. Under these circumstances, it is important to recognize the influence that the President of the Council has in setting the agenda and tone of Council meetings, which can determine whether a measure is successful.

The February Council meeting

The February discussions over the internal implementation of the new banana regime were extremely difficult, partly as a result of the hostile reaction to the proposed regime, both from within the Community and from without. However, the meeting was made even more difficult than expected because of the unprecedented behaviour of a number of member states in withdrawing their support for what had been agreed two months before. The ramifications of this went far wider than just the issue of bananas. Both the Netherlands and Belgium switched their previously held positions under pressure from the dollar banana interests in their respective countries who opposed the December compromise, broke EC precedent, and joined with Germany in requesting further discussion on the details of the accord reached in December. This tactic provoked fury among the Commission and the other Council delegations, notably the UK and France. One Commission official described the Council meeting as 'the most acrimonious Council meeting I've ever seen ... They were roaring and shouting at each other across the table (*Guardian*, 1996). To put back into question the political agreement over bananas would have amounted to reopening December's global compromise package, while undermining the credibility of the Council of Ministers as a decision-making body. Despite the possibility that the December agreement might be overturned, Denmark as Council President decided to put the proposed text with a few minor amendments to a vote, and as in December a qualified majority was sufficient for agreement. Those member states that voted in favour were Spain, France, UK, Ireland, Italy, Denmark, Portugal, Greece, and Luxembourg, constituting 56 votes, while Germany, Belgium and the Netherlands, constituting 20 votes, opposed the measure. Once again, agreement on the banana issue had only been possible through a Qualified Majority, but this was sufficient for the adoption of the legal texts, which paved the way for the introduction of the single market in bananas.

Although Portugal now supported the banana settlement without the complications of the other parts of the December package, the regulations only passed by receiving the support of Denmark who was obliged to defend the integrity of EC procedures by supporting measures that had already been agreed in substance. If Denmark had joined the opposition, the new regime would not have been adopted. In the event, the Danish President of the Council encouraged his junior, who was in the Danish seat to vote for the deal despite having described it as 'protectionist madness' (Europe/Caribbean Confidential, 15 February 1993). The requirement to uphold the proper functioning of EC procedures thus outweighed national self-interest. It seems that the Danish move had been considered in advance as the Danish Parliamentary Committee on EC Affairs had sanctioned the plan almost a fortnight before the vote. The German minister was highly critical of the Danish delegation, claiming that they were only seeking to avoid a crisis within the EC prior to the second Danish referendum on Maastricht in May (Agra Europe, 19 February 1993). Nevertheless, the Danish Council President stated, 'We note with pleasure that the EC has been able to reach a decision on this sensitive issue' (*Agence Europe*, 1993). The legal text and the internal aspects of the December council decision on the single banana regime were adopted on 12 February 1993 as Regulation 404/93 (Official Journal of the European Communities, 1993d). The common organization of the market in bananas came into operation on 1 July 1993, and was due to last until 2002 (Official Journal of the European Communities, 1993e).

The first challenges to the common market organization

The European Court of Justice and the German Constitutional Court

Once the common market organization in bananas had been agreed within the Council of Ministers, those forces that had been pushing for a 'liberal' regime began to explore other avenues of opposition. In May 1993, Germany filed a complaint with the European Court of Justice requesting the annulment of the Council Regulation 404/93. In addition, Germany asked the Court for a preliminary ruling (emergency procedure) to prevent the market organization coming into force as planned, until a decision was made on the merit of the case. The German submission was particularly interesting because, for the first time, a member state brought an action for the annulment of an EC legislative position based on the provisions of GATT. The German government gave numerous reasons for its complaint, including the fact that its special banana protocol had been scrapped, although the legal reasons of the case centred on two main concerns: that the new EC regulation could not take as its basis the Treaty of Rome provisions pertaining to agriculture (majority decisions) because it seeks objectives falling within the scope of development policy, and that the high customs duties were incompatible with the GATT (Official Journal of the European Communities, 1993f). The German action was supported by interventions from Belgium and the Netherlands, while Greece, Spain, France, Italy, Portugal, the UK, and the European Commission supported the defence. The participation of nine of the 12 member states emphasized the importance of this case. Despite the agreement at the February Council meeting, the divisions between the member states, and within the trade itself were apparent. The political compromise had not satisfied those actors that had campaigned against the regime, and as a consequence were determined to explore any avenue, which might provide them with a degree of redress. Thus the action in the European Court of Justice against the new regime, even before the regime itself had come into force, was an attempt to overthrow the political compromise through legal argument. Although the Court actions were unsuccessful it was clear that the divisions within the Council of Ministers in particular would not be easily overcome.

The European Court of Justice rejected demands by the German government, on 29 June, for an injunction to halt the introduction of the new banana regime, stating that the new regime did not cause Germany 'serious and irreparable damage', since the regulations allowed the Commission to rectify difficulties, which might arise. In addition, the Court stated that the urgency of the case had not been proven (*Caribbean Insight*, August 1993; Rapid News Service, 1993; and Official Journal of the European Communities, 1993h). The ruling cleared the way for the introduction of the new regime the day before it was due to come into effect. After the Court had made its preliminary ruling, it finally dismissed the case in October 1994 (European Court of Justice, 1994). Despite the fact that numerous court cases have been brought against the banana regime, the European Court of Justice has never ruled against the fundamental principles underpinning it (see for example cases C-188/12-26, C-122/95 and T-52/99). In addition, German fruit importers attempted to challenge the banana regime through the German court system. Though there were concerns that the Federal Constitutional Court might rule against the regime and thus bring it into conflict with the European Court of Justice, the primacy of European law was upheld and the regime remained intact (Cadot and Webber, 2001, p. 25). However, other legal avenues have proved much more effective in undermining the political compromise achieved in the Council of Ministers.

The General Agreement on Tariffs and Trade

In June 1992, five Latin American banana-producing countries had opened consultations with the EC in the GATT on whether the existing national banana regimes within the Community were GATT compatible, and in February 1993, a GATT Panel began to consider the complaint. During the Panel procedure, Jamaica, Cameroon, Ivory Coast, Senegal and Madagascar represented the ACP countries. Significantly the Windward Islands were unable to participate directly, since they were not members of GATT. Nevertheless, there was a realization that membership was necessary in order that the islands could defend their interests at GATT in the future. By late May, Dominica, St Lucia, and St Vincent had become GATT Contracting Parties, although Grenada was not to become a member until February 1994. However, the applications of Dominica, St Lucia, and St Vincent had not been processed when the GATT Panel ruled against the EC's existing banana regime on 19 May 1993, a decision ratified by GATT's governing council on 16 June.

The Panel recommended that the EC remove the discriminatory quota arrangements that were maintained by the UK, France, Spain, Portugal and Italy (Article XI). In addition, the Panel found that the EC preferential tariff for ACP banana exporters violated Article I (most-favoured nation treatment), in that the benefits of the EC's banana policy were restricted to a small group of countries. The Panel asked the EC to bring its tariff rates for Latin American banana-producing states into line with those for other GATT members (GATT Panel Report, DS32/R). Although the GATT Panel only ruled against the national banana regimes, and not the new single market regime, the ruling was significant as it set a precedent for the future. By ruling against the national regimes, the Panel opened up the possibility of a successful challenge against the new regime. In addition, as the Panel ruled that the preferential tariff for ACP banana importers violated Article I (most-favoured nation treatment), the EC had to reassess its whole trading approach within the Lomé Convention as it was underpinned by tariff rates which discriminated against imports of certain GATT signatories.

The Latin American banana producers welcomed the ruling as a first step to overturning Europe's new banana regime. As Columbia's

Foreign Trade Minister, Juan Manuel Santos, said in a statement, 'This is a very important triumph ... because it strengthens our position in this court battle which we must now continue in its second phase to stop [the new regime]' (Reuter Newswire, 1993). The strategy of the Latin Americans was to use the first ruling to establish various points of principle, which would guide them in their subsequent challenge of the new regime. The EC countered by arguing that the First Panel's decision was no longer valid as it dealt only with the old banana regime, and although the Community blocked adoption of the report, the findings of the first Panel ensured that a second Panel would be convened on the new regime. The US meanwhile was beginning to show an increasing interest in the banana issue, calling for the acceptance of the Panel, and the creation of a second Panel. The US involvement had been restricted by the Presidential elections, but it was known that elements within both the Office of the US Trade Representative and the State Department believed that the European regime went against existing US policy on free trade. Indeed, when in late June 1993 the US Assistant Secretary of State for Latin America and the Caribbean, Donna Hrinak, made the first official public statement on the issue, she suggested that 'We have moved beyond the age where trade preferences are the rule, and any country that wants to benefit from free trade will have to look very seriously at what changes it needs to make in its economic structure to accommodate some of the needs of its trading partners' (Europe/Caribbean Confidential, 2 July 1993). Although, it can be argued that these were ominous words for the future, the US was careful not to overplay its hand, as it did not want to upset the delicate GATT Uruguay Round negotiations that were continuing.

Chapter conclusion

While acknowledging the developing role of the international trading environment in the banana issue, it is important to recognize the highly complex interest-group dynamic within the context of the EC. It can be argued that during the period of negotiations leading up to the creation of the single market in bananas, there was a gradual shift in emphasis away from the policy community, which had been established in the UK, and towards the more complex issue network at the European level. The national policy community had been based on an exclusive membership, stable relations between members, close relationships between groups and government, frequent contact, a high degree of consensus and interdependence between groups and government. While the European issue network had a large number of participants, unstable relations between members, weaker and less regular contacts between groups and governments and much conflict (Marsh and Rhodes, 1992a, p. 251). The transition between the policy community and the issue network had serious ramifications for policy outcomes. However, to properly understand the effects of this shift in interest-groups relations, the criticisms of John (1998) and Dowding (1995) regarding the network approach must be acknowledged.

The criticisms of the approach highlight the problem that networks only tend to explain policy in the context of other factors, and therefore the concept itself can lack explanatory power. In order to address the issue John's (1998) observations can be adopted. He has suggested, 'that network properties have an effect independent of other factors, like group resources. As networks specify a particular structure of linkages the way in which that structure influences communication between actors can affect the way in which issues are processed'. Further, he argues, 'Relationships on policy matters are often an amalgam of professional, propinquitous and friendship associations. Policy-makers relate to each other in different ways, and the network idea captures how different aspects of relationships reinforce each other' (pp. 90–1). It was also recognized that policy network structures have a close relationship with institutions, group structure and resources, and ideas (John, 1998; Daugbjerg and Marsh, 1998; Marsh and Smith, 1996).

The ACP/EC and particularly the Commonwealth Caribbean banana interests were highly effective in their lobbying efforts within the Community. The advantage of being familiar with the European institutions allowed those interests that wanted preferential access to be sustained in the new regime, to gain a strategic advantage over the 'liberal' banana interests. In many ways, the lobbying undertaken by the ACP/EC at the European level was similar to national lobbying, in that 'the most successful groups tend to be those which exhibit the usual professional characteristics – namely resources, advance intelligence, good contacts with bureaucrats and politicians, and an ability to provide policy-makers with useful information and advice' (Mazey and Richardson 1993b, p. 206). In addition, the strategic importance of a number of member states and the European Commission in defending the ACP/EC position was highly significant. Therefore, on one level the effects of the issue network were mitigated by the residual strength of the national policy community, and the effective use of a Euro-level lobbying strategy.

However, it is clear that the policy-making structures and processes of the Community were quite distinct in comparison with the national level. The complex, fragmentary, and more open nature of the European policy process meant that there was not 'the intimate knowledge that often exists between policy actors at the national level', nor was there 'sufficient common interest between them to underpin the development of stable agendas and processes' (Mazey and Richardson, 1993a, p. 23). Therefore, despite the relative effectiveness of the ACP/EC interests at the European level, the close institutional links that existed between the Caribbean banana producers, the UK government and marketing companies were undermined. Indeed, the relative position of the inner and outer circle of actors within the policy community of the UK banana trade was subverted by the openness of decision-making at the European level, and by its multinational character. It can be argued that the 'negotiated order', which existed at the national level was absent at the EC level, and that the characteristics of an issue network began to dominate.

The consequence of a single European market in bananas was that the safeguards for traditional ACP banana suppliers were now less than before. The single market was much larger and more fluid in its construction than the UK market, which meant that the traditional suppliers had less protection against market instability. Further, a European wide Banana Management Committee made up of civil servants from each member state, and chaired by the Commission replaced the institutional mechanisms that had helped stabilize the UK market, particularly the Banana Advisory Committee. Contacts still existed at the national level, but they were less important than in the past. As a consequence what was feared when the UK joined the EEC in 1973 became a reality, with the Caribbean interests being subsumed into a wider and more diverse issue network, which was to have implications for the policy process, policy outcomes and policy change in the future.

7
The Ultimate Challenge: the WTO and the Marginalization of Caribbean Interests

The second GATT challenge and the EU's attempt to co-opt the complainants

Despite the fact that the first GATT Panel ruling against the EU's national banana regimes was not adopted, there was impetus for the establishment of a second Panel in mid-June 1993, to assess the compatibility of the EU's new single market banana regime with the provisions of GATT. In response to this new threat, EU Agriculture Ministers agreed to open negotiations with Costa Rica, Colombia, Guatemala, Nicaragua and Venezuela, the complainants in the case. The EU was prepared to increase the regime's tariff quota by 200 000 tonnes over two years, on condition that the five Latin American countries drop the ongoing GATT dispute prior to the release of the Second Panel report. The negotiations between the EU and the Latin American complainants were the first indication that the ACP in general, and the Commonwealth Caribbean in particular, would be increasingly marginalized in the international debate on the EU's single banana regime. The Commonwealth Caribbean were only third parties in the GATT dispute, and therefore any attempt to reach an accommodation to prevent the Second Panel reporting was going to involve the EU and the Latin American complainants who were directly involved in the case.

The EU proposal sowed dissent between the Latin American complainants, as four of the five positively received the offer, primarily seeing it as a way to avoid lengthy legal proceedings. However, the four in favour of a deal were reluctant to break the unity of the Latin American grouping, and as both Guatemala which had close links with Chiquita, and Ecuador (albeit not a member of GATT) were opposed to any compromise, the four decided to maintain their support for the Panel. As a consequence the Panel Report was published in February 1994, which argued that Regulation 404/93 ran counter to certain GATT rules, including the violation of the principle of most-favoured nation treatment owing to the advantage shown domestic and ACP producers in regard to tariffs, and the distribution of licences which unfairly favoured ACP operators (GATT Panel Report, DS38/R). As soon as the Panel Report was distributed, the EU withdrew its compromise offer, but as it was keen to minimize the international opposition to its banana regime, while increasing the regime's wider credibility, the EU soon renewed its offer to the Latin American complainants. The climate of compromise was reciprocated by Costa Rica, who made clear that agreement was still possible, with Colombia, Venezuela and Nicaragua also open to persuasion. It was apparent that the Panel Report would not be adopted because of a lack of unanimity, and as a result the four Latin American countries felt an arrangement with the EU would be of benefit to them.

After discussions between Directorate General VI (Agriculture) and four of the five GATT complainants in March 1994, a compromise was reached. The Framework Agreement, as it was referred to, involved raising the dollar quota to 2.2 million tonnes by 1995–96, and lowering the tariff from 100 ECU/tonne to 75 ECU/tonne, the latter an added concession demanded by Cost Rica. In addition, the four Latin American countries party to the agreement were allocated 54 per cent of the quota, via country-specific quotas, leaving a 'global' quota of 46 per cent for the remaining third country importers. Further, the Latin American countries were given export licences for 70 per cent of their country quotas in an attempt to reduce the power of the banana companies. In return, the four Latin American signatories agreed not to pursue the adoption of the Second GATT Panel Report, and not to initiate GATT/WTO dispute settlement procedures against the EU's regime for the duration of the agreement (European Commission, 1994). However, Guatemala, was determined to continue its challenge against the EU's regime, and won support for such action from other Latin American governments, including Ecuador, Honduras, Panama and Mexico, who had not been party to the GATT complaint, and felt discriminated against as a consequence. Such perspicacious action on the part of the EU may have eased the pressure on its banana regime in the short term, but in the longer term the opposition of those countries excluded from the Framework Agreement was to precipitate further challenges to the regime.

Conversely, although the Framework Agreement was designed to end legal challenges to the EU's banana regime in the GATT, the reaction of the ACP was not entirely favourable. The additional banana volumes entering the EU as a result of the agreement led to an increase in market supply pressures and precipitated a decline in prices, which adversely affected the returns for ACP banana growers. Indeed, the Framework Agreement along with the subsequent increase in the tariff quota of 353 000 tonnes as a result of the accession of Austria, Finland, and Sweden to the EU on 1 January 1995, meant a fairly significant liberalization of the EU's banana market had taken place, a liberalization that the ACP could do nothing about.

The signing of the Uruguay Round Accords: divisions over bananas continue

As the Framework Agreement was being finalized, the negotiations for the GATT Uruguay Trade Round were being concluded in readiness for the signing of agreements in Marrakesh in April 1994. The European Commission included the new banana regime in the results of the Uruguay Round because a majority in the Council of Ministers had approved the regime, and the Commission considered the Framework Agreement to be an integral part of the regime. However, Germany in particular, contested the Commission's stance concerned that signing the GATT agreement would weaken any legal challenge against the EU's banana regime in the European Court of Justice. Conversely, France feared that Germany with support from other member states could demand the international trade commitment relating to bananas be presented separately, thus increasing the chances of the measure being blocked for incorporation in the Uruguay Round Accords. As a result, France raised the stakes by threatening to prevent approval of the important Government Procurement Agreement with the US, if Germany prevented the adoption of the banana regime as an integral part of the Uruguay Round Agreement.

The problem was that all EU member states had to sign the accord separately along with the Commission, so compromise had to be found if individual states were not to vote against particular aspects of the Uruguay Round. On the morning of 15 April, the day of the official signing ceremony, a compromise deal was reached whereby the Commission would present the implementing regulations for the Uruguay Round in a single package, while accepting that the appended banana tariff schedule would not undermine Germany's opposition to the EU's banana regime. While not resolving the matter fully, the arrangement did allow all 12 member states to sign the GATT Agreement without compromising their differing views on the banana regime. The conclusion of the Uruguay Round was significant in that the agreements established the World Trade Organization (WTO), which set the legal framework for multilateral rules on trade, services, and intellectual property rights, and their enforcement. The WTO was to begin work in January 1995. The creation of a powerful organization to oversee world trade was to prove extremely important in defining the nature of the debate surrounding the EU's single market in bananas, and the interest-group dynamic underpinning it.

The issue of most-favoured nation treatment and the need for a GATT waiver

Even though the EU's banana regime had been incorporated into the accords of the Uruguay Round, and the two GATT Panel rulings had not been enacted, the findings of the Panels had wider ramifications for the Lomé Convention. As the Panels had ruled against the discriminatory tariffication of banana imports as being against GATT's most-favoured nation commitment, the Lomé Convention itself, with its non-reciprocal preferential treatment of ACP goods was put in question. Previously, the EU had thought that the Lomé Convention was an accepted body of international law, and hence there was no reason for a waiver. However, after the GATT Panel rulings the EU and the ACP countries decided that a waiver should be sought and preferably before the end of 1994, as a waiver under the WTO would have been much harder to obtain and to maintain. Thus, in October 1994, in one of the last acts of the GATT under the 1947 rules, the EU formally sought a waiver for the Lomé Convention, and in December 1994 a five-year derogation was granted. The waiver meant that the provisions of Article I of GATT, the most-favoured nation rule, by which tariff concessions must be extended to all other GATT/WTO members on an equal basis, did not apply. The EU was therefore permitted to provide preferential tariff treatment for products originating in ACP states as required by the relevant provisions of the fourth Lomé Convention, without being forced to extend the same preferential treatment to like products of any other GATT/WTO member. Despite the hope on the part of the EU and ACP that the banana issue was now secure from further challenge, the waiver although covering the preferential treatment for products did not cover the way in which that preferential treatment was provided. In the case of the EU's banana regime, the mechanism by which bananas from ACP countries were preferred was considered by some as going far beyond what the scope of the waiver allowed. As a consequence, there was a possibility that the EU's preferential banana import system might be challenged, despite the fact that a waiver had been agreed for the Lomé Convention and its discriminatory tariff arrangements.

The increasing interest of the US in the banana dispute

The US government had taken an interest in the banana dispute at various times during the 1990s, but in the autumn of 1994 that interest became more defined. This was precipitated by the growing feeling on the part of some US companies that the EU's banana regime, together with the Framework Agreement, seriously discriminated against them. The first indication of more serious US opposition to the EU's regime came in August, when a petition was received by the United States Trade Representative (USTR) from 12 senators, calling for a formal inquiry into the regime. A couple of months later, Chiquita and the Hawaii Banana Producers Association (whose bananas are predominately grown for domestic production) sought action from the US government which responded by launching in October an investigation under the unfair trade provisions of Section 301 of the US Trade Act. Section 301 allows the USTR to take action (including unilateral measures) against policies of foreign countries that harm US commerce. The USTR, Mickey Kantor, at the time of taking up the complaint, noted that, 'American banana marketing companies should be able to compete on a fair basis in a European market, just as European firms can here.' While Carl Lindner, President of Chiquita said, 'We applaud the US government's decision to accept this action and compliment Ambassador Kantor for his strong commitment to upholding the principles of free and fair world trade. The US government now becomes a significant, major player in this dispute and will fight to achieve fair treatment of US industry's interests on all fronts' (PrNewswire, 1994).

At the beginning of 1995, the USTR issued a preliminary decision finding that the banana regime did adversely affect US interests, and threatened retaliatory action against imports from both the EU and the Latin American signatories of the Framework Agreement. With the threatened action on the part of the US, the banana dispute began to take on a broader significance that in time was to affect the overall US–EU trading relationship. Further, it is interesting to note that there were now tensions between the US and certain countries of Latin America, which were considered to share the same agenda when it came to opposing the EU's banana regime. In March, the USTR tabled a proposal for changes to the banana regime that Kantor hoped would be the basis of an agreement to end the conflict. The proposal consisted of an increase in the tariff quota, the abolition of the Framework Agreement, and a reallocation of licences in favour of the US banana companies (*Caribbean Insight*, June 1995). Although the proposal was one that considered the options for reform within the context of the existing regime, it was unacceptable to a number of EU states and the banana producing states of the ACP. The opponents of the Kantor proposal believed that the scheme was too expansionist in its remit, and thus would damage the interests of the ACP banana importers.

As a consequence, in August 1995 the USTR indicated that the banana issue would be pursued at the WTO with a view to resolving the dispute, supported by a new Section 301 investigation. This required the USTR to make a determination as to whether EU practices were actionable under Section 301 by no later than 30 days after the conclusion of the WTO dispute settlement process or 27 March 1997, whichever was the earlier. The indication that the USTR would take the EU to the WTO was highly significant, in that a process was begun that was to fundamentally alter the interest-group dynamic within the EU banana trade. In addition, the undertaking on the part of the US to support the WTO action with its own trade legislation provided the US with an additional tool that it could use against the EU if the WTO process proved to be unsatisfactory. Such an approach led to accusations that the US was usurping the role of the WTO by using its own unilateral trading powers.

The US administration, although pushing ahead with the WTO complaint attempted to reassure the Caribbean banana producers that they did not want preferential access to end in the EU, rather to overturn a regime that was unfair to its corporate interests. However, the Caribbean banana-producing countries were not reassured, despite high-level discussions with the US. The US was unyielding in its opposition to certain aspects of the EU's banana regime, which exasperated the Caribbean representatives, who accused the US of not being prepared to negotiate and having already made up its mind to refer the dispute to the WTO. The Caribbean's mood was not improved, when both Costa Rica and Colombia were threatened with trade sanctions if they refused to withdraw from the Framework Agreement. In the US Senate, majority leader Bob Dole made repeated legislative attempts to punish Costa Rica and Colombia for accepting the Framework Agreement. Both countries were highly critical of the US action arguing that any action against them would be inconsistent with America's tradition of rewarding countries for their cooperation in the drug war, and that the actions themselves could force banana growers to cultivate drug crops. Costa Rica and Colombia only managed to avoid sanctions by agreeing to address US exporters' complaints and to cooperate with the US in its opposition to the EU's banana regime.

The motivation for US involvement in the banana issue has been questioned, as it is unusual for the USTR's thinly staffed office to devote resources to a case in which few US jobs are at stake, particularly when only around a dozen cases a year are accepted by the USTR, and even fewer are taken to the WTO. Only a very small amount of bananas are produced in the US, all of which are grown in Hawaii, and even though Chiquita is a significant US concern with an annual revenue of around three billion dollars, most of its 40 000 workers are based in Honduras and Guatemala. However, it seems that as Chiquita was anxious to make up for losses sustained in the Far Eastern and Eastern European markets as well as in its Latin American operations, the company hoped that an opening of the EU market would help mitigate some of its incurred losses. From 1992 to 1994 the company had suffered over $400 million in losses, with its share price falling from $40 to $11 (*Time Magazine*, 2000). In order to create a momentum for action Chiquita laid the entire blame for its losses on the European banana regime. Indeed, it has been suggested that Chiquita believed that Europe's banana regime was introduced in order 'to break or reduce the power of the multinational US banana companies. Convinced that it would never get its way in Europe' (Cadot and Webber, 2001, p. 21). As a consequence, Carl Lindner and Chiquita believed that only with US government support would the company be able to challenge the regime.

Two arguments have been put forward in an attempt to explain the extent of US government involvement in the banana dispute. First, it has been suggested that the US government was determined that the banana case should set the correct precedent for future WTO actions. In essence, the US wanted to be sure 'that WTO rules would be respected and that the WTO would not lose its credibility as a mechanism to halt protectionism' (Gunn Clissold, 2001, p. 3). Within this context it could be argued that the banana dispute's importance had less to do with the actual issue of disagreement and much more to do with the fact that it was the first major dispute between the world's two most powerful trading blocs within the WTO. Indeed, with festering disagreements between the two parties over hormone treated beef and genetically modified food, the banana dispute was seen as a test case for possible future action within the WTO.

Another, perhaps more powerful suggestion has been made that financial donations from Carl Lindner, a staunch Republican, and his American Financial Corporation, the parent company of Chiquita, to both Democrats and Republicans was important in persuading the US to take action against the EU's banana regime. For example, in 1993–94 Chiquita contributed just under one million dollars in 'soft money' to both parties and it has been alleged that half of that sum was donated in November and December 1994 just after the launch of the Section 301 investigation (Common Cause, 1995, p. 1). Indeed, financial donations from Lindner and his associates worth hundreds of thousands of pounds continued throughout the decade, much of it as 'soft money', and much of it being donated during crucial periods of the dispute process (*Time Magazine*, 2000). The manner of the donations is significant as 'soft money' contributions remain 'outside the limits and prohibitions of federal law, [and include] large individual or political action committee contributions and direct corporate or union contributions' (Common Cause, 1995, p. 10). In addition, the financial dimension was complemented by strong support from certain high profile US politicians. Individuals such as Trent Lott, the former Republican majority leader of the Senate, John Glenn, at the time a Democratic Senator from Ohio, Terence McAuliffe, the leading Democratic fundraiser and now Democratic National Chairman, and Newt Gingrich, the former Republican majority leader of the House of Representatives all had close connections with Chiquita. In addition, Bob Dole used Carl Lindner's corporate jet for his 1996 presidential campaign, while Lindner himself was a guest of the White House, sleeping in the Lincoln Bedroom on occasion (*Time Magazine*, 2000). Carl Lindner has declined to comment on the alleged link between political donations and government action, while the US government itself has argued that such events are nothing more than coincidence. However, the importance of private financial donations in influencing government policy seems to be an important element in the interest group dynamic, but its precise significance is difficult to quantify, as the nature of policy formulation is so complex, with a large number of different influences at work.

The role of Chiquita is important in illustrating the flexibility of approach that companies can employ when defending their commercial interests. When the predecessor of Chiquita, the United Fruit Company, was involved in the ACP banana trade it resented any government interference, as the company could influence the nature of that trade directly. However, after Chiquita sold Fyffes in 1986, the parent company no longer had a direct role in the ACP trade, and as a consequence had to adopt other techniques to further its interests in a part of the trade, which the company was no longer involved. Thus, when the EU's banana regime was established providing preferential access for ACP producers, the company was quite willing to co-opt US government assistance in order to challenge the privileged position of the ACP. The flexibility of Chiquita's approach in defending its interests goes some way to account for the company's market resilience over the last century.

Within the US, however, it would be wrong to assume that all Congressional representatives, and the other large multinational banana companies were opposed to the EU regime. The Black Congressional Caucus was supportive of the Caribbean banana producers, and during the height of the WTO crisis in the autumn of 1998 called for a boycott of Chiquita bananas. In addition, unlike Chiquita, both Dole and Del Monte (now a Chilean-owned company, based in Florida) were more accommodating to the EU's banana regime. Such a stance had much to do with the fact that since the introduction of the regime, both Dole and Del Monte increased their market share from 12 and five per cent respectively in 1992 to around 16 per cent each in 1998, while Chiquita's share fell from over 30 per cent to less than 20 per cent in the same period (FruiTrop, October 1999). In terms of the approach of Dole and Del Monte to the EU's banana regime, Dole favoured changes to the way it was administered, but did not support the US action, while Del Monte had modified its production, transportation and distribution systems in preparation for the new regime, and was quite happy with the fundamentals of the system. The distinct approaches taken by the multinational banana companies in relation to the EU's banana regime is important, as it highlights the complex set of interests that exist within the banana trade which transcend general assumptions.

The first WTO Panel: a challenge to the basis of the EU regime

The first moves to challenge the EU's banana regime at the WTO were taken in September 1995, when the US filed a petition at the WTO supported by Guatemala, Honduras and Mexico. The US believed that the EU had not done enough to meet the concerns of those parties critical of the regime, and as a consequence felt it necessary to activate the WTO's dispute settlement procedures. More fundamentally, the USTR felt that the EU had a case to answer, maintaining that the regime protected the economic interests of certain European firms at the expense of non-EU companies, something the GATT waiver did not cover. Meanwhile, the Latin American complainants felt that the EU's banana regime unfairly penalized their banana exports, particularly when it came to the Framework Agreement. However, this first petition was dropped when Ecuador, the world's largest banana exporter, entered the WTO and sought to join the dispute against the EU's regime. A second petition was then filed in February 1996, which superseded the first and now included Ecuador as one of the complainants. The scene was therefore set for the first trade dispute involving the EU and US under the new dispute procedures of the WTO.

The WTO was designed to be a strong and independent body providing the means for resolving trade disputes. The most significant change from the GATT was the dispute settlement process contained in the Understanding on Rules and Procedures Governing the Settlement of Disputes. The Dispute Settlement Body (DSB), consisting of WTO members, administers it. After consultations, the DSB can establish a panel to examine the issues raised by the complainants, and to pass judgement on whether the measures under consideration conform to international trade law. If there is an appeal, the DSB then appoints an Appellate Body to consider the matter. The decision of the Appellate Body is fundamentally different from that of the panel under the GATT 1947 dispute settlement rules, in that an Appellate Body report has to be adopted by the DSB and unconditionally accepted by the parties to the dispute unless the DSB decides by negative consensus not to adopt the report. Such negative consensus is highly unusual, as it would need the benefiting party to reject the favourable decision of the Panel. Under the new system, any ruling is therefore adopted despite the opposition of the defendants, unlike in the GATT where a defendant was able to prevent the ruling being adopted, as adoption required unanimity. The new system thus shifted the balance of the dispute settlement process away from the defendant and towards the complainant, which meant any changes to the EU's banana regime that were stipulated by the WTO had to be implemented.

Within the dispute settlement process, consultations were undertaken between the parties to the dispute (the US, the EU and the four

Latin American countries) during March and April 1996. However, as little progress was made in narrowing the differences during that time the US and the other complainants asked for the creation of a dispute panel, a request that the DSB acceded to on 8 May. The Panel consisted of Kym Anderson, Director of the Centre for International Economic Studies in Australia, Christian Haberli, executive director of the GATT/WTO division of the Swiss Ministry of Economic Affairs, and Stuart Harbinson, permanent representative of Hong Kong to GATT/WTO, and the Chairman of the Panel. The ACP banana producing countries were extremely disappointed with the composition of the panel, believing that none of its members truly represented the interests of developing countries in the dispute. Of more significance, however, was the fact that the ACP countries were only allowed third party rights at the panel hearings, which meant that they were grouped together with countries such as Canada, India, Japan and Thailand, who had no direct interest in the dispute (WT/DS27/R/ECU). The significance of the third party status for the ACP countries was that for the first time they were excluded from direct involvement in a process, which was considering the future status of their banana exports. In the past, the banana-producing interests of the ACP were able to directly access the policy process both at the national and European levels, in order to make sure their interests were secured. However, the WTO had the power to demand changes to the EU's banana regime, irrespective of the views held by the ACP.

At the Panel hearings in September and October, both the EU and the ACP states, the latter doing so under their third party status, set out a legal defence for the provisions of the EU's banana regime, while the complainants, along with Paraguay, presented arguments against the regime. There was a perception on the part of the Caribbean that during the hearings the Panel was receptive to those arguments that suggested the EU's regime was a restriction on free trade, while dismissing submissions which argued that the regime was an important mechanism in promoting economic development. In addition, the legal defence set out by the Caribbean was blunted somewhat by the fact that only permanent government employees were allowed to sit in on Panel hearings. As a consequence, a number of advisers to the Caribbean banana-producing countries, including those with legal experience, were barred from the panel hearings after the US delegation protested at their presence. Three officials were excluded who had been accredited by St Lucia, but were informally representing 12 countries in the ACP group, while a lawyer representing St Vincent, a former deputy USTR was also ejected. Only Ambassador Edwin Laurent of the Eastern Caribbean Mission was allowed to remain (author's interviews). Small states such as St Lucia and St Vincent were unable to employ the necessary expertise on a permanent basis, and had legal advisers when required. The ejection of these advisers from the Panel hearings angered Ambassador Laurent, who subsequently argued, 'Small countries like mine have no power ... All that is on offer is rough justice' (*Caribbean Insight*, 20 April 1997). The exclusion of a number of accredited representatives of the small Caribbean states exacerbated the feeling that the nature of the WTO discriminated against the particular needs and circumstances of the smaller contracting parties of the organization. The perception that the WTO was insensitive to the needs of small less-developed states grew during the time, which the EU's banana regime was being considered at the WTO. Indeed, it can be argued that concerns over the way in which the high-profile banana case was dealt with at the WTO helped to precipitate the more general opposition to the organization that manifested itself during the Seattle trade talks in December 1999.

The publication of the WTO's final ruling came in May 1997, which upheld several elements of the complaint lodged by the US and the four Latin American countries. The Panel found that the EU's banana regime went against Articles I: 1, III: 4 and X: 3 of the GATT, and Article 1.2 of the Licensing Agreement, as regards the discriminatory licensing system being against the interests of third country and non-traditional ACP banana producers and importers. Further, the Panel found that the regime was contrary to Article XIII of the GATT, with reference to the discriminatory Banana Framework Agreement tariff quota allocations, and the quota-specific allocations for ACP imports. The Panel also ruled that the regime was at variance with Articles II and XVII of GATS (General Agreement on Trade in Services) in that it discriminated against distributors of Latin American and non-traditional ACP bananas. The banana ruling was the first case won under the new General Agreement on Trade in Services, and confirmed the broad scope of the coverage of GATS and its significance in eliminating barriers in distribution and other service sectors. The Panel did rule that the EU could continue to give preferential access to its markets for traditional ACP bananas, but the Panel recommended 'that the Dispute Settlement Body request the European Communities to bring its import regime for bananas into conformity with its obligations under GATT, the Licensing Agreement and the GATS' (WT/DS27/R/ECU). The Appellate Body heard an unsuccessful appeal in July, and in September, two weeks after the Appellate Body report was released, the DSB adopted the ruling. The EU undertook to reform its banana regime to meet the WTO ruling, and was given until 1 January 1999 to do so, much to the annoyance of the US who thought that too long a period for compliance.

The rulings of the Panel and the Appellate Body, meanwhile, were strongly criticized by Caribbean politicians and officials. For example, the Prime Minister of Dominica, Edison James, argued, 'We feel betrayed by the WTO, because we joined the Organization believing that its primary purpose was to bring about improved living standards and equity and fairness in international trade.' While Ambassador Laurent claimed

> The experience of the case has exposed blatant shortcomings in the [WTO disputes] system. These must be addressed in any reform, including the necessity to take into account the impact of decisions especially when, as in this case, the affected countries have vulnerable and fragile economies. It is already too late for our bananas case, maybe the right improvements can yet be made to a system which would be helpful to the participation of small developing countries and reassure them that the system is not structurally weighted against them.' (*The Courier*, No. 166, 1997, p. 60)

From the Caribbean perspective, the banana case at the WTO illustrated the narrow remit of the organization in terms of the development/liberal trade dichotomy, and the risk of marginalization of small states at the WTO. Although there is some merit to these arguments, the former issue has to be qualified, as the WTO did not rule against preferential access *per se*, but just the nature of the system that sustained that access. It could be argued that in reality the principle of preferential access, and the way in which that access was safeguarded, were so closely linked that the ruling against the latter negated the former, but it was hoped that reforms to the regime would be possible under the Lomé Convention waiver, which would secure the position of ACP bananas in the European market.

However, it is important to recognize that the ruling by the WTO was a seminal moment in defining the changing nature of the interest group dynamic within the UK and EU banana trades. There was now an actor, which had the power to override the traditional interest-group dynamic that had defined the nature of the UK banana trade, and latterly the EU banana trade during the twentieth century. The EU had no choice but to accept the Panel ruling and change the nature of its banana regime, a change which superseded any concerns the European Commission, the European Parliament, the member states, the banana producers, and the banana companies may have had. A new level of arbitration thus undermined the usual avenues of influence. Under these circumstances it can be argued that the WTO was establishing itself as an important issue network, with particular characteristics that determined the nature of relations between the actors involved and the subsequent policy outcomes. In order to properly understand the difference between the issue network at the European level and the issue network at the global level, the observations of Daugbjerg and Marsh (1998), Dowding (1995), John (1998), and Marsh and Smith (1996) of the network approach need to be acknowledged.

Policy network structures have a close association with institutions, group structure and resources, ideas, and personal relationships, which all provide networks with independent properties. The WTO is primarily a legally-based organization, unlike the EU, which has a strong political dimension. The WTO also has a much narrower remit than the EU in terms of its responsibilities, and is underpinned by a different ideological rationale. Further, it is important to recognize that the WTO is a body that involves national governments, or in the case of the EU a single supranational trading entity. As a consequence those interests that represented banana growers and banana companies were excluded from this higher level of arbitration, and were therefore obliged to continue their lobbying efforts at the national and regional level, in order to make sure that their interests were not neglected at the WTO. In addition, the basis of the relationship between the states at the WTO and those within the EU is quite different, which helped to determine the way in which the banana issue was processed in each issue network.

The interest-group dynamic in the new organization was therefore more legalistic and stratified than in the other arenas of influence, with the result that the traditional actors involved in the ACP trade saw their interests superseded. However, it is important to appreciate that the effect the WTO had on ACP interests was partially due to the nature of the banana issue, in that the dispute was primarily between the US and the EU, which meant that the ACP only had third party status. As a consequence, the ACP were marginalized in the dispute settlement process, which meant that they were grouped together with countries who had no direct stake in the issue under consideration.

The WTO process did not discriminate against the interests of the ACP states *per se*, but rather the particular nature of the issue under adjudication meant that the ACP's influence was constrained.

The EU reforms its banana regime: an attempted accommodation between the WTO and the Lomé Convention

As with the negotiations for the design of the EU's original single market regime in the late 1980s and early 1990s, the method of policy formulation was similar, although the dynamics of the process were different. Unlike in 1992 when a new regime had to be designed from scratch, the changes needed in 1998 were less fundamental. In addition, the Commission was more experienced in handling the banana portfolio, with the regular contacts within the Banana Management Committee proving most useful in judging what kind of changes would be acceptable to member states. As a consequence, the actual discussions for a revised regime were less controversial than those for the original regime. Although there were strong criticisms of the US involvement in the process, after its representatives suggested that the European Council should vote on a US designed proposal (Agra Europe, 26 June 1998). Despite such interference the Inter-Services Group prepared proposals, subsequently adopted by the European Commissioners, which entailed abolishing the import licence system which discriminated between ACP and dollar operators, while retaining a revised quota system designed to sustain duty-free access for ACP banana producers. Although a number of states at the February 1998 Agriculture Council meeting wanted a tariff-only solution, no nation specifically ruled out the Commission compromise. However, those countries that had taken the EU's regime to the WTO were already indicating that the revised proposals did not go far enough in meeting WTO compliance.

Despite such criticism, the European Parliament and the Economic and Social Committee considered the proposals, and after further discussions at ministerial and official level the proposals were placed before the Agriculture Council at the end of June. As in December 1992, the UK was President of the Council, and with the Commission wanted to secure a single package deal which forced member states to compromise, thus making the passage of the banana proposal more likely (for details of package see Council of the European Union General Secretariat, 1999). The Council subsequently reached agreement on the package by a Qualified Majority.

Under the banana agreement the tariff quota remained unchanged, although the distribution of it was altered with over 90 per cent being allocated to Ecuador, Costa Rica, Colombia and Panama, the four main EU banana-supplying countries. In addition, there were no longer specific quota allocations for traditional ACP bananas, just a global ACP quota. As a consequence, the Commonwealth Caribbean countries had no guaranteed quantitative access in the European market. The operators were able to import from any source, unlike under the previous rules where the Caribbean producers had a quota assigned to them. Such a change meant that there was the potential for competition between traditional ACP suppliers for a share of the EU market, with no guarantee that any individual state would be able to export its traditional volumes of bananas.

The special incentive through the licence system for operators to import ACP or EU bananas was also ended. Under the old arrangement ACP/EU operators automatically held dollar licences whether they could use them or not, and if not they could sell them on. The practice of selling import licences was heavily criticized for being open to abuse by those who had no intention in trading in dollar bananas, creating a highly profitable trade in licences. In the reformed regime, a three-year reference period was the basis for establishing operating rights and licence distribution. Under this reference period ACP banana importers had licences to import dollar bananas, but there was no longer the right to claim dollar licences, so if all the licences were not used future licence distribution was reduced. Thus in the longer term the commitment to import ACP bananas into the EU had the potential to be undermined, particularly if ACP importers were unable to sustain their levels of dollar banana imports. The Commission and the Presidency were both pleased with the changes, believing that the banana reforms would make the regime WTO compliant, while also honouring the EU's commitments to the ACP banana producers under the Lomé Convention. The new banana regime came into force at the beginning of 1999, and was due to last at least until the end of 2004 (Official Journal of the European Communities, 1998a).

The second WTO Panel: a challenge to the rule-driven framework

Through the first half of 1998 attempts were made by the US to persuade the EU to make further changes to the revised regime, which the US thought would make it more acceptable to the WTO. However, when these efforts were rebuffed the USTR Charlene Barshefsky on 7 July asked the EU whether the WTO Panel could be reconvened on an expedited basis to assess whether the new regime was WTO consistent. The EU resisted such demands during the autumn, believing that no case could be brought until the precise regulations of the EU regime were finalized in late October (Official Journal of the European Communities, 1998b). As a consequence of this perceived stalling on the part of the EU, members of the US Congress demanded that unilateral action should be taken by their government to force the EU to alter its regime. The role of domestic political pressure in the US should again be recognized as an important influence in encouraging a more pro-active stance by the US government on this issue. As part of the Congressional campaign, a bill was introduced in the House of Representatives requiring retaliatory measures to be prepared. The bill was only withdrawn after the USTR outlined plans at a meeting of the WTO's Dispute Settlement Body (DSB) in October for unilateral action to be taken under Section 301 of the Trade Act against the EU for alleged inaction to comply with the WTO ruling. The EU condemned such action as being illegal under WTO law. The EU argued that sanctions were only allowed when authorized by the DSB.

Despite the standoff between the EU and the US, Ecuador broke ranks with the US and the other Latin American complainants to begin the process of reconvening the WTO Panel, engaging in consultations at the WTO on 23 November 1998. Ecuador was critical of the behaviour of the US and EU for ignoring its interests, while exploiting the banana dispute for their own ends. Ecuador was better able to act unilaterally than the other Latin American complainants, as Chiquita has no significant interest in Ecuador, whose banana interests are dominated by the Ecuadorian owned NABOA company. While Ecuador was undertaking its own action, the EU, in an unprecedented move asked the DSB on 15 December to set up a Panel to examine the EU's reformed banana regime. Usually it is the complainants who request the establishment of a Panel, but in this case the EU wanted to ensure that the US arbitrated the dispute within the WTO in order to avoid the imposition of unilateral sanctions. Further, on 18 December, Ecuador requested the re-establishment of the original Panel to examine whether the new EU regime was WTO compatible.

By the end of December 1998 there were signs that the dispute was beginning to dominate EU/US trade relations, despite previous efforts of both sides to isolate the issue while strengthening their cooperation in other areas. It was hoped that at a meeting on 18 December 1998, between US President Bill Clinton and EU Commission President Jacques Santer and EU President-in-Office Austrian Chancellor Viktor Klima, the US President would give some political direction to resolve the banana dispute, but the White House was distracted with impeachment hearings and a new Iraqi crisis. Instead, the dispute worsened on 21 December when the USTR published a list of 16 products on which it was threatening to impose 100 per cent duties 'as early as February 1st' or 'not later than March 2nd' (*Inside Europe*, 21 December 1998). The products included, pecorino cheese, bath preparations (though not bath salts), handbags, knitted sweaters, lead-acid storage batteries, and chandeliers. The US maintained that such action was permitted by the WTO because the EU had failed to amend its banana regime to be fully consistent with WTO rules, and that the increase in tariffs would be equivalent to the harm caused by the EU regime. The list, which covered trade to the value of US$520 million, was to be applied on European goods except for those from Denmark and the Netherlands on the basis that the two countries had voted against the revised banana regime at the EU Council meeting in June. The US followed this course of action, because they feared that the normal WTO process would take too long, thus restricting the USTR's ability to take action. Despite the hope that the WTO would effectively promote a new approach to global trade, the realities of diplomatic horse-trading transcended any high ideals that may have existed. The determination of the US to force the EU to design a regime that met its requirements risked usurping the role of the WTO as the final arbiter in international trade disputes.

At the heart of the dispute between the EU and the US was an interpretation over two articles of the Dispute Settlement Understanding. The EU believed that in the circumstances Article 21.5 should take precedence, in that any doubt over the compatibility of the revised regime should be decided through recourse to the dispute settlement procedures. The US meanwhile believed that it had a right to impose sanctions under Article 22, which allows a member of the WTO to ask for authorization to suspend trade concessions when a third party has not implemented WTO findings. The US was concerned that if Article 21.5 took precedence, implementing measures could be continually changed if challenged with no recourse to Article 22 and the right to receive compensation or to suspend trade concessions (author's interview). The problem was that this was the first case in which compliance had been disputed and it took the WTO into uncharted legal waters. WTO rules permit retaliation, but they were ambiguous about how compliance should be determined. Therefore there were no authoritative rules laying out the relationship between Articles 21.5 and 22 of the Dispute Settlement Understanding. (In a subsequent Panel, it was ruled that the US trade legislation used as the basis for imposing sanctions in trade disputes is compatible with world trade rules, but that the US should only use the legislation in compliance with WTO rules and procedures (WT/DS152/R)).

Despite the threat of sanctions the DSB established the Panels requested by Ecuador and the EU on 12 January 1999, and were due to complete their work in April, although this was at least a month after US sanctions were scheduled to be applied. As a consequence, the US prepared to ask the DSB on 25 January to approve its trade sanctions. However, when the US attempted to get WTO approval, Dominica and St Lucia, supported by the Ivory Coast, effectively delayed the examination of the US request for authorization of sanctions by blocking the adoption of the agenda, the first time this had happened. Under WTO consensus rules, meetings cannot proceed if the agenda is not accepted. The representatives of Dominica and St Lucia argued that it was illogical for the WTO to consider the US request at a time when a Panel had just been established to rule on WTO conformity of the EU's revised banana regime. In an associated press release it was argued

> that the Dispute Settlement Body cannot be seen to undermine the dispute settlement process, which lies at the very foundation of the multilateral system. As founding members of the WTO, the islands were concerned that a dangerous precedent might be set, if the US was permitted to act on a unilateral determination as to whether the EU's regime is WTO compatible. (Embassies of the Eastern Caribbean States and Mission to the European Communities, 26 January 1999)

Although blocking the DSB agenda was only a temporary expedient, and had no direct bearing on the final outcome of the banana issue, it was an important gesture on the part of two small states highlighting the fact that their rights and interests had not been fully recognized during the time the WTO had considered the banana issue. As regards the banana dispute itself, such action on the part of Dominica and St Lucia can be seen as a last act of defiance before the US and Latin American complainants finally got their way. Nevertheless, the US was deeply critical of the move and accused the EU of colluding with the two Caribbean states, an accusation strongly denied by the EU and the islands. With the agenda blocked, the meeting was adjourned to allow the WTO director-general to find a compromise to break the deadlock.

A compromise plan was agreed between the EU and the US on 29 January that postponed the unilateral imposition of US sanctions against EU products until 12 March at the earliest. In return the Panel created to consider the validity of the EU's revised banana regime would also examine the US request for sanctions, and to set the value of any penalty. Although the threat of sanctions had been postponed, some EU member states remained concerned about the wider ramifications of the dispute. Italy in particular, strongly criticized the effect it was having on the wider trading environment, a view supported by a number of European companies whose products were at risk from US sanctions. There was a belief in some quarters that the EU's commitment to safeguard preferential access for ACP bananas was damaging European economic interests, and a result there was a realization that defending the banana regime was becoming more trouble than it was worth (author's interviews).

There was an expectation that on 2 March the WTO Panel would report on the amount of sanctions that the US could apply on EU goods, with Washington planning to ask the WTO's dispute settlement body the following day to authorize sanctions based on the recommendations of the Panel. However, the arbitrators gave the US and EU only an initial report on how they intended to proceed and requested additional information from both sides. In response, the USTR announced that the US Customs Service would begin 'withholding liquidation' on imports valued at US$520 million of selected products from the EU. In a move that the EU maintained broke WTO rules, US customs on 3 March ordered importers of the products on the sanctions list to post bonds of 100 per cent of the goods' value, although the US would refrain from collecting higher duties until the release of the arbitrators' final decision. The US used the bond mechanism to ensure that the delay in the WTO arbitrators' decision did not result in delaying its timetable for the unilateral imposition of sanctions.

The final decision from the WTO Panel considering Ecuador's complaint came on 6 April 1999, and found that the EU's revised banana regime was still inconsistent with WTO rules in a number of respects. In particular, the Panel found against the reference period for the distribution of import licences, arguing that it maintained the distortions of the previous regime, and that the separate ACP quota was in violation of Article XIII of GATT. At the same time authorization was given for US sanctions, which the arbitrators agreed should be implemented up to a total of $191.4 million, which is just over a third of the amount the US was originally claiming (WT/DS27/ARB). The Panel established on behalf of the EU refused to make any judgements citing the precedence of the Ecuador panel and the lack of information provided by the EU (WT/DS27/RW/EEC).

On 9 April the office of the USTR published a revised list of European products, which would be subject to a suspension of concessions, and on 19 April the WTO Dispute Settlement Body authorized the action. It is ironic that after the second WTO Panel, the immediate result was not a liberalization of the EU's banana regime, but an increase in trade protectionism on the part of the US to punish the EU for its perceived intransigence, a move authorized by the WTO itself. The operation of the WTO's dispute settlement system proved to be more complicated, both politically and technically, than was the expectation when the WTO was established, highlighting the fact that even a legally-based trading organization was not above domestic political considerations. However, despite the complicated, and at times controversial, events that surrounded the second WTO Panel, it is important to remember that the interests of the ACP banana producers were once more under threat. After the first WTO Panel, the ACP banana interests had been able to use its network of influence at the national and European levels to secure a revised EU regime, which sustained their preferential access. However, once the banana issue returned to the WTO, the ACP interests were again marginalized as a result of the nature of the new dispute settlement system.

The account of networks by Marsh and Rhodes (1992a), supplemented by the work of John (1998), Daugbjerg and Marsh (1998), and Marsh and Smith (1996), provides the basis for understanding the changes in the nature of the interest group relationships at the national, European, and international levels. However, an additional approach is needed to help understand how the influence of the traditional interests was altered by the structure of the different levels of decision-making. In order to assess the precise dynamics of this trend, an adaptation of Grant's (1978) 'insider/outsider' group paradigm is useful, in the form of May and Nugent's (1982) account of 'thresholder' groups, where groups oscillate over time between insider and outsider strategies. The value of the insider/outsider distinction is that it focuses attention on changes in status and strategy when the nature of the political environment undergoes change. The approach can also highlight the choices that have to be made by groups and government and on the exchange relationships that develop between them.

It can be argued that with the development of the WTO as an issue network to challenge the role of the other policy networks at the national and European levels, the traditional ACP banana interests took on the characteristics of thresholder groups. Within the policy networks at the national, and to a lesser extent at the EU level, the ACP interests were able to influence the decision-making process directly as the actors were considered to be legitimate by politicians and civil servants and were consulted regularly. The status of the ACP interests was secured through the pursuit of a broad political strategy (after Whiteley and Winyard, 1987), although an insider strategy was important in helping to gain insider status (after Grant, 1978). However, it should be recognized that pursuing an insider strategy was sometimes not sufficient to achieve insider status, and that the logic of accommodation restricted the ACP's room for manoeuvre (Jordan, Maloney and McLaughlin, 1992). At the EU level in particular, the traditional ACP interests were marginalized on certain issues, for example the establishment of the Framework Agreement, and the market liberalization as a result of the accession of new members to the EU. Nevertheless, overall it can be argued that the ACP interests defending the concept of preferential access were able to sustain their insider status, through the pursuit of an effective strategy. As Grant (1995) has suggested, 'While not denying the force of the logic of the bargaining process in a policy community, groups can make choices which can either improve an initially weak bargaining position or undermine an initially strong position' (p. 16).

However, within the context of the WTO the ACP banana interests became outsider groups, with the ACP states being relegated to third party status, and the banana-producing representatives having no direct role in the process. In this context, the issue of strategy and status was less important as the ACP interests were unable to gain proper recognition at the WTO because of the nature of the issue under consideration. Both status and strategy were pre-determined within the framework of WTO rules, and so there was little opportunity for the ACP states to adopt a particular strategy to improve their standing within the dispute settlement process. The ACP interests became outsiders within the WTO not through choice, but through design. Therefore, as the banana dispute moved between the two issue networks at the European and international levels, the banana interests of the ACP oscillated between having insider and outsider status. The more distant the decision-making process became, the more damaging were the policy outcomes for the ACP.

The politics of fatigue: a final settlement

There was a feeling of inevitability when the WTO Panel gave its judgement. On 21 April, the EU decided not to appeal against the ruling, and undertook to amend the regime. With no appeal forthcoming, the Panel Report was adopted by the DSB in early May. The European Commission then set about the task of reforming the EU's banana regime once more. The divisions between EU member states over the banana issue were as deep as ever, with one group of countries including Germany, Sweden, the Netherlands, Finland, Austria and Luxembourg supporting the idea of a tariff-only system, which would eliminate the problem of licence allocation, while another group consisting of France, Spain, Greece and Portugal strongly opposed this approach, arguing that it was essential to retain a quota system for the higher cost ACP/EU producers. The UK, meanwhile, indicated that it was prepared to accept a tariff-based approach provided the Caribbean producers were protected in other ways. The difference of opinion between the member states was compounded by the crisis within the European Commission over the allegations of corruption, which led to the resignation of the Santer cabinet. The caretaker Commission that followed did not believe it had the authority to table a reform proposal without stronger political direction from member states.

The Commission's position was made even more difficult by the wide differences of opinion between the other actors involved in the EU's banana trade. The Latin American countries and operators wanted to safeguard their high export earnings in the EU market through the maintenance of a tariff rate quota, but disagreed on how it should be operated. The US meanwhile, wanted a reference period for the distribution of licences, which would be as generous as possible to its domestic commercial interests, but ultimately wanted the EU to move to a flat rate tariff. While, the Caribbean states were determined that a tariff rate quota system should be retained, in order to preserve guaranteed access for ACP bananas at a remunerative price, in a stable market (Eurolink, 2 June 1999). In addition, there was no consensus about which of the alternatives would be compatible with WTO rules.

After detailed consultations the European Commission finally adopted a proposal to revise the EU's banana regime at the beginning of November. The intention was to bring the regime into line with WTO commitments, while meeting the EU's obligations under the Lomé Convention, and protecting the interests of EU producers and consumers. The proposal was based on two stages. The first stage entailed a transitional tariff rate quota (TRQ) system, which would maintain both the current GATT bound quota and the autonomous quota, both with a tariff of 75 euro/tonne and open to all suppliers. The preferred option for the distribution of licences was a system based on a historical reference period, although if this proved unacceptable a 'first come, first served system' could be introduced. In addition, a new third quota would be open to all suppliers, although ACP bananas would be accorded a 275-euro/tonne preference. The distribution of this quota would be undertaken by auction. After a period of transition, a tariff-only system would enter into force in January 2006, with the ACP receiving an appropriate tariff-preference (European Commission, 1999). The Commission hoped that the transitional nature of the regime would ease the adjustment to a flat tariff system, and would enable the ACP and the EU banana-supplying countries to make the necessary adaptations to have some chance of survival. Within this context the Commission envisaged some additional help for those countries most dependent upon bananas, either through the successor arrangements to the Lomé Convention, or through EU structural funds. However, the Commission made clear that if no resolution of the banana dispute were possible, the existing arrangements would be replaced with a flat tariff.

Indeed, the intractability of the banana dispute meant that little progress was made in reaching an agreement. After eight months of intensive discussion between the European Commission and the WTO complainants, the auctioning system was rejected, as it was not favoured by any of the major parties to the dispute as they were unable to decide on the reference period for licences. As a consequence, in early July 2000 the Commission proposed, 'It will continue to study a transitional system of tariff quotas, but at this stage on a "first come, first served basis" for the three tariff quotas'. The Commission also asked the Council of Ministers to provide it with the authority to begin negotiations under Article 28 of the GATT (to establish a new tariff level) with the relevant suppliers, 'in order to implement a flat tariff system, in case no solution can be found on the tariff quota basis' (European Commission, 2000). In early October, the General Affairs Council accepted the Commission's proposal for reform, despite strong opposition from the European Parliament, who believed the provisions within it would not safeguard vulnerable ACP producers. More importantly, however, both the US government and Chiquita objected to the proposal with a Chiquita spokesman claiming it was 'patently illegal', while USTR Barshefsky recommended a continuation of negotiations

(*Caribbean Insight*, 13 October 2000; Commission of the European Communities, 2000; European Parliament, 2000; and Banana Trade News Bulletin, October 2000).

The patience of the European Commission and Council was now wearing thin. The pressures within the EU had been growing for any kind of resolution to be found, as the wider economic interests of the Union were being further damaged. For example two European firms sought compensation from the EU for alleged damages as a result of the banana dispute between the EU and US (Eurolink, 6 September 2000). In addition, Ecuador received the support of the WTO's Dispute Settlement Body to apply sanctions worth $201.6 million on trade with the EU because of the banana regime (Eurolink, 23 April 2000). While the US threatened to impose further sanctions on EU goods, if a settlement was not found, through the 'carousel' system whereby sanctions on goods are rotated over time (Banana Trade News Bulletin, July 2000). Indeed the threat of introducing a carousel meant that the highly important and symbolic Scottish cashmere trade was now a likely target for the imposition of a 100 per cent tariff rate.

The Caribbean's position through this period of negotiation was to reiterate the importance of the banana export trade to a number of its island economies. In addition, the Caribbean argued in the strongest terms possible that both the 'first come, first served' system, which would have ended guaranteed access for its bananas into the EU market, and the tariff-only regime were unacceptable. In an attempt to actively defend its interests the Commonwealth Caribbean put forward its own plan, known as the 'Chiquita-Fyffes' proposal. The accord, with apparent support from the US government, attempted to secure Caribbean interests by adapting the Commission's own proposal while meeting some of the concerns of the companies. However, although the proposal gained support from some quarters, the plan fell owing to American attempts to distort and dilute its core principles (Banana Trade News Bulletin, February 2000 and Eurolink, 10 July 2000).

Indeed, the banana interests in both the Caribbean and more widely in the ACP saw their position being marginalized in the negotiations, for a number of reasons. First, the French and Spanish producers who had been allies of the ACP lobbied for the 'first come, first served system', thus undermining the united front that had existed between the EU and ACP banana producers in the past (Eurolink, 4 October 2000). Secondly, a number of the WTO complainants indicated that in the absence of an agreement on bananas they would block the EU's request for a WTO waiver for the newly agreed Cotonou Agreement between the EU and the ACP, the successor to the Lomé Convention (Banana Trade News Bulletin, October 2000). The WTO complainants hoped that by threatening such action, the unity of the ACP would fragment between those that produced bananas and those that did not, and that the greater prize of the Cotonou Agreement would make both the EU and the ACP more willing to come to an agreement over bananas. The final and most important issue was that the EU was obliged to undertake discussions with the WTO complainants, and the US in particular, to make sure that any changes to the regime were acceptable to them. This was necessary in order to prevent any further action at the WTO being taken, and to end the US sanctions on certain EU imports, which were in place. The need to find a solution to the dispute thus outweighed the concerns the ACP had regarding whether the outcome of the negotiations would adequately safeguard their market access.

The pressure exerted by the US and Chiquita finally paid off at the beginning of April 2001. After almost 16 months of discussion, it was revealed that the EU and the US had reached a settlement regarding the banana dispute. Under the agreement, the EU consented that the distribution of licences would be based on historical trading patterns, rather than the 'first come, first served' system suggested by the Commission in July 2000. In addition, the Commission reduced the import quota for ACP bananas by 100 000 tonnes to 750 000 tonnes, while the autonomous quota favouring dollar bananas was increased from 353 000 tonnes to 453 000 tonnes. The third quota category also primarily for dollar bananas remained at 2.2 million tonnes. The EU further committed itself to move to a tariff-only system in 2006. In return, the US removed its $191 million of sanctions imposed on the EU in April 1999 and agreed to support the EU's attempt to obtain a WTO waiver to allow for the continuation of the exclusive ACP quota until 2006 (Official Journal of the European Communities, 2001 and Office of the United States Trade Representative Press Release, 11 April 2001). The new import rules took effect at the beginning of July 2001. The EU's Agriculture Commissioner Franz Fischler showed his relief that an agreement had been found when he stated 'the decision shows the determination of the Commission to end this never ending story. We are delivering' (*Caribbean Insight*, 4 May 2001).

The agreement particularly benefits Chiquita, who will gain most from the quota changes; an indication of this became apparent when the company's share price rose by 50 per cent on the news of the settlement (*Financial Times*, 12 April 2001). Dole and the independent banana-producing country of Ecuador were originally unhappy with the compromise, as both had been in favour of a settlement, which would have discounted past performance. Indeed, earlier in the negotiating process, Ecuador's ambassador to the EU complained that the EU and Ecuador had been 'virtually taken hostage' by the US government (*Caribbean Insight*, 13 October 2000). However, after reassurances from the Commission regarding technical aspects of the new regime, Ecuador swung behind the agreement. As for the Caribbean producers, even though they will be guaranteed sales above current levels in the agreement, the medium-term future looks bleak. Indeed, a statement from Caribbean producers warned that the transition period to a flat rate tariff was 'too short' and 'imposes a daunting and possibly insurmountable challenge to compete the restructuring of our banana industries and economies' (*Caribbean Insight*, 27 April 2001). The EU has been forced to favour those interests that have opposed the regime at the WTO at the expense of the ACP, in order to secure an end to the dispute, which was damaging the wider trading interests of the EU. With the solution to the banana dispute being a tariff-only arrangement for the EU market, it is questionable whether such a system will be able to meet the obligations in the new Banana Protocol attached to the Cotonou Agreement. The protocol commits the EU 'to examine and where necessary take measures aimed at ensuring the continued viability [of the ACP] banana export industries and the continuing outlet for their bananas on the Community market' (Protocol 5, The Second Banana Protocol, *The Courier*, September 2000, pp. 156–7).

Coda: The fracturing of Caribbean interests

The developments within the context of the WTO have dominated the politics of the European banana trade for most of the 1990s, and the increasing marginalization of the interests of the Commonwealth Caribbean are apparent. However, what is less obvious when considering the international trade issues are the effects that the EU's banana regime and the WTO actions have had on the unity of the Caribbean interests themselves. The growing divisions between the marketing companies and the banana growers, between the banana-producing islands, and between the banana growers are indicative of the serious pressures that have been exerted on the industry over the last decade.

The nature of the relationship between the banana companies and the growers of the Commonwealth Caribbean has changed over the last decade. The banana companies have adapted to the EU regime and have developed a wider sourcing of bananas, with the help of the licence system that underpinned the regime until the end of 1998. With 30 per cent of the tariff quota reserved for established operators of ACP and EU bananas, the companies were able to access considerable volumes of dollar bananas. Despite the fact that Fyffes had some dollar sourcing in the UK banana market prior to 1993, the company has since expanded its marketing contracts in Central America and Ecuador, and also in European producing areas such as the Canary Islands. At the present time around 50 per cent of Fyffes' banana sourcing comes from the dollar area. In addition, the company has purchased interests in a number of European fruit companies which has led Fyffes to become a major banana concern across Europe, accounting for around 20 per cent of the EU's banana trade (author's interview). Despite the fact that Fyffes has an interest in Belize, Jamaica, Suriname, and the Windward Islands, the company could survive without ACP bananas in a more liberal EU regime.

The Jamaica Producers Group Limited, successor to the Jamaican Banana Growers Association, which has dominated the Jamaican industry since the early 1970s, has also made attempts to both diversify its banana sourcing, and develop its non-banana interests. Perhaps most significantly has been the purchase by Dole of 35 per cent of Jamaica Producers' UK operations in 1994. This provided Jamaica Producers with additional bananas from Latin America to supplement its core supplies from Jamaica and Costa Rica. For Dole, buying into Jamaica Producers meant that the company now had an interest in ACP bananas, and could therefore benefit from the EU banana-licensing system. In addition, the Jamaica Producers Group, with the support of Dole, has attempted to diversify its business away from bananas into other product areas such as general produce and agri-processing. As with Fyffes, ACP bananas are now less important to Jamaica Producers than in the past, and an indication of this came in November 1998, when the company threatened to withdraw from banana production on Jamaica, unless fundamental changes were implemented (author's interview). The approach of both Fyffes and Jamaica Producers in diversifying and deepening their commercial interests beyond ACP bananas means that the two companies are now less beholden to its traditional areas of supply. The flexibility that companies have to alter their investment strategies compares starkly with the position of nation-states that cannot so easily adapt their economies to meet the new challenges within the international trading system.

The situation in the Windward Islands is a little different, as the Windward Islands Banana Development and Exporting Company Limited (WIBDECO), the successor of WINBAN, entered into a joint venture with Fyffes to buy Geest's banana interests in December 1995. WIBDECO, in which the four island governments and the respective banana associations have an interest, was keen to develop its role in the industry at all levels, in order that it could share the benefits of the EU's banana licensing system (author's interview). However, despite an undertaking that the Windward Islands growers themselves would benefit from WIBDECO having a direct interest in the marketing of bananas, the same kind of influences that have affected Jamaica are also apparent in the Windward Islands.

With the onset of the EU's single market in bananas, there was a concerted attempt to improve the productivity, quality, and reliability of banana production in the Windward Islands. The basis for change came with the Cargill Report in 1995, commissioned by the European Commission, and the UK Overseas Development Administration, which set out a package of financial management and technical advice for each island to meet the requirements of the increasingly important supermarket sector (Cargill Technical Services, 1995). The Certified Growers Programme introduced in 1997 to meet the requirements of production and field hygiene required by supermarkets has increased the percentage of bananas within quality specification. However, the long-term price instability in the EU banana market, particularly during 1995 and 1996, and the growing demand for production specifications removed from the industry the part-time banana farmers, with a consequent reduction in production levels (author's interviews). In the spring of 1998, a Banana Production Recovery Plan was instituted in an attempt to increase banana volumes to meet the Windward Islands' supply obligations. However, even though prices held up, production continued to fall. Between 1993 and 2000 banana production fell from 242 452 tonnes to 140 499 (WIBDECO Annual Report, 1997, *Caribbean Insight*, 24 August 2001). The situation in the Windward Islands worsened in 2001, with banana production in the year to August totalling 56 580 tonnes, down from 89 082 tonnes in the same period the year before. WIBDECO's CEO Bernard Cornibert summed up the plight of the industry when he warned, 'there is a critical level at which production cannot survive for very long. I think we are probably at that level now. We are almost at the bottom' (*Caribbean Insight*, 28 September 2001). The general market pressures centred on the needs of the supermarket sector have played their part in altering the nature of the banana industry in the Windward Islands, and indeed elsewhere in the Caribbean. The demand for higher production standards has produced improvements in the quality of the fruit, but this has been done at the expense of reducing the banana export industry's value to the islands as a whole, in terms of lost employment and lost production.

Chapter conclusion

The period from 1993 has consisted of a series of challenges against the EU's banana regime, which have undermined the banana interests of the Commonwealth Caribbean. The creation of the WTO Dispute Settlement Process has meant that the Commonwealth Caribbean has become a peripheral player in defending a regime that they so successfully lobbied for. Rather, the EU has been obligated to meet the legal requirements stipulated under WTO law. The institutional nature of the present international trading environment superseded national and regional commitments to retain long-term trading relationships. Commonwealth Caribbean lobbying has continued at the national and European levels, but there is now a new level of arbitration in the form of the WTO, which has reduced the effectiveness of lower level action. As the EU's banana regime was not theirs to defend, the Commonwealth Caribbean became third parties in a dispute between the two great trading areas of the world, the US and the EU. The increasing role of the US government along with Chiquita Brands International was also important in that the banana dispute took on a significance that bore little relation to its actual importance, with ramifications for the future operation of the WTO, the power of multinational companies, the place of small island states in a more integrated international economy, and the nature of the US–EU trading relationship. In short, the 1990s have seen a significant marginalization of Commonwealth Caribbean banana interests, whereby the very future of their industry is now in serious question.

8
Conclusion

The study was undertaken to investigate and analyse the detailed political interactions of the Caribbean banana trade, as an important contemporary issue within the context of the international trading system. At the centre of the study was an evaluation of the relationship between the traditional actors in the trade, namely governments (and government departments), private corporate interests and producers. The study assessed the different means by which the various interest groups have responded to one another in a highly complex trading environment shaped by a number of influences. It was intended that revealing such relationships would help us to further our understanding of the nature of the political process. Within this context, there was a consideration as to why the Caribbean banana trade developed in the way it did, and why in the past thirty years the traditional actors within the trade have seen their influence and importance decline.

The study highlighted the complex nature of the relationships involved in the Caribbean banana trade since its inception, and the political and economic trends, which have affected the character of those relationships. Indeed, the four key themes identified at the beginning of the study have assisted in explaining the trends apparent within the Caribbean banana trade. The trends were those of corporate ownership and monopoly power, colonial responsibility, the gradual diminution of national control of the UK's trading policy and the beginning of a re-focusing of political and economic commitments from the colonies and former colonies towards Europe, and the influence of an empowered world trading organization and the marginalization of those interests that have defended the merits of preferential access in international trade.

The first theme of corporate ownership and monopoly control proved to be important, although not to the extent as might have been expected. The dominant American corporate interests in the Jamaican banana trade at the turn of the century were the catalyst for attempts by the colonial interests to counterbalance this dependency, a situation that persisted to a greater or lesser extent over the next 40 years. However, the distinction in attitudes between the various colonial interests to the issue of corporate ownership and monopoly control has been demonstrated. As was seen, the greatest resistance to American corporate dominance of the banana export trade on Jamaica came from those who were directly affected by the nature of corporate ownership on the island. When there was a unity of purpose amongst those banana-growing interests, an effective lobbying force was created which precipitated UK government action on occasion to reduce the influence of American corporate interests on Jamaica. However, it is also clear that such unity of purpose was not a regular occurrence, and the issue of American corporate control of the Jamaican industry was never addressed in a coordinated manner. The UK government was less preoccupied with the nature of monopoly control and corporate ownership, than with the fact that Jamaica had a viable and large-scale export industry that helped to provide the island with a degree of social cohesion. The interest group dynamic at this time had certain attributes of the group approach, such as the need of groups to consult over specific, technical, complex, and managerial decisions (Richardson and Jordan, 1979); the ability of groups to retain policies that are beneficial to them (Bachrach and Baratz, 1970; Crenson, 1971; Rose, 1976); and the role of personal networks (Baggott, 1995). However, the relationship between the actors had not yet developed into a policy community as defined by Richardson and Jordan (1979), where a 'regularised and routinised' relationship exists between the actors involved in a particular area of policy.

It is clear that the issue of corporate ownership and monopoly control of banana sourcing has become less important for the UK more recently, with the development of the Windward Islands banana export trade, and the growing range of other banana sourcing, particularly from Latin America, which is overseen by a number of different companies. In addition, the nature of ownership *per se* has become less of an issue in recent years with the decline in colonial ties and the increasing importance of regional and global trading patterns. However, even though corporate ownership and monopoly control is no longer an issue for the UK, it is still very much an issue for the banana growers themselves. In Jamaica and the Windward Islands, domestic interests now primarily control the banana industry, but many banana growers still resent the monopoly control that exists. Such a division between the interests of the UK, and of the banana growers is both indicative of the fragmentation of the traditional interests involved in the Caribbean banana trade, and the fact that concerns over monopoly power are the same whether a company is foreign owned or domestically owned.

As would be expected when considering the interactions involved in an aspect of international trade, the second theme of colonial responsibility was extremely important, albeit with certain reservations. The colonial authorities, in attempting to promote economic and social stability on Jamaica and the Windward Islands, did provide financial and technical assistance for the development of their banana export industries, but significantly the authorities were dependent upon commercial interests making a clear commitment to the endeavour before any real assistance was forthcoming. Further, the assistance given by the colonial authorities was not without its provisos, with both Jamaica and the Windward Islands required to adhere to particular safeguards and responsibilities. In addition, it can be argued that once the commercial interests had secured their position on the islands, the colonial authorities were reluctant to interfere in the day-to-day running of the trade for fear of putting at risk the companies' involvement. As Crenson (1971) argues, actors can exercise influence simply by being there. Politicians are aware of groups and the attitudes they are likely to adopt in a given situation and will often avoid action that is likely to provoke the groups into greater activity. It is apparent that colonial action was necessary but not sufficient for the establishment of a banana export industry on the Caribbean islands in question, and indeed the division of responsibility between government action and commercial opportunity has continued to define the nature of the trade.

The limits of colonial responsibility are further illustrated when considering the most important measure instituted by the UK government, that of preferential access via Imperial Preference for colonial banana exports to the UK. It is important to recognize that such a fundamental change in the structure of the trade had little to do with colonial responsibility in safeguarding market access for Jamaican bananas, and much more to do with protecting the rather narrower economic interests of the UK itself. In addition, it needs to be appreciated that the decision to introduce a more restrictive form of trade would not have been taken had the international trading environment been more secure. As Grove argues, 'the departure from free trade in 1932 has been called a stroke of fate rather than an act of policy' (1962, p. 45).

Furthermore, it has been demonstrated that once preferential access was introduced and Jamaica became the dominant banana supplier for the UK, the colonial authorities were obliged to secure the viability of that source, and their policies were in turn determined by that dependence. Indeed, the authorities began to show a greater concern for the state of banana production on Jamaica than in the past. This is exemplified by a consideration of the differences in approach during the two world wars. During the First World War before preferential access, the UK government did little to safeguard the welfare of Jamaican growers even though banana exports, and therefore banana production, were greatly reduced. In contrast, after the introduction of preferential access when banana exports to the UK were halted during the Second World War, the UK government in cooperation with the colonial administration of Jamaica made great efforts to secure financial support for the island's banana growers.

The effect that independence had on the nature of the relationship between the now former-colonies and the UK government regarding the banana issue was not immediate, with its effect only being felt over the longer term, despite the fact that there was pressure from inside and outside government to liberalize the UK's banana import policy. The close relationship between the Colonial Office and the grower interests on Jamaica and the Windward Islands was strong enough to prevent any significant change. This policy inertia confirms Christoph's (1975) contention that there is a tendency for officials to identify with those interests with which they have regular contact, and promote those interests within government circles, and the assertion of Bachrach and Baratz (1970) and Rose (1976) that once a policy has been adopted, in this case preferential access, the groups who benefit, be they bureaucrats or 'outside' groups, will make every effort to retain their benefits. Furthermore, although the particular relationship between the Colonial Office (now the Foreign and Commonwealth Office) and the banana interests of Jamaica and the Windward Islands has weakened over time, the Ministry of Agriculture has sustained the commitment owing to its own more recently developed relationship with the traditional banana interests.

Notwithstanding the close cooperation that developed between the UK government and the banana interests on Jamaica and the Windward Islands, the umbrella of preferential access shared by the Caribbean islands led to a period of intense competition between them, which precipitated a period of instability within the trade. The importance of colonial ties as a conservative force is demonstrated by the fact that the government was unable to discriminate between the Windward Islands and Jamaican banana-exporting interests when problems of over supply arose. As a consequence an accommodation between the various commercial and grower interests became necessary in the guise of the Banana Advisory Committee. The eventual development of a formalized interest group relationship within the UK banana trade was interpreted in terms of Richardson and Jordan's group approach, and their contention that the nature of interest-group behaviour regarding a particular policy area is one 'of a regularised, routinised relationship, which appears to be the normal response to problems that automatically reappear on the agenda' (1979, p. 98). The group approach explained the particular dynamics of the trade at the time, and by considering in detail the circumstances that led to the establishment of a policy community, a number of criticisms of the group approach (Christiansen and Dowding, 1994; John, 1998; and Smith, 1992) were addressed. The study revealed the distinction between what constituted a policy community as opposed to a close relationship, highlighted the process by which a policy community was established, and illustrated the important role that state institutions played in the group approach.

Despite the operation of the Banana Advisory Committee, the concept of colonial responsibility was attenuated, as colonial legacies became less relevant. The UK government became more prepared to frame its banana policy towards encouraging increasing consumer demand, rather than having its banana policy determined by the likely import volumes from Jamaica and the Windward Islands. The assessment of the reasons for the change in the UK banana import policy addressed a further criticism of the group approach as highlighted by John (1998), that it is descriptive rather than explanatory, with little consideration of why decisions emerge when they do. By evaluating the merits of negotiated order (Heclo and Wildavsky, 1974 and Strauss *et al.*, 1976) and the role of 'outside' groups in influencing the policy agenda (Richardson and Jordan, 1979), it became apparent that the nature of the policy process allowed the recognized interests to conduct their business, but also provided other groups with different priorities the opportunity to influence policy and thus alter the relative position of the traditional interests in the established community. Further, despite the fact that preferential access was retained, its importance was reduced because bananas from the Windward Islands and Jamaica became less able to meet consumer demand, which meant that their position in the market and the strength of their interests were automatically weakened.

The third theme of the study was the gradual diminution of national control of the UK's trading policy, and the beginning of a re-focusing of political and economic commitments from the colonies and former colonies to Europe, since the establishment of the European Economic Community (EEC). As would be expected there have been important ramifications for those traditional interests within the Caribbean banana trade. Membership of the EEC and the signing of the Banana Protocol of the Lomé Convention, meant that not only did the UK have to adjust to the new network of influences, but also Jamaica and the Windward Islands themselves had to cooperate with unfamiliar actors, some of whom had interests that were at complete variance to their own. The actors who now had an interest in the UK banana trade included the other EEC member states, the European Commission, the European Court of Justice, and the traditional banana suppliers and marketing companies of the other member states. As Streeck and Schmitter argue, the European policy process is characterized by 'a profound absence of hierarchy and monopoly among a wide variety of players of different but uncertain status' (1991, p. 159). Marsh and Smith (2000) suggest the operation of a network can be influenced by other networks, which may in turn affect policy outcomes. However, despite the influence of the European dimension, national banana markets were able to retain their essential character because of the disparate legacies that every member state had in terms of its particular banana sourcing. Thus the UK was able to maintain overall control of its banana market favouring those producers with colonial ties, even though the tools for doing so were slightly different than before.

In order to explain the changing nature of the interest-group dynamic between the traditional relationships at the national level, and the new challenges at the European level, an additional theoretical perspective to supplement the group approach was used. The network approach of Marsh and Rhodes (1992a) suggests that with an emphasis on different policy networks, the nature of interest-group relationships can be determined, with consequent ramifications for the policy process, policy outcomes and policy change. It is suggested that a gradual change could be seen within the decision-making environment with the traditional UK banana interests being forced to readjust their focus from a policy community to an issue network, with a resultant effect on policy outcomes. However, it is important to recognize that overall the traditional actors within the UK banana trade were able to

withstand the pressures from the European level, as national preferences were allowed to continue.

The enacting of the Single European Act in 1987, which committed the
European Community (EC) to eliminate internal frontier controls, meant
that the 12 highly distinctive banana regimes of the member states had to
be organized into one. The nature of the process during which a single
banana regime was adopted highlights the significant differences in
approach to policy-making between the national and European levels.
The Jamaican and Windward Islands interests in cooperation with the
wider Commonwealth Caribbean and Francophone African banana-producing interests were highly effective in lobbying for continued preferential access within the EC, assisted by strong support from the former
European colonial powers, against those interests which were calling for a
more liberal regime. As Mazey and Richardson (1993b) have asserted, 'in
order to be effective Euro-lobbyists, groups must be able to coordinate
their national and EC level strategies, construct alliances with their coun-
terparts, and monitor changing national and EC policy agendas' (pp.
191–2). The banana issue showed the importance of colonial legacies,
together with a familiarity of European processes, in preventing the introduction of a liberal banana-trading regime in Europe.

It has been demonstrated, however, that despite the apparent success of
those interests defending preferential access and the commitments under
the Lomé Convention, the creation of the single market in bananas fundamentally changed the structure of banana imports into the
Community, and in turn reduced the influence of those interests associated with the UK banana trade. The single market was larger and more
fluid than that of the national regimes, so safeguards for traditional
Caribbean and African banana suppliers were now less secure than in the
past. Further, a European-wide Banana Management Committee made up
of civil servants from each member state, and chaired by the Commission
replaced the institutional mechanisms that had helped stabilize the UK
market, particularly the Banana Advisory Committee. The apprehension,
which existed in 1973, now became a reality, with the undermining of
the close bonds between the UK government, the former colonial
Caribbean banana producers and marketing companies. The central
actors involved in the UK banana trade were now subsumed into a
broader and more complex interest-group relationship with implications
for the policy process, policy outcomes, and policy change.

It is argued that during the period of negotiations leading up to the
creation of the single market in bananas, there was a gradual shift in
emphasis away from the policy community, which had been established

in the UK, and towards the more complex issue network at the European level. The transition between the policy community and the issue network had serious ramifications for policy outcomes. However, in order properly to understand the effects of this shift in interest-groups relations, and to provide the network approach with a degree of explanatory power, it was necessary to adopt the criticisms of Dowding (1995) and John (1998) regarding the network approach. There was recognition that network properties had an effect independent of other factors like group resources, and that policy network structures were closely related with institutions, group structure and resources, and ideas.

The fourth theme of the study was the influence of an empowered world trading organization, and the marginalization of those interests that have defended the merits of preferential access for bananas imported into the European Union (EU), against those who have argued for a liberal trading regime. A number of attempts were made since the mid-1950s to overturn the concept of preferential access, but these proved unsuccessful as there was sufficient support within the traditional interest-group dynamic to sustain the concept, both in the national and subsequently European markets (Bachrach and Baratz, 1970; Crenson, 1971; Christoph, 1975; Rose, 1976). However, by the early 1990s, there was a critical body of international opinion opposed to what some considered to be the EU's highly discriminatory banana regime, which found its voice within the context of the World Trade Organization (WTO), the successor of the General Agreement on Tariffs and Trade (GATT).

The rulings by the WTO Dispute Settlement Body against the EU's banana regime were highly significant in altering the nature of the interest-group dynamic. The traditional interest-group relationships, which had underpinned the UK banana trade, and latterly the EU banana trade, were now superseded. Once the WTO had given its opinion, the EU had no alternative but to acquiesce, and reform its banana regime, irrespective of any concerns the European Commission, the European Parliament, the member states, the banana producers, and the banana companies may have had. The WTO, as an institutional mechanism, had therefore established itself as an important issue network which was able to influence the nature of the relationships between the actors involved in the dispute settlement process, and determine, at least in general terms, policy outcomes.

However, it was important to distinguish between the characteristics of the issue network at the international level and the issue network at the European level. The basis of the relationship between the actors at the WTO and those within the EU was quite different, which determined the way in which the banana issue was processed in each issue network. The networks approach of Marsh and Rhodes (1992a) supplemented by the work of John (1998), Daugbjerg and Marsh (1998), and Marsh and Smith (1996 and 2000) helped to interpret the changes in the nature of the interest-group relationships at the national, European, and international levels. However, in order to explain how the influence of the traditional interests was altered by the structure of the different levels of decision-making, a supplementary paradigm of explanation was needed. The precise dynamics of the trend between the different levels of decision-making was explained by May and Nugent's (1982) account of 'thresholder' groups, where groups oscillate over time between insider and outsider status.

It can be argued that the ACP banana interests adopted the characteristics of thresholder groups. Within the policy networks at the national, and to a lesser extent at the EU level, the ACP interests were able to influence the decision-making process directly, through the pursuit of certain strategies (Grant, 1978 and 1995; Jordan, Maloney and McLaughlin, 1992; Whiteley and Winyard, 1987). The ACP interests were held to be legitimate by politicians and civil servants and were consulted on a regular basis. However, within the context of the WTO the ACP states were only given third party status, with the banana-producing representatives having no direct role in the process. The status of the ACP states was pre-determined because of the particular rules of the WTO, and as a consequence the ACP states were not in a position to improve their standing within the dispute settlement process by adopting a particular strategy. As the banana issue moved between the EU and the WTO, the banana interests of the ACP oscillated from having insider status, to a position of being outsiders. The less involvement the ACP states had in the decision-making process, the less favourable were the policy outcomes for them.

The Windward Islands and Jamaica, as well as the other ACP banana producers, were now in a position whereby their historical patterns of influence were fundamentally undermined, meaning that that they could no longer depend on political commitments undertaken by their former colonial powers to sustain their traditional market access. Within this context, it is important to recognize the influence of American commercial interests in this process. Chiquita Brands International, formerly the United Fruit Company, which had sold its interest in Fyffes some years before, and with it a stake in the traditional preferential supplies of the UK market, was now undermining those supplies by lobbying the US government to take action in the WTO. The flexibility of Chiquita's approach in exploiting a wide range of political arenas (Jordan and Richardson, 1987) and pressure points (Baggott, 1994) is important in highlighting the different methods a private company can undertake to further its commercial interests. The United Fruit Company who dominated the UK banana trade for the first half of the twentieth century, was now as Chiquita Brands International attempting to partially re-establish that dominance, by attacking those banana sources that had once been so fundamental to its operations. The power and influence of commercial organizations in superseding and undermining the interests of nation-states is important and should be acknowledged.

The broader relevance of the study can be found within the context of the changing EU–ACP relations, the operation of the WTO and the developing liberal discourse in international trade. The study highlighted the changes that have taken place in the relationship between the EU and the African, Caribbean, and Pacific (ACP) states within the context of the Lomé Convention and latterly the Cotonou Agreement. The pressures that have undermined the commitments in the Banana Protocol are apparent with regard to the other protocols covering rum, sugar, and beef and veal, which are also undergoing change. In more general terms the trends seen within the study help to explain why the nature of the ACP–EU relationship is transforming, from one based on the pillars of preferential trade and aid which underpinned the Lomé Convention, to one based on more liberal Regional Economic Partnership Agreements as stipulated within the Cotonou Agreement.

The study also has relevance when addressing the issue of the WTO's position within the international trading system. The case of the EU's banana regime which sustained preferential access for former-colonial banana producers was the first case in which compliance with a WTO ruling was disputed, highlighting how unclear the WTO's rules on compliance were. In addition, the banana case was the first to be ruled non-compliant with the General Agreement on Trade in Services (GATS). The ruling on GATS confirmed the broad scope of the agreement and its potential to eliminate barriers in distribution and other services in the future. Further, the banana issue helped to put concerns over environmental and employment standards at the centre of the new round of WTO negotiations on further trade liberalization, and has made less developed states and those groups and individuals with an interest in the international trading environment more aware of the importance of the WTO.

Indeed, the WTO itself has become more sensitive to the concerns of small states and private interests as a consequence of the banana case.

The exclusion of private legal advisers representing the Caribbean during the first WTO Panel in 1996 was highly controversial, provoking accusations that the organization did not appreciate the particular difficulties facing small states when it came to legal representation at the WTO. Since then the attitude of the WTO has changed, with a ruling arguing that sovereign states should be allowed to choose the composition of their own delegations (WT/DS54/R). This is significant, as it will now allow small states without the resources to employ full time legal representation to co-opt outside help when they are involved in WTO disputes and by doing so have a greater voice when important matters are being decided. In addition, the WTO has become more accepting of the views of private groups during Panel and Appellate hearings. In the banana case, those with an interest in the issue such as companies, banana growers and non-governmental organizations (NGOs) were excluded from directly giving evidence and consequently there were accusations that the WTO lacked accountability and legitimacy. However, as a result of deliberations during the 'Shrimp-Turtle' case, the WTO accepted for the first time that private organizations could submit evidence directly to a Panel or Appellate Body (WT/DS58/AB/R). Again, such a concession may well improve the position of small states within the WTO with evidence from other parties bolstering their own position.

The WTO has also attempted to encourage the integration of developing countries within the organization. Measures such as technical cooperation, which includes training, seminars and workshops, have been instituted in an effort to help developing countries adjust and participate effectively within the multilateral trading system. In particular, there has been an attempt to improve states' knowledge of multilateral trade rules and WTO working procedures and negotiations. Further, there was a special seminar organized by the WTO in October 2000, to explore ways in which the peculiar features of trade and production in small economies could be overcome (Eurolink, 1 November 2000). These discussions were followed up by a report by the WTO on the Eastern Caribbean in June 2001, which assessed the region's trading needs (WTO Press Release/TPRB/167, 7 June 2001). It is open to debate whether there have been or will be any tangible improvements in the economies of the Caribbean as a consequence of these modest developments within the WTO. However, what is clear is that after the banana dispute the multilateral trading system will never be the same again.

Appendix: Banana Imports to the United Kingdom and the European Union

Table A1   United Kingdom Banana Imports 1904–25 *(thousands long tons)*

	Jamaica	Canary Islands	Central America & Colombia	Others	Total
1904	7.2	23.7	4.8	–	35.7
1910	11.6				81.7
1911	8.4				90.0
1912	0.9				93.6
1913	7.8	25.9	56.1	0.2	90.0
1914	15.6				120.7
1915	6.1	37.9	65.1	0.1	109.2
1916	2.7				81.7
1917	7.5				29.9
1918	4.4				9.8
1919	37.1				65.6
1920	29.3				108.0
1921	18.6				127.4
1922	24.2	35.5	88.2	–	147.9
1923	37.5	32.1	89.3	–	158.9
1924	22.9	35.5	92.2	0.4	151.0
1925	32.2				161.3

Note: a dash indicates no bananas sent to the UK; a gap indicates incomplete data

Table A2   United Kingdom banana imports 1926–40 *(thousands long tons)*

	Jamaica	Canary Islands	Brazil	Cameroons	Others [1,2]	Total
1926	48.0	34.7	–	–	98.9	181.6
1927	26.4	24.2	6.1	–	113.5	170.2
1928	36.7	21.4	11.9	–	103.8	173.8
1929	53.8	16.4	18.1	–	111.9	200.2
1930	79.4	13.0	19.2	–	89.4	201.0
1931	93.4	12.0	19.7	–	91.5	216.6
1932	143.9	7.0	19.5	–	59.0	229.4
1933	88.8	7.0	28.0	–	89.0	212.8
1934	138.8	4.6	23.2	0.9	61.0	227.7
1935	211.0	3.8	24.5	3.0	26.8	269.1
1936	194.2	4.3	25.9	5.6	44.0	274.0
1937	263.2	6.4	24.8	4.8	4.2	303.4
1938	232.8	7.8	30.6	5.6	28.2	305.0
1939	211.6	4.3	23.7	16.7	44.2	300.5
1940	66.0					193.0

Notes: 1   Honduras, Costa Rica and Colombia
         2   Small amounts from Gold Coast and French Africa (late 1930s)
         –   indicates no bananas sent to the UK; a gap indicates incomplete data

Tables A3   United Kingdom banana imports 1945–65 *(thousands long tons)*

	Jamaica	Windward Islands	West Cameroon	Others[1, 2]	Total
1945	1.0	–	–	–	1.0
1946	52.3	–	4.0	26.8	83.1
1947	59.0	–	28.2	14.7	101.9
1948	79.1	–	48.3	18.7	146.1
1949	88.5	–	63.0	13.4	164.9
1950	65.7	0.1	59.2	13.1	138.1
1951	43.2	3.5	65.7	51.1	163.5
1952	57.6	8.2	73.4	27.5	166.7
1953	117.4	15.5	84.4	42.5	259.8
1954	138.6	19.7	75.8	55.3	289.4
1955	136.5	21.8	68.9	79.5	306.7
1956	145.7	34.3	67.1	67.9	315.0
1957	145.6	47.5	68.8	51.9	313.8
1958	121.4	58.4	73.6	55.0	308.4
1959	133.2	88.5	57.0	55.3	334.0
1960	137.8	88.6	70.3	47.4	344.1
1961	135.9	101.9	78.4	48.5	364.7
1962	145.0	110.0	74.9	37.8	367.7
1963	147.2	124.1	63.8	22.4	357.5
1964	157.7	139.2	22.3	27.8	347.0
1965	182.2	170.1	8.6	11.3	372.2

Notes: 1   Brazil and the Canary Islands
2   Small amounts from Spanish West Africa and Dominican Republic

Table A4   United Kingdom banana imports 1966–87 *(thousands long tons)*

	Jamaica	Windward Islands	ACP/EC[1]	Dollar[2]	Other[3]	Total
1966	181.9	150.3	6.2	1.0	–	339.4
1967	177.6	148.6	2.3	1.2	–	329.7
1968	151.7	166.3	1.1	6.3	–	325.4
1969	148.7	181.7	1.7	6.0	–	338.1
1970	136.0	138.9	29.4	8.7	–	313.0
1971	122.1	121.0	49.4	11.7	–	304.2
1972	118.9	115.1	55.7	16.0	–	305.7
1973	109.4	89.1	50.6	48.3	–	297.4
1974	72.0	100.3	65.0	62.2	–	299.5
1975	68.1	89.3	72.7	70.1	–	300.2
1976	75.2	115.1	70.2	40.6	–	301.1
1977	76.6	107.3	61.5	47.1	–	292.5
1978	73.6	128.2	51.5	58.0	–	311.3
1979	66.5	98.2	47.0	87.9	–	299.6
1980	34.3	67.3	51.5	154.3	–	307.4
1981	17.1	102.0	44.7	156.8	–	320.6
1982	20.7	101.6	36.9	154.5	–	313.7
1983	23.3	115.7	48.3	115.5	–	302.8
1984	11.1	133.3	48.0	111.3	0.6	304.3
1985	12.4	144.4	46.1	105.1	2.2	310.2
1986	20.1	195.6	54.6	56.8	0.9	328.0
1987	32.3	174.3	58.3	73.9	–	338.8

Notes: 1   Belize, Suriname, Cameroon, Ivory Coast, Dominican Republic, Canary Islands, Barbados, Ghana, Martinique, Uganda
2   Costa Rica, Honduras, Guatemala, Colombia, Ecuador, Mexico, Panama, Brazil, Chile
3   Intra-EC trade (country of origin unknown), Bermuda, Malaysia, Nauru

Table A5   United Kingdom banana imports 1988–2000 *(thousands tonnes)*

	Jamaica	Windward Islands	ACP/EC	Dollar	Other	Total
1988	31.7	232.3	60.3	23.0	40.9	388.2
1989	39.1	214.4	59.3	21.6	99.6	434.0
1990	63.1	243.5	56.2	27.0	80.4	470.2
1991	68.9	200.9	51.8	37.4	130.6	489.6
1992	75.4	218.2	60.1	44.8	146.7	545.2
1993	77.0	212.8	87.9	75.7	118.8	572.2
1994	76.5	157.1	114.7	93.0	184.4	625.7
1995	83.5	182.8	120.1	96.0	233.6	716.0
1996	89.5	192.2	130.4	88.1	249.1	749.3
1997	77.1	136.1	127.2	116.8	274.3	731.5
1998	62.1	136.7	107.1	171.9	310.6	788.3
1999	50.6	131.9	146.0	200.9	228.4	757.8
2000	40.9	143.9	178.0	191.3	195.2	749.3

Sources for all tables: Black, 1984, p. 108. Davies, 1990, p. 264. Imperial Economic Committee, Third Report. Fruit, 1926, p. 243. Jamaica Banana Commission, 1936, p. 2. MAF 86/149. McFarlane, 1964, p. 83. Rodriquez, 1955, p. 35. Statistics (Commodities and Food) Accounts and Trade, ESD, DEFRA. Tripartite Banana Talks, 1966, Annex One. West India Committee Circular, 24 August 1916, 6 March 1930 and 24 February 1938.

Table A6   European Community banana imports 1988–2000 (*thousands tonnes*)

	ACP[1]	EC[2]	Dollar[3]	Total
1988	514.1	757.1	1643.9	2915.0
1989	544.4	738.9	1716.1	2999.4
1990	621.9	737.5	2024.2	3383.6
1991	596.4	699.5	2285.9	3581.8
1992	680.2	705.8	2366.7	3752.6
1993	748.1	643.7	2218.9	3610.7
1994	726.9	584.6	2102.3	3413.8
1995[a]	764.0	658.2	2405.1	3827.3
1996	796.1	684.6	2398.8	3879.6
1997	692.8	810.5	2462.9	3966.3
1998[b]	616.4		2444.9	3062.2
1999[b]	677.0		2541.7	3224.3
2000[b]	757.7		2541.8	3312.8

Notes: a   Expansion of EU from 12 to 15 member states
       b   EU-dependent exports are no longer registered as extra trade
       1   Ivory Coast, Cameroon, Suriname, Somalia, Jamaica, St Lucia, St Vincent,
          Dominica, Belize, Cape Verde, Grenada, Madagascar, Dominican Republic, Ghana
       2   Greece, Spain, France (Martinique and Guadeloupe), Portugal
       3   Colombia, Costa Rica, Nicaragua, Venezuela, Ecuador, Honduras, Guatemala,
          Panama, Mexico, Philippines.

Source: Statistics (Commodities and Food) Accounts and Trade, ESD, DEFRA.

Interviews

David Jessop, Caribbean Council for Europe/West India Committee, London, 3 July 1998 and 12 October 1999.

Gordon Myers, European Representative, Caribbean Banana Exporters Association, London, 14 October 1998.

John Ellis, Chairman Fyffes UK, London, 4 November 1998.

Claire Wenner, EuroPA, Political Lobbyist, Peterborough, 18 November 1998.

Ray Hillbourne, Former Executive Director of Geest Industries, Hedge End, 20 November 1998.

Alistair Smith, Banana Link, London, 25 November 1998.

Ted Lyndon, Sales Director, Geest Bananas, Southampton, 9 December 1998.

Junior Lodge, Jamaica Marketing Company, London, 15 December 1998.

Rt Hon. John Gummer MP, 1972: Parliamentary Private Secretary to Minister of Agriculture; 1985–88: Minister of State, Ministry of Agriculture, Fisheries and Food; 1989–93: Minister of Agriculture, Fisheries and Food, London, 17 December 1998.

Janet Purnell, Trade Policy and Tropical Foods Division, Branch B, Ministry of Agriculture, Fisheries and Food, London, 11 January 1999.

Willem C.C. Kokkeel, Vorstand, Atlanta Aktiengsellshaft, Bremen, Germany, 26 January 1999.

Wolfgang Ahlers, Syndikus, Atlanta Aktiengsellshaft, Bremen, Germany, 26 January 1999.

Leonard Van Geest, L.V. Geest Farms, New Milton, Hampshire, 2 February 1999.

Dickon Poole, Marketing Manager, Del Monte Fresh Produce (UK) Ltd., Paddock Wood Distribution Centre, Paddock Wood, Kent, 4 February 1999.

David Reid, Chief Executive Officer, JP Fruit Distributors Limited, Dartford, 11 February 1999.

Steve Chaplin, Associate Director, JP Fruit Distributors Limited, Dartford, 11 February 1999.

Hon. Bowen Wells MP, Chairman of the International Development Select Committee, House of Commons, London, 18 February 1999.

Sir Shridath Ramphal, formerly Minister of Foreign Affairs, Guyana. At present Chief Negotiator for the Caribbean Community in the post-Lomé Four negotiations, London, 19 February 1999.

Carl B. Greenidge, Deputy Secretary General of the African, Caribbean and Pacific States Secretariat, Brussels, 8 March 1999.

Sherryll M. Lashley, Expert, Commodity Protocols, African, Caribbean and Pacific States Secretariat, Brussels, 8 March 1999.

Philippe Binard, European Community Banana Trade Association, Brussels, 9 March 1999.

Ché Odlum, Political Attaché, Embassies of the Eastern Caribbean States and Missions to the European Communities, Brussels, 9 March 1999.

Jesus Melero Martinez, Directorate General 6, Unit 3 (including bananas), European Commission, Brussels, 9 March 1999.

Gundula Azeez, Directorate General 6, Unit 3 (including bananas), European Commission, Brussels, 9 March 1999.

Alexia Davison, Directorate General 8, Unit A4, European Commission, Brussels, 10 March 1999.

HE Edwin Laurent, Ambassador, Embassies of the Eastern Caribbean States and Missions to the European Communities, based in Brussels, via telephone conversation, 11 March 1999.

Kathy Ann Brown, Legal Expert, Caribbean Regional Negotiating Machinery, London, 17 March 1999.

George Williams, High Commissioner of Dominica, London, 19 March 1999.

Mark Thomas, Technical Adviser, Dominica Banana Marketing Corporation, Roseau, Dominica, 13 April 1999.

Charles Savarin, Leader of the Freedom Party, Roseau, Dominica, 13 April 1999.

William Rapier, Former Chairman, Geest Industries (WI) Ltd, Castries, St Lucia, 19 April 1999.

Francis Leonce, Former Managing Director, Geest Industries (WI) Ltd, Castries, St Lucia. 19 April 1999.

Tony Smith, General Manager, St Lucia Banana Corporation, Castries, St Lucia, 20 April 1999.

A.F. Rodriguez, Former Director, Antilles Products Limited and Geest Industries (WI) Ltd, Castries, St Lucia, 20 April 1999.

Julius Polius, Director of Agricultural Services, Ministry of Agriculture, Forestry, Fisheries and the Environment, Castries, St Lucia, 20 April 1999.

Peter Serieux, Managing Director, Tropical Quality Fruit Company Limited, Castries, St Lucia, 20 April 1999.

Elias John, President, St Lucia National Farmers' Association, Rodney Bay, St Lucia, 21 April 1999.

Wilberforce Emmanuel, Director, Windward Islands Farmers' Association and St Vincent Banana Growers' Association, Kingstown, St Vincent, 23 April 1999.

Wayne Sandiford, Economic Adviser, Organisation for Eastern Caribbean States, St Lucia, 26 April 1999.

Garnet Didier, Director, Dominica Banana Marketing Corporation and President of the Windward Islands Banana Developing and Exporting Company, Roseau, Dominica, 27 April 1999.

Gregory Shillingford, Managing Director, Dominica Banana Marketing Corporation, Roseau, Dominica, 27 April 1999.

Hon. Edison James, Prime Minister of Dominica, Government House, Roseau, Dominica, 28 April 1999.

Edwin Carrington, Secretary General, Caribbean Community, Georgetown, Guyana, 29 April 1999.

Gloria Francis, Former Protocols Expert, ACP Secretariat, Bagatelle, Barbados, 5 May 1999.

John Ferguson, Donor Coordinator, Windward Islands Banana Industry, attached to the Delegation of the European Communities, Bridgetown, Barbados, 5 May 1999.

Marshall Hall, Chief Executive, Jamaica Producers Group, Kingston, Jamaica, 12 May 1999.

Charles Johnston, Jamaica Freight and Shipping Company and Chairman, Jamaica Producers Group, Kingston, Jamaica, 17 May 1999.

Patsy Lewis, Department of Government, University of the West Indies, Mona Campus, Kingston, Jamaica, 17 May 1999.

Ren Gonsalves, Managing Director, Jamaican Banana Board, Kingston, Jamaica, 18 May 1999.

Aubrey French, Director, Jamaica Producers Group, Kingston, Jamaica, 20 May 1999.

Herbert Hart, Former Managing Director, Jamaica Producers Group, Kingston, Jamaica, 20 May 1999.

Ambassador John Pringle, Jamaica High Commission, London, 12 July 1999.

Patrick Foley, Former Director, Antilles Products Limited, Jobstown, County Dublin, 21 July 1999.

Geoffrey Spikins, Former Captain, Fyffes shipping fleet, Ashurst, near Southampton, 30 September 1999.

Bill Salmond, Corporate Affairs Director, Geest Bananas, Southampton, 12 November 1999.

Alex Mason, Trade Policy and Tropical Foods Division, Branch B, Ministry of Agriculture, Fisheries and Food, London, via telephone conversation, 25 January 2000.

Malcolm Borthwick, Caribbean Banana Exporters Association, London, via telephone conversation, 25 January 2000.

Bibliography

ACP Secretariat, 'Comparative analysis of the ACP and French positions on the common rules necessary for the management of the market for bananas in the Single European Market', June (Brussels, 1991).

Adler, E. and Haas, P. 'Epistemic communities, world order and the creation of a reflective research program', *International Organization*, 46(3) (1992) pp. 367–90.

Agence Europe, 'New bananas regime is adopted', 16 February (1993).

Agra Europe, information service on European and international agricultural policy and trade for all major agricultural commodities (London: www.agra-net.com).

Alderman, G. *Pressure Groups and Government in Great Britain* (Harlow: Longman, 1984).

Antilles Products Limited, General Minute Book, located at WIBDECO (St Lucia).

Arp, H.A. 'Technical regulation and politics: the interplay between economic interests and environmental policy goals in EC car emission legislation', in J.D. Liefferink, P.D. Lowe and A.P.J. Nol (eds), *European Integration and Environmental Policy* (London: Belhaven, 1993).

Averyt, W.F. *Agropolitics in the European Community: Interest Groups and the Common Agricultural Policy* (London: Praeger, 1977).

Bachrach, P. and Baratz, M.S. *Power and Poverty: Theory and Practice* (New York: Oxford University Press, 1970).

Baggott, R. 'Pressure groups in Britain: change and decline?' *Talking Politics*, Autumn, 1(1) (1988) pp. 25–30.

Baggott, R. 'The measurement of change in pressure group politics', *Talking Politics*, Autumn, 5(1) (1992) pp. 18–22.

Baggott, R. *Pressure Groups: A Question of Interest* (Sheffield: PAVIC Publications, 1994).

Baggott, R. *Pressure Groups Today* (Manchester: Manchester University Press, 1995).

Ball, A. and Millard, F.A. *Pressure Politics in Industrial Societies: A Comparative Introduction* (Basingstoke: Macmillan – now Palgrave – 1986).

Banana Trade News Bulletin, published by Banana Watch (Dublin) and Banana Link (Norwich).

Baumgartner, F.R. and Leech, B.L. *Basic Interests: The Importance of Groups in Politics and in Political Science* (New Jersey: Princetown University Press, 1998).

Beaver, P. *Yes! We Have Some: The Story of Fyffes* (Stevenage: Publications for Companies, 1976).

Beckford, G. 'Issues in the Windward–Jamaica Banana War', in N. Girvan and O. Jefferson (eds) *Readings in the Political Economy of the Caribbean* (Kingston: New World Group, 1971).

Benelux Economic Union, 'Memorandum of the Governments of the Three Benelux Countries', Commission for Foreign Economic Relations, September (1990).

Bennington, J. and Harvey J. 'Transnational local authority networking within the European Union: passing fashion or new paradigm?' in D. Marsh (ed.) *Comparing Policy Networks* (Buckingham: Open University Press, 1998).

Bentley, A.F. *The Process of Government* (Cambridge, MA: Belknap, 1967).

Black, C.V. (ed.) *Jamaica's Banana Industry: A History of the Banana Industry with Particular Reference to the Part Played by The Jamaica Banana Producers Association Ltd* (Kingston: The Jamaica Banana Producers Association, 1984).

Bomberg, E. 'Issue networks and the environment: explaining European Union environmental policy', in D. Marsh (ed.) *Comparing Policy Networks* (Buckingham: Open University Press, 1998).

Butt Philip, A. *Directory of Pressure Groups in the European Community* (Harlow: Longman, 1991).

Cadot, O. and Webber, D. 'Banana Splits and Slipping over Banana Skins: The European and Transatlantic Politics of Bananas' (European University Institute Working Paper No. 2001/3, 2001).

Cairney, P. 'Advocacy coalitions and policy change' in J. Stanyer and G. Stoker (eds) *Contemporary Political Studies* (Oxford: Blackwell, 1997).

Cargill Technical Services Limited, 'Proposals for restructuring the Windward Islands banana industry', prepared for the Overseas Development Administration, British Development Division in the Caribbean, Barbados at the request of OECS/WIBDECO (Surrey, 1995).

Caribbean Banana Exporters' Association, 'The Community Banana Market and 1992', paper given at the West India Committee Conference, Lancaster House, September (London, 1988).

Caribbean Banana Exporters' Association, 'Joint response of the Caribbean Banana Exporters Association and their marketing partners to the United Kingdom Government proposals on common arrangements for bananas based on a European quota for dollar source imports', 2 May (London, 1990).

Caribbean Banana Exporters' Association, 'Caribbean Banana Production: The Case Against Tariffication', 21 May (London, 1992).

Caribbean Banana Exporters' Association, 'A Single Market for Bananas', April (London, 1993).

Caribbean Insight (Caribbean Council for Europe: London).

Castles, F. *Pressure Groups and Political Culture* (London: Routledge, 1967).

Cavanagh, M. 'Offshore health and safety policy in the North Sea: policy networks and policy outcomes in Britain and Norway', in D. Marsh (ed.) *Comparing Policy Networks* (Buckingham: Open University Press, 1998).

Cawson, A. *Corporatism and Welfare* (Heinemann: London, 1982).

Cawson, A. *Organised Interests and the State: Studies in Meso-Corporatism* (Beverly Hills: Sage, 1985).

Cawson, A. 'Interests, groups and public policy-making: the case of the European consumer electronics industry', in J. Greenwood, J.R. Grote and K. Ronit (eds) *Organized Interests and the European Community* (London, Sage, 1992).

Christiansen, L. and Dowding, K. 'Pluralism or State Autonomy? The Case of Amnesty International (British Section): the Insider/Outsider Group', *Political Studies*, XLII (1994) pp. 15–24.

Christoph, J.B. 'High Civil Servants and the Politics of Consensualism in Great Britain', in M. Dogan (ed.) *The Mandarins of Western Europe* (New York: Wiley, 1975).

Chronicle of the West India Committee (London: West India Committee).

Colonial Reports on Dominica, Grenada, Jamaica, St Lucia, and St Vincent (London: HMSO).

Commission of the European Communities, *Directorate-General for Development, Ten Years of Lomé: A Record of ACP-EEC Partnership* (Brussels, 1986).

Commission of the European Communities, 'Setting up the internal market in the banana sector, Report compiled by a Commission ad hoc 'Bananas' Interdepartmental Working Party working to Commission guidelines', Commission working document, SEC (92) 940 final, 12 May (Brussels, 1992a).

Commission of the European Communities, *Proposal for a Council Regulation (EEC) on the Common Organisation of the Market in Bananas*, COM (92) 359 final, 7 August (Brussels, 1992b).

Commission of the European Communities (CEC) *Report on the Operation of the Banana Regime* [SEC (95) 1565 final: 11/10/95] (Brussels, 1995).

Commission of the European Communities, *Communication from the Commission to the Council on the 'First Come, First Served' Method for the Banana Regime and the Implications of a 'Tariff Only' System*, COM (2000) 621 final, 4 October (Brussels, 2000).

Common Cause, 'Banana Republic' press release (Washington, 1995).

Companies House, 00128094 (Geest Industries Limited); 00266840 (Geest Bananas Limited); 00515647 (Antilles Imports Limited); 00557743 (Geest Overseas Limited).

Council of the European Union General Secretariat, '2110th Council Meeting, Agriculture', 9558/98 (Presse 214) 26 June (Brussels, 1999).

The Courier, Journal of ACP and EU Affairs (Brussels: Commission of the European Communities).

Cox, G., P. Lowe and Winter, M. 'The state and the farmer: perspectives on agricultural policy', in G. Cox, P. Lowe and M. Winter (eds) *Agriculture: People and Policies*, (London: Allen and Unwin, 1986).

Crenson, M.A. *The Un-Politics of Air Pollution: A Study of Non-Decision making in the Cities* (London: Johns Hopkins Press, 1971).

Current Year Law Book 1983 (London: Sweet and Maxwell Ltd/Stevens and Sons Ltd, 1984).

Dahl, R. *Dilemmas of Pluralist Democracy* (London: Yale University Press, 1982).

The Daily Gleaner newspaper (Kingston, Jamaica).

Daugbjerg, C. 'Similar problems, different policies: policy networks and environmental policy in Danish and Swedish agriculture', in D. Marsh (ed.) *Comparing Policy Networks* (Buckingham: Open University Press, 1998).

Daugbjerg, C. and Marsh, D. 'Explaining policy outcomes: integrating the policy network approach with macro-level and micro-level analysis', in D. Marsh (ed.) *Comparing Policy Networks* (Buckingham: Open University Press, 1998).

Davies, P. *Fyffes and the Banana: Musa Sapientum – A Century of History, 1888–1988* (London: Athlone, 1990).

Lord Denning, 'The Denning Report', November (London, 1970).

The Denning File, containing various minutes and memoranda, JAMCO (London).

Department of Agriculture and Forestry, *Annual Report on Agricultural Development* (Dominica, 1952).

The Dominica Tribune newspaper (Roseau, Dominica).

Dowding, K. 'Model or metaphor? A critical review of the policy network approach', *Political Studies*, 43 (1995) pp. 136–58.

Dunlop, C. 'Epistemic Communities: A Reply to Toke', *Politics*, 20(3) (2000) pp. 137–44.

Dyett, H. *ACP Diplomacy: The Caribbean Dimension* (Georgetown, Guyana, 1998).

Eberlie, R. 'The Confederation of British Industry and policy-making in the European Community', in S. Massey and J.J. Richardson (eds) *Lobbying in the European Community* (Oxford: Oxford University Press, 1993).

Embassies of the Eastern Caribbean States and Missions to the European Communities, 'Windward Islands object to sanctions request in WTO', Press Release, 26 January (1999).

Etienne, T. 'Radio Address by Minister for Agriculture, Trade and Natural Resources following Banana Talks in London', January (1973).

Eurolink newsletter (Brussels: Organisation of Eastern Caribbean States Joint Mission).

Europe/Caribbean Confidential (London: Caribbean Council for Europe).

European Commission, 'Commission Announces Resolution of Banana Dispute with Latin American Countries' (IP/94/265, 29 March), EC Spokesman's Service (Brussels, 1994).

European Commission, 'Commission Proposes Modifications to the Banana Regime' (IP/96/206, 6 March), EC Spokesman's Service (Brussels, 1996).

European Commission, 'Commission proposes to modify the EU's Banana Regime' (IP/99/828; 10 November), EC Spokesman's Service (Brussels, 1999).

European Commission, 'Commission gives new impetus to resolve banana dispute' (IP/00/07, 5 July), EC Spokesman's Service (Brussels, 2000).

European Court of Justice, *Mr Charmasson v Minister for Economic Affairs and Finance (Paris) (preliminary ruling requested by the Council d'Etat de France) Judgement of the Court*, 10 December (including Opinion of Advocate General), Case 48/74 (1974) pp. 1397–1404.

European Court of Justice, *United Brands Company and the United Brands Continental B. V. v Commission of the European Communities Judgement of the Court*, 14 February, (including Opinion of Advocate General), Case 27/76 (1978) pp. 207–351.

European Court of Justice, *Chris International Foods Limited v. Commission of the European Communities*, Order of the Court, 23 February, Cases 91 and 200/82 (1983) pp. 417–29.

European Court of Justice, *Federal Republic of Germany v. Commission of the European Communities*, Case C-280/93 (1994) (Full Court 5/10/1994).

European Court of Justice, *Application for annulment of the first indent of Article 1(1) of Council Decision 94/800/EC of 22 December 1994 concerning the conclusion on behalf of the European Community, as regards matters within its competence, of the agreements reached in the Uruguay Round multilateral negotiations (1986-1994) (OJ 1994 L 336, p. 1), to the extent that the Council thereby approved the conclusion of the Framework Agreement on Bananas with the Republic of Costa Rica, the Republic of Colombia, the Republic of Nicaragua and the Republic of Venezuela*, Case C-122/95, 10 March (1998).

European Court of Justice, *Application for compensation for the loss which the applicant has suffered as a result of the Commission introducing, under Regulation (EC)*

No 2362/98 of 28 October 1998 laying down detailed rules for the implementation of Council Regulation (EEC) No 404/93 regarding imports of bananas into the Community (OJ 1998 L 293, p. 32), provisions which are alleged to conflict with World Trade Organisation (WTO) rules and certain general principles of Community law, Case T-52/99, 20 March (2001).

European Parliament, 'MEPs infuriated by Commission proposals for banana deal', News Report, 11 July (Brussels, 2000).

European Standing Committee A, *European Document No. 8372/92, Relating to the Common Market Organisation for Bananas*, 9 December (London: HMSO, 1992).

Financial Times, 'Banana imports rule change soon', 21 September (1984).

Financial Times, 'US and EU agree on banana imports' 12 April (2001).

Finer, S.E. *Anonymous Empire* (London: Pall Mall, 1966).

Finer, S.E. 'The Political Power of Organised Labour', *Government and Opposition*, 8 (4) October (1973) pp. 391–406.

Food and Agriculture Organisation, *Committee on Commodity Problems, Current Banana Situation and Outlook* (CCP/Bananas/66/2, January) (Rome, 1966).

Food and Agriculture Organisation, *The World Banana Economy, Commodity Bulletin*, Series 50 (Rome, 1972).

Food and Agriculture Organisation, *World Banana Economy Statistical Compendium*, FAO Economic and Social Development Paper No. 31 (Rome, 1983).

Food and Agriculture Organisation, *Intergovernmental Group on Bananas, Tenth Session*, Banana Statistics, July (Rome, 1988).

Food and Agriculture Organisation, *Policy Developments and Prospects for Coordinated International Action on Bananas*, Committee on Commodity Problems, BA 91/5, April (Rome, 1991).

Francis, G. 'Present situation and Future Prospects of ACP Bananas in the ECU Market', paper presented at the First International Symposium on the Current Status of Future Prospects of the ECU Banana Market (Tenerife, 1989).

Franklin, M. 'Food policy formation in the UK/EC', in S. Henson and S. Gregory (eds) *The Politics of Food* (University of Reading: Department of Agricultural Economics and Management, 1994).

Franklin, M. and Myers, G. *A Single European Market for Bananas*, a report for the West India Committee, January (1992).

The Fruit, Flower, and Vegetable Trades' Journal (St Albans, Hertfordshire).

FruiTrop in *Banana Trade News Bulletin*, No. 18, November (Norwich: Banana Link, 1999).

Galbraith, J. K. *The New Industrial State* (Harmondsworth: Pelican, 1974).

General Agreement on Tariffs and Trade, *EEC-Member States' Import Regimes for Bananas*, DS32/R, 19 May (1993).

General Agreement on Tariffs and Trade, *EEC-Import Regime for Bananas*, DS38/R, 11 February (1994).

Gonzales, A. 'The future of the EU-Caribbean Links', *The Courier*, no. 161 (1997) pp. 72–3.

Grant, W. 'Insider groups, outsider groups and interest group strategies in Britain', (University of Warwick: Department of Politics Working Paper No. 19, 1978).

Grant, W. *Pressure Groups, Politics and Democracy in Britain* (Hemel Hempstead: Philip Allan, 1989).

Grant, W. *Pressure Groups, Politics and Democracy in Britain* (London: Harvester Wheatsheaf, 1995).

Greenwood, J., Grote, J.R. and Ronit K. *Organised Interests and the European Community* (London: Sage, 1992).

Grossman, L. 'British Aid and Windwards Bananas: The Case of St Vincent and the Grenadines', *Social and Economic Studies*, 43(1) (1994) pp. 151–79.

Grove, J. W. *Government and Industry in Britain* (London: Longman, 1962).

The Guardian, 'Why Europe is divided by the banana split', 10 January (1996).

Gunn Clissold, G. 'Can the Windward Islands Survive Globalisation?' Caribbean Briefing Paper, March (2001).

Haas, P. (ed.) *When Knowledge is Power* (Berkeley: University of California, 1990).

Haas, P. 'Introduction: epistemic communities and international policy co-ordination', *International Organization*, 46(1) (1992) pp. 1–35.

Hall, D. *A Brief History of the West India Committee* (London: Ginn and Co. Ltd, 1971)

Hansard (London: HMSO).

Hart, A. 'The banana in Jamaica: export trade', *Social and Economic Studies*, 3(2) (1954) pp. 212–29.

Hart, H.T. *Memorandum on Banana Industry*, 28 March (Kingston, 1968).

Heclo, H. 'Issue networks and the executive establishment', in A. King (ed.) *The New American Political System* (Washington: AEI, 1978).

Heclo, H. and Wildavsky, A. *The Private Government of Public Money* (London: Macmillan, 1974).

Hogwood, B. *From Crisis to Complacency: Shaping Public Policy in Britain* (Oxford, Oxford University Press, 1986).

Holbech, B. 'Policy and Influence: MAFF and the NFU', *Public Policy and Administration*, 1(3) (1986) pp. 40–7.

Imperial Economic Committee, *Report of the Imperial Economic Committee on Marketing and Preparing for Market of Foodstuffs Produced in the Overseas Parts of the Empire*, 8 volumes (London: HMSO, 1925–7).

Inside Europe (London: Caribbean Council for Europe).

Jackson, S. 'Bananas and '1992': the Battle to Preserve Protected Trade from the Caribbean', *Trocaire Development Review*, Dublin (1991) pp. 57–71.

Jamaica Banana Producers Association Dossier, including Memorandum and Articles of Association, and Share Trustees at the Company's inception. Provided by Aubrey French, Director, Jamaica Producers Group, Kingston, Jamaica.

Jamaica Banana Producers Association File, detailing the development of the Company from its origins to the Banana Commission of 1936. Donated by Herbert Hart, Former Managing Director, Jamaica Producers Group, to the West India Collection, University of the West Indies, Kingston, Jamaica.

Jamaica Banana Commission Report (Kingston, Jamaica, 1936).

Jamaica Commission of Enquiry into the Banana Industry Report (Kingston, Jamaica, 1959).

JAMCO (Jamaica Marketing Company) 'JAMCO Accountability, 1970-1991' (London, 1991).

John, P. *Analysing Public Policy* (London: Pinter, 1998).

Jordan, G., Maloney, W. and McLaughlin, A. *'Insiders, outsiders and political access'* (University of Aberdeen: British Interest Group Project Working Paper No. 3, 1992).

Jordan, A.G. and Richardson, J.J. *Government and Pressure Groups in Britain* (Oxford: Clarendon, 1987).

Judge, D. 'Parliament and interest representation', in M. Rush (ed.) *Parliament and Pressure Politics* (Oxford: Clarendon, 1990).

Kassim, H. 'Policy networks, networks and European Union policy-making: a sceptical view', *Western European Politics*, 17 (1994) pp. 15–27.

Kepner, D. and Soothill, J.H. *The Banana Empire. A Case Study of Economic Imperialism* (USA: Russell and Russell, 1963).

Kimber, R. and Richardson, J.J. (eds) *Pressure Groups in Britain* (London: Dent, 1974).

Kogan, M. *Education Policy-Making* (London: Allen and Unwin, 1975).

Kohler-Koch, B. 'Germany: fragmented but strong lobbying', in M.P.C.M. Van Schendelen (ed.) *National Public and Private EC Lobbying* (Aldershot: Dartmouth, 1993).

Kohler-Koch, B. 'Changing Patterns of interest intermediation in the European Union', *Government and Opposition*, Spring, 29(2) (1994) pp. 166–80.

Krenzler, H.G. and G. Wiegand 'EU–US Relations: More than Trade Disputes?' *European Foreign Affairs Review*, 4 (1999) pp. 153–80.

Latham, E. *The Group Basis of Politics* (New York: Octagon, 1953).

The Law Reports, *The Public General Acts Passed in the Twenty Second and Twenty Third Years of the Reign of His Majesty King George the Fifth and the Church Assembly Measure, Import Duties Act*, 29 February (London: HMSO, 1932).

Lijphart, A.L. *The Politics of Accommodation, Pluralism and Democracy in the Netherlands* (Berkeley and Los Angeles: University of California Press, 1968).

Lindblom, C. 'The science of 'muddling through'', *Public Administration Review*, 19, Spring (1960) pp. 79–88.

Lindblom, C. *The Policy-Making Process* (New Jersey: Prentice-Hall, 1968).

Lindblom, C. *Politics and Markets* (New York: Basic Books, 1977).

Litvak, I.S. and Maule, C.J. 'Transnational Corporations and Vertical Integration: The Banana Case', *Journal of World Trade Law*, 11 (1997) pp. 537–49.

Lyons, R. 'European Union Banana Controversy', *Florida Journal of International Law*, 9 (1994) pp. 165–88.

MacKenzie, W.J.M. 'Pressure groups in British government', *British Journal of Sociology*, June, 6(2) (1955) pp. 133–48.

Marsh, D. (ed.) *Pressure Politics: Interests Groups in Britain* (London: Junction Books, 1983).

Marsh, D. and Rhodes, R.A.W. (eds) *Policy Networks in British Government* (Oxford: Clarendon Press, 1992a).

Marsh, D. and Rhodes, R.A.W. (eds) *Implementing Thatcherite Policies: Audit of an Era* (Buckingham: Open University Press, 1992b).

Marsh, D. and Smith, M. 'Understanding Policy Networks: Towards A Dialectical Approach', paper presented at the Political Science Workshop, Department of Politics, University of York (1996).

Marsh, D. and Smith, M. 'Understanding Policy Networks: towards A Dialectical Approach', *Political Studies*, 48 (1) (2000) March, pp. 4–21.

May, S. and Plaza, G. *The United Fruit Company in Latin America* (New York: National Planning Association, 1958).

May, T. and Nugent, N. 'Insiders, outsiders and thresholders', paper presented to Political Studies Association Annual Conference, University of Kent (1982).

Mazey, S. and Richardson, J.J. 'British pressure groups in the European Community: the challenge of Brussels', *Parliamentary Affairs*, January, 45(1) (1992) pp. 92–107.

Mazey, S. and Richardson, J.J. 'Introduction', in Mazey and Richardson (eds) *Lobbying in the European Community* (Oxford: Oxford University Press, 1993a).

Mazey, S. and Richardson, J.J. 'Interests Groups in the European Community', in Richardson, *Pressure Groups* (Oxford: Oxford University Press, 1993b).

Mazey, S. and Richardson, J.J. 'Pressure Groups and the European Community', *Politics Review*, September, 3(1) (1993c) pp. 20–4.

McFarlane, D. 'The Future of the Banana Industry in the West Indies', *Social and Economic Studies*, 13(1) (1964) pp. 38–93.

McInerney, J. and Lord Peston (eds) *Fair Trade in Bananas? International Trade Policies in Bananas and Proposals to Alter Existing Policies in Line with the Single European Market* (University of Exeter: Report No. 239, December, 1992).

McLeay, E. 'Policing policy and policy networks in Britain and New Zealand', in D. Marsh (ed.) *Comparing Policy Networks* (Buckingham: Open University Press, 1998).

Mills, M. and Saward, M. 'All very well in practice, but what about the theory? A critique of the British idea of policy networks', in P. Dunleavy and J. Stanyer (eds) *Contemporary Political Studies* (Belfast: Political Studies Association, 1994).

Ministry of Overseas Development, *Report of the Tripartite Economic Survey of the Eastern Caribbean*, January–April 1966 (London: HMSO, 1967).

Mitchell, W.C. 'Interest Groups: Economic Perspectives and Contributions', *Journal of Theoretical Politics*, 2(1) (1990) pp. 85–108.

Moon, J.L. and Richardson, J.J. 'Policy making with a difference? The technical and vocational education initiative', *Public Administration*, Spring, 62(1) (1984) pp. 22–33.

Mourillon, V.J.F. *The Dominica Banana Industry from Inception to Independence 1928–1978* (Roseau, Dominica: Tropical Printers Limited, 1979).

Nugent, N. *The Government and Politics of the European Union* (Macmillan: Oxford, 1994).

Nurse, K. and Sandiford, W. *Windward Island Bananas. Challenges and Options under the Single European Market* (Jamaica: Friedrich Ebert Stiftung, 1995).

Odegard, P.H. 'A Group Basis of Politics: A New Name for an Ancient Myth', *Western Political Quarterly*, 11, September, (1958) pp. 689–702.

Office of the United States Trade Representative 'US Government and European Commission Reach Agreement to Resolve Long-Standing Banana Dispute', Press Release, 11 April (Washington, 2000).

Official Journal of the European Communities, *Commission Decision of 17 December 1975 relating to a proceeding under Article 86 of the EEC Treaty (IV/26699-Chiquita)*, No. L 95/1-95/20, 9 April (1976).

Official Journal of the European Communities, *Resolution on ACP bananas, The ACP–EEC Joint Assembly*, No. C 186/46-47, 24 July (1989).

Official Journal of the European Communities, *Resolution on ACP bananas, The ACP–EEC Joint Assembly*, No. C 211/55/5 and 60/1, 17 August (1992).

Official Journal of the European Communities, *Commission Decisions C (92) 3381 and 3382 of 28 December 1992*, C1/4, 5 January (1993a).

Official Journal of the European Communities, *Opinion of the Economic and Social Committee on the Commission Regulation (EEC) on the common organisation of the market in bananas*, C 19, 25 January (1993b).

Official Journal of the European Communities, *Legislative Resolution embodying the opinion of the European Parliament on the Commission proposal for a Council regulation on the common organisation of the market in bananas,* C 21, 25 January (1993c).

Official Journal of the European Communities, *Council Regulation (EEC) No 404/93 of 13 February 1993 on the common organisation of the market in bananas,* No L 47/1, 25 February (1993d).

Official Journal of the European Communities, *Commission Regulation (EEC) No 1442/93 of 10 June 1993, laying down detailed rules for the application of the arrangements for importing bananas into the Community,* No L 142/6, 12 June (1993e).

Official Journal of the European Communities, *Action brought on 14 May 1993 by the Federal Republic of Germany against the Council of the European Communities (Case C-280/93),* No C 173/17, 24 June (1993f).

Official Journal of the European Communities, *Actions brought by German, Belgian, Dutch, and Italian companies against Council Regulation No. 404/93,* various submission dates, No C 188/12-26, 10 July (1993g).

Official Journal of the European Communities, *Order of the Court of 29 June 1993, in Case C-280/93 R: Federal Republic of Germany v. Council of the European Communities,* No C 199/13, 23 July (1993h).

Official Journal of the European Communities, *Council Regulation No. 1637/98 of 20 July 1998 amending Regulation (EEC) No 404/93 on the common organisation of the market in bananas,* L 210/28, 28 July (1998a).

Official Journal of the European Communities, *Council Regulation (EC) No. 2362/98 of 28 October laying down the detailed rules for the implementation of Council Regulation (EEC) No 404/93 regarding imports of bananas into the Community,* L 293/31, 31 October (1998b).

Official Journal of the European Communities, *Council Regulation (EC) No. 896/2001 of 7 May laying down the detailed rules for applying Council Regulation (EEC) No 404/93 as regards arrangements for importing bananas into the Community,* L 126/6, 8 May (2001).

O'Loughlin, C. *Economic and Political Change in the Leeward and Windward Islands* (London: Yale University Press, 1968).

Parker, N.A. 'The United Fruit Company in Jamaica', *Jamaica Review,* 1(2) (1925) pp. 6–10.

Parsons, R.M. 'Elders and Fyffes – a short history of the company and its famous banana boats', *Ships Monthly,* three parts, April, May, and June (1988).

Pedler, R.H. 'The Fruit Companies and the Banana Trade Regime', in R.H. Pedler and M.P.C.M. Van Schendelen (eds) *Lobbying the European Union: Companies, Trade Associations and Issue Groups* (Aldershot: Dartmouth, 1995).

Price Commission, *Prices and Distribution of Bananas* (London: HMSO, 1975).

Principle Agreement between The Jamaica Banana Producers Association Limited and the United Fruit Company, 31 December 1936. Provided by Aubrey French, Director, Jamaica Producers Group, Kingston, Jamaica.

PrNewswire, 'Chiquita applauds US intervention in banana dispute', 17 October (1994).

Public Record Office Files held at Kew:
CO 852/31/8: Banana Commission, 1936.
CO 852/31/10: Banana Commission Report.
CO 852/70/12: Jamaica Bananas, 1937.
CO 852/255/7: Bananas, 1939.
CO 852/317/7: Cameroon Bananas, 1940.

CO 852/333/4: Bananas, 1940.

CO 852/593/1: Banana Main File, 1945.

CO 852/594/4: Windward Islands, 1945.

CO 852/902/2: Windward Islands Bananas, 1948.

CO 852/902/3: Windward Islands Bananas, 1949.

CO 852/1147/11: Jamaica Bananas, 1950.

CO 852/1148/3: Windward Islands Bananas, 1950–51.

CO 1031/1558: CD and W scheme to aid the banana industry, St Lucia, 1954–57.

CO 1031/1559: CD and W scheme to aid the banana industry, St Vincent, 1954–56.

CO 1031/1563: CD and W scheme for the development of the banana industry, Grenada.

DO 200/19: Jamaica and Windward Islands banana crop and trade with UK, 1962–63.

DO 200/21: Jamaica and Windward Islands banana crop and trade with UK, 1963.

FCO 23/334: Import quotas for bananas: Cabinet Committee deliberations, 1967.

FCO 23/335: Import quotas for bananas: Cabinet Committee deliberations, 1967–68.

FCO 23/336: Import quotas for bananas: Cabinet Committee deliberations, 1968.

FCO 23/338: Import quotas for bananas: Cabinet Committee deliberations, 1968.

MAF 86/149: Import of bananas, September 1939–December 1944.

MAF 86/151: Return of banana imports to the private trade, April 1951–December 1953.

MAF 152/12: Fruit and Vegetable control policy, 1939–1940.

MAF 286/3: Briefings to the Prime Minister on meat rationing and bananas, 1940.

Putman, R.D. 'Diplomacy and Domestic Politics: The Logic of Two-Level Games', *International Organisation*, 42(3) Summer (1988) pp. 427–60.

'R. *v.* Secretary of State for Trade ex parte Chris International Foods Limited', Queen's Bench Division, Crown Office List, CO/1020/82 (London).

Ramsaran, R. *Negotiating the Lomé IV Convention*, (Institute of International Relations, University of the West Indies, 1990).

Rapid News Service, 'Commission welcomes European Court decision on banana regime', 29 June (1993).

Ravenhill, J. *Collective Clientelism: The Lomé Conventions and North-South Relations* (New York: Columbia University Press, 1985).

Read, R. 'The EC Internal Banana Market: The Issues and the Dilemma', *World Economy*, 17 (2) (1994) pp. 219–35.

Report of the Tripartite Economic Survey of the Eastern Caribbean, January–April 1966, (London: HMSO, 1967).

Reports on the Agricultural Department: Grenada (St Georges', Grenada).

Reports on the Agricultural Department: St Lucia (Castries, St Lucia).

Reports on the Agricultural Department: St Vincent (Kingstown, St Vincent).

Reuter Newswire, 'Colombia hails GATT banana decision', 25 May (1993).

Rhodes, R.A.W. *The National World of Local Government* (London: Allen and Unwin, 1993).

Rhodes, R.A.W. *Beyond Westminster and Whitehall* (London: Unwin Hyman, 1988).

Rhodes, R.A.W. *Understanding Governance: Policy Networks, Governance, Reflexivity and Accountability* (Buckingham: Open University Press, 1997).

Richardson, J.J. 'Interest group behaviour in Britain: continuity and change', in Richardson (ed.) *Pressure Groups* (Oxford: Oxford University Press, 1993).

Richardson, J.J. and Jordan, A.G. *Governing Under Pressure: The Policy Process in a Post-Parliamentary Democracy* (Oxford: Blackwells, 1979).

Richardson, J.J., Maloney, W.A., and Rudig, W.L. 'The dynamics of policy change', *Public Administration*, Summer, 70 (2) (1992) pp. 157–75.

Roberts, G. *A Dictionary of Political Analysis* (London: Longman, 1971).

Roche, J. *The International Banana Trade* (Cambridge: Woodhead Publishing Limited, 1998).

Rodriquez, D.W. *Bananas: An Outline of the Economic History of Production and Trade with Special Reference to Jamaica*, Commodity Bulletin No. 1 (Kingston, Jamaica: Department of Agriculture, 1955).

Rose, R. 'On the Priorities of Government: A Developmental Analysis of Public Policies', *European Journal of Political Research*, 4(3) (1976) pp. 247–89.

Rudden, B. and Wyatt, D. (eds) *Basic Community Laws* (Oxford: Clarendon Press, 1980).

Sabatier, P. 'An advocacy coalition model of policy change and the role of policy orientated learning therein', *Policy Sciences*, 21(2) (1988) pp. 129–68.

Sabatier, P. 'The Advocacy Coalition Framework: Revisions and Relevance for Europe', *Journal of European Public Policy*, 5(1) (1998) pp. 98–130.

Sabatier, P. and Jenkins-Smith, H. (eds) *Policy Change and Learning: An Advocacy Coalition Approach* (Oxford: Westview, 1993).

Sabatier, P. and Jenkins-Smith, H. *An Advocacy Coalition Lens on Environmental Policy* (New York: Suny Press, 1997).

Sabatier, P. and Jenkins-Smith, H. 'The Advocacy Coalition Framework: An Assessment, in P. Sabatier (ed.) *Theories of the Policy Process* (Oxford: Westview, 1999).

Sandiford, W. 'Adjustment Initiatives in the Windward Islands Banana Industry', (Eastern Caribbean Central Bank: Research and Information Department, 1997).

Sandiford, W. 'The Proposed Amendments to the European Banana Regime: Would the Windward Islands be no worse off?' (St Lucia: OECS Secretariat, October 1998).

Sandiford, W. *On the Brink of Decline: Bananas in the Windward Islands* (Grenada: Fedon Books, 2000).

Saul, S.B. 'The Economic Significance of Constructive Imperialism', *Journal of Economic History*, XVII(2) June (1957) pp. 173–92.

Schmitter, P. and Lehmbruch, G. (eds) *Trends Towards Corporatist Intermediation* (Beverly Hills: Sage, 1979).

Select Committee on Agriculture, *Arrangements for the Importation of Bananas into the United Kingdom: Interim Report* (London: HMSO, 1992).

Select Committee on Agriculture, *Arrangements for the Importation of Bananas into the United Kingdom: Second Report* (London: HMSO, 1993a).

Select Committee on Agriculture, *Response by the Government to the Second Report from the Agriculture Committee, 'Arrangements for the Importation of Bananas into the United Kingdom' (HC 452)*, First Special Report (London: HMSO, 1993b).

Select Committee on European Legislation, *Bananas*, Sixth Report (London: HMSO, 1993).

Select Committee on European Legislation, *Bananas: Post-Enlargement Arrangements*, Eighth Report (London: HMSO, 1995).

Select Committee on European Legislation, *Banana Regime: Proposed Changes*, 15th Report (London: HMSO, 1996).

Select Committee on International Development, *The Renegotiation of the Lomé Convention*, Fourth Report, Two Volumes, Report and Proceedings of the Committee and Minutes of Evidence and Appendices (London: HMSO, 1998).

Select Committee on Overseas Development, *The United Kingdom's Entry into Europe and Economic Relations with Developing Countries*, Volume Two, Report (London: HMSO, 1973).

Select Committee on Overseas Development, *The United Kingdom's Entry into Europe and Economic Relations with Developing Countries*, Second Special Report (London: HMSO, 1974).

Select Committee on Overseas Development, *The Renegotiation of the Lomé Convention*, Two Volumes, Report (London: HMSO, 1978).

Self, P. and Storing, H. *The State and the Farmer* (London: Allen and Unwin, 1962).

Smith, M.J. 'From policy community to issue network: salmonella in eggs and the new politics of food', *Public Administration*, Summer, 69(2) (1991) pp. 235–55.

Smith, M.J. 'The agricultural policy community: the rise and fall of a closed relationship', in D. Marsh and R. Rhodes (eds) *Policy Networks in British Government* (Oxford: Clarendon, 1992).

Smith, M.J. *Pressure, Power, and Policy* (Hemel Hempstead: Harvester Wheatsheaf, 1993).

Somsen, H. 'State discretion in European Community environmental law: the case of the Bathing Water Directive', State Autonomy in the European Community research seminar, Christ Church, Oxford (1994).

Spector, J. 'European Economic Community and the West Indian banana industry', *West India Chronicle*, 82(1437) (1967) pp. 499–500.

Spence, D. 'The role of the national civil service in European lobbying: the British case', in S. Mazey and J.J. Richardson (eds), *Lobbying the European Community* (Oxford: Oxford University Press, 1993).

Stemman, R. *Geest 1935–1985* (London, 1986).

Stevens, C. 'The Caribbean and Europe 1992: Endgame?' *Development Policy Review*, 9 (1991) pp. 265–83.

Stevens, C. 'Trade with Developing Countries: Banana Skins and Turf Wars', in H. Wallace and W. Wallace (eds) *Policy Making in the European Union* (Oxford: Oxford University Press, 2000).

Stewart, J.D. *British Pressure Groups* (Oxford: Clarendon, 1958).

Stockley, A.H. *Consciousness of Effort: The Romance of the Banana* (printed for private circulation, 1937).

Strauss, A.L. *Negotiations, Values, Contexts, Processes and Social Order* (London: Jossey Bass, 1987).

Strauss, A., Schatzman, L., Ehrlich, D., Bucher, R., and Abshin, S. 'The Hospital and its Negotiated Order' (1963) reprinted in F. Charles *et al.* (eds) *Decisions, Organisations, and Society* (Penguin in association with the Open University Press, 1976).

Streeck, W. and Schmitter, P.C. 'From National Corporatism to Transnational Pluralism: Organised Interests in the Single European Market', *Politics and Society*, 19(2) (1991) pp. 133–64.

Sutton, P. 'From neo-colonialism to neo-colonialism: Britain and the EEC in the Commonwealth Caribbean', in A. Payne and P. Sutton (eds) *Dependency under Challenge. The Political Economy of the Commonwealth Caribbean* (Manchester University Press, 1984).

Sutton, P. 'The banana regime of the European Union, the Caribbean, and Latin America', *Journal of International Studies and World Affairs*, 39(2) (1997) pp. 5–36.

Thagsen, R. and Matthews, A. 'The EU's Common Banana Regime: An Initial Evaluation', *Journal of Common Market Studies*, 35(4) (1997) pp. 615–38.

Thomson, R. *Green Gold: Bananas and Dependency in the Eastern Caribbean* (London: Latin America Bureau, 1987).

The Times, 'Banana imports protected by 1939 Act', 22 July (1983).

Time Magazine, 'Big Money and Politics: Who gets hurt?' 7 February (2000).

Treaty concerning the Accession of the Kingdom of Denmark, Ireland, the Kingdom of Norway and the United Kingdom of Great Britain and Northern Ireland to the European Economic Community and the European Atomic Energy Community, including the Act concerning the Conditions of Accession and the Adjustments to the Treaties (with Final Act) (Brussels, 22 January 1972).

Treaty establishing The European Economic Community (Rome, 25 March 1957).

Tripartite Banana Talks, 'Minutes of the meetings held during July 1966 between Jamaica, the Windward Islands, and the UK Government', London. Located at the Dominica Documentation Centre, Roseau, Dominica (1966).

Truman, D. *The Governmental Process* (New York: Alfred Knopf, 1962).

The United Kingdom and the European Communities, *Command 4715. Presented to Parliament by the Prime Minister by Command of Her Majesty* (London: HMSO, 1971).

Visser, J. and Ebbinghaus, B. 'Making the most of diversity? European integration and transnational organisation of labour', in J. Greenwood, J.R. Grote and K. Ronit (eds) *Organized Interests and the European Community* (London: Sage, 1992).

Welch, B. 'Banana Dependency: Albatross or Liferaft for the Windwards', *Social and Economic Studies*, 43(1) (1994) pp. 123–49.

West India Committee, Minutes of Executive Committee Meetings (London).

West India Committee, *The Commonwealth Caribbean and the EEC* (London, 1967 and 1970).

West India Committee Circular (London: West India Committee).

West India Committee in conjunction with the Commonwealth Secretariat, '1992 and the Caribbean: Issues and Opportunities, Lomé IV and Beyond', papers given at a conference on the implications for the Caribbean of the Single European Market, Barbados, November (1989).

West India Royal Commission, appointed to inquire into the Depression of the Sugar Industry in the West Indian Colonies, and into their General Condition in connection therewith (London: HMSO, 1898).

West India Royal Commission Report (London: HMSO, 1945).

Whiteley, P.F. and Winyard, S.J. *Pressure for the Poor* (London: Methuen, 1987).

Wilks, S. and Wright, M. *Comparing Government–Industry Relations: Western Europe, the United States and Japan* (Oxford: Clarendon Press, 1987).

Williamson, P.J. *Corporatism in Perspective* (London: Sage, 1989).

Wilson, G.K. *Special Interests and Policy Making* (London: Wiley, 1977).

Windward Islands Banana Development and Export Company Limited, Annual Report (1997).

Windward Islands Banana Growers' Association, *Report on the visit of the Windward Islands Governments and WINBAN to London from 11th to 31st July 1966* (Castries, St Lucia: WINBAN Office, 29 August 1966).

Windward Islands Banana Growers' Association, *WINBAN News* (Castries, St Lucia).

World Trade Organisation, *European Communities – Regime for the Importation, Sale and Distribution of Bananas, Complaint by Ecuador*, Report of the Panel, WT/DS27/R/ECU, 22 May (1997a).

World Trade Organisation, *European Communities – Regime for the Importation, Sale and Distribution of Bananas, Request for Consultations by Panama*, WT/DS105/1, 24 October (1997b).

World Trade Organisation, *Report of the Panel Indonesia – Certain Measures Affecting the Automobile Industry*, WT/DS54/R, 2 July (1998a).

World Trade Organisation, *WTO Appellate Body, United States – Import Prohibition of Certain Shrimp and Shrimp Products*, WT/DS58/AB/R, 12 October (1998b).

World Trade Organisation, *European Communities – Regime for the Importation, Sale and Distribution of Bananas-Recourse to Arbitration by the European Communities under Article 22.6 of the DSU*, Decision by the Arbitrators, WT/DS27/ARB, 9 April (1999a).

World Trade Organisation, *European Communities-Regime for the Importation, Sale and Distribution of Bananas-Recourse to Article 21.5 by Ecuador*, Report of the Panel, WT/DS27/RW/ECU, 12 April (1999b).

World Trade Organisation, *European Communities-Regime for the Importation, Sale and Distribution of Bananas-Recourse to Article 21.5 by the European Communities*, Report of the Panel, WT/DS27/RW/EEC, 12 April (1999c).

World Trade Organisation, *United States and Sections 301–310 of the Trade Act of 1974*, WT/DS152/R, 22 December (1999d).

World Trade Organisation, *WTO Members of the Organization of Eastern Caribbean States – OECS: June 2001*, Press Release, Press/TPRB/166, 7 June (2001).

Worrell, D., Bourne, C. and Sophia, D. (eds) *Financing Development in the Commonwealth Caribbean* (London: Macmillan – now Palgrave – 1991).

Wright, M. 'Policy community, policy network and comparative industrial policies', *Political Studies*, 36 (1988) pp. 593–612.

Index

conflict with Jamaica Banana
Producers' Association, 46–50,
61–2, 64–7
issue of war-time controls, 54–6
purchase of Elders and Fyffes, 30–1,
34
see also United Brands and Chiquita
Brands
United Kingdom policy on bananas,
26–7, 28–30, 32–7, 40, 43–4, 48,
53, 55, 58, 60, 63, 68, 77, 79, 81,
87, 91, 94, 102, 124–5, 137, 166,
175–8
as President of the EC Council,
131–7, 158
see also individual government
departments
United States, 130, 148–54, 158, 159,
166–70, 173, 182
sanctions against EU, 160–4, 168;
removal of, 169
United States Trade Representative,
141, 148, 149, 150, 160, 161,
163–4
Section 301 Action, 148–9, 160

Venezuela, 130, 144

War, First World, 35–6, 177
War, Second World, 7, 177
banana rationing, 62–3
colonial dimension, 56–7, 59
Government import ban, 56–60;
end of ban, 60–3
Guaranteed Purchase Scheme, 59
restrictions ended, 67–72
Wells, Bowen, 125
West Germany
see under Germany
West India Commission (1898), 27
West India Committee, 28, 80, 120
West Indies Transatlantic Freight
Conference, 75
WINBAN Agreement, 88, 90
Windward Islands, 1–2, 12, 20, 59,
74, 77, 78, 79, 81, 82, 85–9, 93–5,
98, 104, 108, 114, 115, 118,

121–2, 171, 172, 175, 176, 178,
179, 180, 182
exports to Canada, 74
first banana shipment to UK, 76–7
GATT Contracting Parties, 140
increasing production (1950s), 81
traditional industries in decline, 77
UK financial assistance, 81
UK government shipping assistance, 77–9
see also individual islands
Windward Islands Banana
Development and Exporting
Company (WIBDECO), 172
Windward Islands Banana Growers'
Association (WINBAN), 81, 95,
107
World Trade Organization (WTO), 2,
13, 15, 147, 165, 166, 181, 182,
183
agenda blocked, 162
Appellate Body, 153, 155–6, 184
as a powerful actor, 156–7
bananas as a test case, 150–1
compared with EU, 15–16, 157
conflict between Articles 21.5 and
22, 161–2
Dispute Settlement Body (DSB),
153, 156, 160, 162, 164, 166,
168, 181
ejection of Caribbean representatives, 154–5, 184
first banana Panel established, 154
first Panel report, 155; reaction to,
156; insensitivity of, 155
second banana Panel established,
160, 162–3
second Panel report, 163–4
settlement of banana dispute, 169
structure and operation, 153
third party status, 154, 157, 165,
182
waiver, 168, 169

Yaoundé Convention, 103

Zemurray, Samuel, 50